D0053724

Hermeneutics and Social Science

European Perspectives
A Series of the Columbia University Press

Zygmunt Bauman is professor of sociology in the University of Leeds. He was educated at the University of Warsaw, where he taught until March 1968. Between 1968 and 1971 he was professor of sociology at Tel Aviv and Haifa. As a visiting professor he has taught at the University of Manchester, the Australian National University, the University of California at Berkeley, and Yale University.

Hermeneutics and Social Science

Zygmunt Bauman

Columbia University Press
New York   1978

Published in 1978 in Great Britain by Hutchinson & Co. (Publishers) Ltd
and in the United States of America by Columbia University Press

Library of Congress Cataloging in Publication Data

Bauman, Zygmunt.
  Hermeneutics and social science.

  (European perspectives)
  Bibliography: p.
  Includes index
  1. Hermeneutics. 2. Social sciences. I. Title.
BD241.B33   1978   300′.1   78–877
ISBN 0–231–04546–8

Printed in Great Britain

Contents

Introduction: the challenge of hermeneutics

This book is concerned with the various responses of social science to the challenge of hermeneutics.

Hermeneutics (from the Greek *hermēneutikós*, 'related to explaining'; 'explaining' is used here in the sense of 'clarifying', of rendering the obscure plain, the unclear clear) was for many centuries a subdiscipline of philology. Since most of the texts considered essential in the Christian world were available in contradictory versions, bearing traces of sloppiness and absent-mindedness in an endless chain of anonymous copyists, the question of authenticity, of the true version versus distorted ones – could not but turn into a major concern of scholars. Hermeneutics was originally developed to answer this question. Employing mostly philological methods, hermeneutics occupied itself with critical scrutiny of contending texts, with the re-possession of the authentic version – the 'true meaning' of the document – as its ultimate objective. At that stage, recovering the true meaning was seen as identical with demonstrating the authenticity of the text. For obvious reasons, historiography was the most keen and grateful client of hermeneutics.

It was in the sixteenth century that hermeneutics emerged from relative obscurity and swiftly moved into the very centre of scholarly argument. It owed its sudden eminence to the Catholic–Protestant debate regarding the authentic text of the Bible and what was understood as essentially the same problem, the true meaning of its message. The practical urgency of the matter, which had acquired much more than merely technical significance, propelled hermeneutics into a central position in the humanities. 'Philological critique' attracted the most brilliant and creative historians and philosophers. Its prestige was boosted by an impressive series of unquestionable accomplishments (going back to Lorenzo Valla) in exposing the falsity of documents whose authenticity had not been doubted for centuries. Hermeneutics raised the critique of historical sources to the rank of methodical scholarship. In this capacity it became, and remained even when its initial motives lost much of their urgency, an indispensable branch of historiography. For different, but obvious reasons, its technical refinement has been also prompted by the jurists' concern with their interpretation of law.

It was not in this capacity, however, that hermeneutics became a challenge to the social sciences in general, sociology in particular. As long as the task of 'clarifying' which hermeneutics set for itself was seen as, above all, a search for the original, undistorted message of written sources, hermeneutics was rightly viewed simply as a tool, however powerful and indispensable. A tool helps to solve problems; it does not create them. By the end of the eighteenth century, however, a fateful shift took place. The philosophical reflection on the activity and results of hermeneutics moved beyond the mere critique of texts and began to ask difficult questions about the nature and the objectives of historical knowledge as such; indeed, of social knowledge in general.

Slowly, and at the beginning imperceptibly, the sense ascribed to the meaning sought by hermeneutical inquiry began to change. The texts dealt with by early hermeneutics were more often than not anonymous; even if the name of an author had been attached to them, they acquired enough weight of their own through the centuries to render them largely autonomous from their creators. The available knowledge of the lives of the genuine or putative authors was on the whole still less reliable than the extant texts themselves; it could hardly contribute to their clarification. An almost total concentration on the text itself, as the only guide to its meaning, was the most obvious response. Philology, rather than psychology, was the obvious framework for the quest for authenticity.

Perhaps more important still was the essential harmony of the task so defined with the cognitive predisposition of the era. The perception of the author as the legitimate 'owner' of his ideas was only beginning to capture the imagination. Artists were still regarded as craftsmen guided by the anonymous rules of the guild rather than by thoroughly individual and 'private' feelings and visions. The middle of the eighteenth century saw a genuine revival of classical aesthetics – with its emphasis on the work of art itself, its form and structure, its harmony, its inherent logic – and utter lack of interest in author's intentions. To Winckelmann, by far the most influential theorist of the time, beauty – this innermost meaning of the work of art – was a matter of the inner proportions of the artistic product; the product could communicate no information beside that contained in its finished form. This aesthetics had no room for the personality of the author; it considered bad any art which bore too visible an imprint of its author's individuality. Winckelmann's theory of art, and indeed the enlightened opinion of his time, saw eye to eye with the credulous and over-confident pre-Kantian view of knowledge in general – as a skilful, but essentially unproblematic reflection of the world 'as it is'.

Kant's discovery of the crucial role of the subject in the process of all cognition (which itself came in the wake of the socio-political establishment of the individual as the sole lawful owner of everything pertaining to his social identity) was soon followed by the discovery of the artist behind every work of art, a thinking and feeling personality behind each creation. To find the meaning of a work of art, wrote W. H. Wackenroder in 1797, one has to contemplate the artist rather than his products, to the point of 'embracing all his characteristic individuality'. Not much later, Novalis spoke confidently of the 'inner universe' of the artist whose representation of the work of art is. In the words of Shelley, the artist turns into the 'legislator of the world'. With personal freedom fast becoming the inviolable canon of the new aesthetics (as, indeed, of the dominant world-view of the new era), there was little point in searching for meaning in the text while neglecting the author. With authors repossessing their texts, readers were denied the authority of their judgement.

The new image of the artist and his work (as, indeed, of all human creation) was recorded in the intellectual history of the western world under the name of Romanticism. Though the artistic theories of Romanticism hardly outlived the intense poetic and visual-artistic movements they accompanied, they had lasting effects on the later developments of the social sciences. In particular, they were instrumental in the fateful transformation of the subject-matter and strategy of hermeneutics.

It was a Romantic discovery that the work of art (like human creation in general) was, above all, a purposive system. The text, the painting, the sculpture came to be seen as visible embodiments of ideas which, though represented in the result, were not exhausted by it. They were fully at home only within the artist's experience, and it was there they could be discovered, if they could be discovered at all. The work of art seemed suddenly less important as a reflection of reality 'out there' than as a reflection of a design of the author, his thoughts and emotions. It became evident that the genuine meaning of the text could not be found by immanent analysis. One had to go beyond the text. Lest the true meaning of the text should elude him, the reader must plumb the impenetrable depth of the author's spiritual experience. In this effort the reader could not be guided by hard and fast rules. There are few laws of uniformity in the act of creation; the work of art acquires its value from the individuality, uniqueness, irregularity of the experience from which it is born. Unless the reader was capable of similar experience, the meaning of art would forever remain for him a closed book. To grasp the meaning, the reader had to employ his imagination, and be sure that his imagination is rich and flexible enough to be truly commensurate with that of the artist.

To remain true to its task, hermeneutics had now to extend its concerns beyond the faithful description and structural analysis of the text. It had to interpret, to advance hypotheses regarding the hidden meaning of the text. The text itself could only advise the reader as to the plausibility of his interpretation; it could not offer conclusive proof that the choice had been right. Indeed, one could establish whether descriptions were true or false; but one could at best speak of the 'plausibility' or 'implausibility' of interpretations. The methods of philology, so helpful in the test of authenticity, could not suffice when the real meaning was perceived to be located somewhere 'beneath' the text proper, of an entirely different nature from the text itself. Philological critique remained an integral part of hermeneutics, though of an auxiliary status. The main attention of hermeneutics shifted to the truly 'frontier' area, the interpretation of meaning. There the methodological questions arose which presented difficulties never confronted before, and which threatened to undermine the very foundation of social science.

Social science developed, throughout the nineteenth and well into the twentieth century, 'in the shadow of the triumphs of natural science'.[1]* These triumphs were spectacular and convincing. In the dazzling splendour of technological accomplishment for which natural science rightly claimed credit and from which it drew ever-renewed supplies of confidence, shadowy corners of doubt were barely discernible. The preachers of the new social science, cut to the measure of the new self-reliant age, dreamt of emulating, in social knowledge, 'the same kind of sensational illumination and explanatory power already yielded up by the sciences of nature'.[2]

The visible achievements of natural science were too headstrong

*Superior figures refer to the Notes, pages 247–59.

and intoxicating for their enthusiasts to waste time in hole-picking – or, indeed, in reflecting upon the suitability of the natural scientists' approach for the study of social life. Neither was the time propitious (at any rate at the beginning) for meditating on the exact nature and intrinsic limits of the 'scientific method' as such; philosophers of science came nowhere near the level of subtlety and self-awareness reached much later by philosophers of science like Bachelard or Popper. This was an age of exuberance, and the optimistic self-image which befits such an age did not allow for obstacles to human mastery over the world other than those temporarily erected by the sinful sluggishness of human inventiveness and ingenuity.

One feature revealed by even the most superficial look at the natural-scientific success story was the spectacular absence in the scientific accounts of the category of 'purpose'. Natural science gradually developed a language in which exhaustive accounts could be given without any reference to 'will', 'purpose', 'intention'. This new quality of scientific language had been expressed by Comte as the supercession of the 'theological' or 'metaphysical' by the 'positive'; the many who were unaware of Comte's terminology would speak of the triumph of secular sobriety over religious illusion. Not that the natural scientist had to be an agnostic in order to produce scientific results; but his results were scientific in so far as they talked about 'what had to happen' and left no room for an essentially voluntaristic 'divine purpose' which, in principle, could deprive phenomena of their observed and recorded regularity. Natural science could be defined almost by the absence of miracles and, indeed, of anything bizarre and extraordinary, suggestive of a conscious, deliberative, scheming and intending subject. In this approach the 'understanding' of phenomena collapsed into 'explaining'. Without 'meaning' in the sense of purpose, 'understanding', i.e. the intellectual grasp of the logic of phenomena, was one with their 'explanation', i.e. the demonstration of the general rules and specific conditions which made the occurrence of given phenomena inevitable. Only this kind of 'understanding' seemed compatible with a science of society aspiring to emulate the magnificent accomplishments of the science of nature.

To this emerging concept of a 'natural science of the social', hermeneutics, inspired by the Romantic vision of creation, presented a serious challenge. Indeed, it questioned the very possibility that we could cleanse our knowledge of the social by taking away the consideration of purpose. True, we ought to stop the vain search for 'design' and 'objective' in nature; if there was such a design and such an objective, it would not be ours, human, in the first place – and thus it was futile to hope that we would ever be able to grasp it. This, however, does not apply to human affairs. Here the presence of design and objectives is unquestionable. Men and women do what they do on purpose. Social phenomena, since they are ultimately acts of men and women, demand to be understood in a different way than by mere explaining. Understanding them must contain an element missing from the explaining of natural phenomena: the retrieval of purpose, of intention, of the unique configuration of thoughts and feelings which preceded a social phenomenon and found its only manifestation, imperfect and incomplete, in the observable consequences of action. To understand a human act, therefore, was to grasp the meaning with which the actor's intention invested it; a task, as could be easily seen, essentially different from that of natural science.

Whoever agreed with this suggestion of hermeneutics was immediately confronted with a number of fundamental difficulties. The most haunting was the legitimate doubt that the study of the social could ever rise to the level of precision and exactitude, the 'explanatory power', which had come to be associated with science. The Romantic image of the work of art served as a pattern for the model of social action in general; the acts of writing and of reading, of acting and of interpreting action, seemed to belong to the same family and to bear a strong family resemblance. To understand the work of art was to recover the artist's design, a labour of art in itself; to interpret any human act was to re-create the actor's web of motives and intentions. Both cases required above all the forging of affinity into shared experience, a sort of sympathetic self-identification with another human being. Like the essentially voluntaristic, design-oriented act which was to be understood, the imaginative sympathy which was to bring about such an understanding could not be reduced to a set of rules which eliminated the role played by subjective purpose and purpose-subordinated decisions. Thus understanding was an art, rather than a science.

The artistic rather than scientific nature of understanding was a natural obstacle to the consensus of interpretations, a first essential step in the construction of a communal activity called science. Even during the periods of rift and dissent which punctuate the history of every science, its practitioners can derive comfort and confidence from the belief that there are, or can be found, some specific rules of conduct which will command communal agreement and thereby secure a communal consensus for the result. The notion of such rules does nor square well with the image of artistic creation. Faced with the necessity to choose between several competing interpretations, practitioners of hermeneutics could not easily refer to impersonal rules which could govern thoroughly a personal act of sympathetic insight and self identification. The constitution of the consensus of interpretation appeared to present complications unheard of in the science of nature.

This difficulty, considerable in itself, was a relatively minor irritant compared with the complexity of the question of truth. The nineteenth-century image of science went beyond the aim of reaching a consensus that specific results were valid 'beyond reasonable doubt'. It was an integral part of the image, and an important reason for the prestige natural science enjoyed, that the validity of results had a foundation more solid and lasting than the consensus of science's current practitioners; that, in other words, the rules which found a consensus here and now can as well support a reasonable hope that the results are conclusive, final. The results of natural science were seen, in principle, not just as universally accepted, but as true, that is, likely to be accepted forever. This belief was based on the laboriously observed impersonality of the operations which led, in communally controllable fashion, to the formulation of results. However important the role of individual genius, insight, lucky accident or flash of inspiration in *articulating* the new idea, there must be a set of universal rules (which specifically did not hinge on unique, personal factors) employed in *validating* the claim of the idea to the status of truth. Science was seen as an utterly legal-rational, therefore impersonal and democratic, activity. Discovery was a matter of genius or talent, but validation was founded on rules which could be applied by everybody who mastered the publicly accessible skills, and which therefore avoided the differences arising from the personalities of scientists. Validation was, therefore, thoroughly impersonal; as personal factors did not intervene in its process, there were no obvious reasons to doubt that whatever had been validated would remain valid for successive generations of scholars.

It was obvious, however, that the validation of the interpretations of meaning could not easily be raised to the level of impersonality or, indeed, the hoped-for a-temporality, achieved by natural-scientific findings. Hermeneutics saw 'understanding' as residing in a sort of 'spiritual unification' of the writer and the reader, the actor and his interpreter. Unification, whether achievable or not, was bound to start from a specific, always to an extent unique, historical and biographical position. Even if interpreters could find the means to neutralize the personal differences between them, they would still remain 'historically enclosed' by the volume and type of experience made available to them by tradition. Consensus, therefore, would not guarantee truth. The resources used in validating their interpretations could, at best, be impersonal only within the given stage of history. Impersonality was not, in this case, equivalent to a-temporality. On the contrary, the impersonality of the act of interpretation (and, consequently, the chance of a consensus between interpreters) could only be conceived as resting on the shared participation of interpreters in the same historical tradition; on their drawing resources from the same pool of shared historical experience. It seemed that the consensus could only be temporary, tradition-bound, and therefore organically incapable of meeting the standards of truth. The very foundation of its attainment and validation, as consensus, precluded its treatment as a-temporal and conclusive.

In short, the challenge of hermeneutics to the idea that social sciences should measure up to the standards of cogency and authority of the natural sciences consisted of two problems: that of consensus and that of truth. Accordingly, social science, in asserting its scientific status, was bound to prove that its rules of consensus and its standards of truth for the interpretation of meaning could attain a cogency comparable to that achieved in the study of nature. This book is dedicated to a discussion of the most eminent attempts to offer such a proof.

To be sure, the continuous efforts to parry the challenge of hermeneutics do not exhaust the history of sociology. A powerful current within social science (dominant in the nineteenth century, and by no means marginal in the twentieth) is either oblivious to the challenge or stubbornly belittles its seriousness. This current derives its confidence from the assumption that no significant difference exists between the situations in which the natural and social sciences operate. The assumption is defended on one of two grounds: that 'subjective meanings', intentions, motives and similar 'internal' experiences are not accessible to observation and therefore ought to be left out of scientific study, whose only legitimate object is observable behaviour; or that subjective factors present no methodological problem of their own, since they can be fully reduced to external phenomena, amenable to normal scientific treatment. The right to deny the challenge of hermeneutics is justified by the view that the subjective aspect of social life either presents no special problem to scientific study, or – inasmuch as it does – ought to be left where it belongs, in the domain of poetry or philosophy. It is not the task of this book to deal with the school of sociology which stems from this attitude. Only such standpoints have been selected for analysis which admit that the subjective aspect of social, as distinct from natural, phenomena does present a problem of unusual complexity but which, however, hope to find a solution which will either neutralize its impact or will reconcile social science to its inescapable fate: the necessity to remain tradition-bound and to proclaim admittedly relative and temporal assertions. These standpoints consider relativity of knowledge as a problem particularly acute in the study of the social.

The unintended effect of my criteria of selection is that this book favours ideas developed within the predominantly German intellectual tradition, while paying relatively less attention to the French. The French fathers of modern social science took little notice of the peculiarity of social reality as conditioned by the subjective character of social action, and were largely unconcerned with the resulting complexity of research strategy. They remained strikingly unimpressed by the soul-searching analyses of philosophical hermeneutics; indeed, one can follow the development of French sociology from Saint-Simon to Durkheim, Halbwachs or even Mauss while neglecting the presence, across the Rhine, of concerns which the hermeneutical tradition forced social scientists to regard as their own. Neither Comte nor Durkheim, nor the most eminent among their heirs, were seriously worried by the danger of relativity in the study of the social; still less were they inclined to suspect that relativity might be a chronic affliction resistant to all known medicine. Believing that social facts are 'things' like all others, i.e. that they exist in their own right as real entities 'out there', outside the realm of individual experience, they naturally concluded, first, that one can study social realities without necessarily looking at the processes of their social production and, second, that whoever does this study with proper method and diligence will certainly arrive at the same results. This is, after all, how the activity of the natural sciences was seen in the nineteenth century. Faithful to the unbroken French rationalist tradition, they regarded true knowledge as, above all (if not solely), the question of method and of its systematic application. The cognizing reason and the object of its scrutiny were not made of the same stuff nor subject to the same laws. Autonomous and attentive only to the rules of logic, reason (including its sociological brand) was viewed as immune by and large to the historical or other constraints (indeed, historical concreteness) typical of its object. Reason, in short, was not a part of the social reality it was bent on studying.

This was, exactly, the assumption challenged by the German intellectual tradition, in which reflections upon hermeneutic activity and problems played a dominant part. There, the interpretation of social reality came to be revealed as a conversation between one historical era and another, or between one communally founded tradition and another; even an 'inside', immanent study of one's own social reality was accordingly regarded as a particular case of the tradition-bound activity of understanding. To anyone concerned with reaching an objectively valid knowledge of the social, relativism was a real danger, which could not be staved off simply by discarding wrong methods, or by being sceptical towards uncontrolled assumptions and 'evidencies'. Both partners of the conversation called 'understanding' or 'interpretation' were historically specific and tradition-bound, and the study of the social could only be seen as an endless process of re-evaluation and recapitulation, rather than a bold step from ignorance to truth. In an excellent characterization by Isaiah Berlin, Germany during the Romantic era held that human forms of life 'could be felt, or intuited, or understood by a species of direct acquaintance; they could not be taken to pieces and re-assembled, even in thought, like a mechanism compounded of isolable parts, obedient to universal and unaltering causal laws'. Due to contingencies of their own history, going back at least to the Reformation, German thinkers of the era 'were acutely aware of the differences between their world and the universalism and scientific rationalism deeply embedded in the outlook of the civilisations west of the Rhine'.[3]

It can be shown that the heretofore technical discipline of hermeneutics had been given its new philosophical depth and theoretical relevance mainly by the powerful vision of Hegel's philosophy. No philosophical system before Hegel was nearly as successful in condensing reason and its object, knowledge and history, into a monolithic unity; and in presenting their separation and opposition as merely a moment of development, to be transcended when history runs its course. In Hegel's philosophy, consciousness of each historical era is a stage in the progress of reason coming to know itself and gradually discovering itself as the only 'essence' of being: 'The whole process of History . . . is directed to rendering this unconscious impulse a conscious one.' Through the historical activities of peoples, Reason 'completes itself into a self-comprehending totality'. The effort aimed at self-comprehension is, simultaneously, the consummation of Reason.[4] History and its understanding become essentially the same process; the understanding of the past, the effort to penetrate and to capture the meaning of human deeds is itself history. Acting as an agent of this understanding, the historian is subject to the logic of history. He has no transcendental ground from which to contemplate the process of which he is irretrievably a part. He can see as much as can be seen from his position in the process.

This realization has been reflected in philosophical hermeneutics in the notion of 'hermeneutic circle'. Understanding means going in circles: rather than a unilinear progress towards better and less vulnerable knowledge, it consists of an endless recapitulation and reassessment of collective memories – ever more voluminous, but always selective. It is difficult to see how any of the successive recapitulations can claim to be final and conclusive; still more difficult would be to substantiate this claim. The plight came to be seen as specific to the study of the social, presenting the 'understanding' sciences with problems unknown to the science bent on mere 'explaining'.

The development of hermeneutical ideas through the nineteenth century reached its culmination in the work of Wilhelm Dilthey, where they found their most profound and – in a sense – extreme expression. A brilliant philosopher and a masterly historian, Dilthey arrived, it seemed, as far as one could go with the notion of the historical, and tradition-bound nature of understanding. As the most thorough exploration of the activity of understanding led Dilthey to abandon his initial hope of providing history with a finite set of stern methodological, truth-generating rules – the inherent 'inconclusiveness' of understanding seemed to be conclusively demonstrated. This challenge had to be faced, or else social science would have to surrender its claim to scientific results. This book is concerned with the major strategies employed by those who agreed that the question of valid knowledge of the social cannot be resolved without facing the queries raised by hermeneutical reflection.

We shall start from the discussion of strategies developed by Marx, Weber, and Mannheim. All the conspicuous differences between them notwithstanding, the three great sociologists share one prominent feature: they all worked, by and large, within the Hegelian theme of 'history coming to understand itself'; or, more simply, history bringing to pass conditions in which not just an interpretation of its diverse manifestations but the *true* interpretation becomes possible, or inescapable. They all agreed that these conditions did not exist in the past; but all three looked hopefully to the present, or to the immediate future, for a cognitive situation qualitatively different, and sharply better than all past vantage points of interpretation. All three found their conviction, that a true knowledge of the social is accessible, in the already accomplished, or imminent transformations of the fabric of society: they viewed the merger of understanding and science as an end to which both cognition and its object must move.

Karl Marx translated the Hegelian theory of history and knowledge from the philosophical language to the language of sociology. This had been done already before Dilthey drew full methodological conclusions from Hegelian theory enclosed in the philosophical discourse alone. Though preceding Dilthey chronologically, Marx was, therefore, ahead of Dilthey in realizing that the problem of true understanding of a history which is itself historical can be resolved, if at all, as a sociological problem: as such it is a transformation of human community which renders it both amenable to, and capable of, objective understanding. Max Weber, unlike Karl Marx, was confronted with the work of Dilthey in which the historicality of understanding had been explored to the full and presented as, in fact, the perpetual predicament of humanities. Weber had, therefore, to engage directly the question of the scientific nature of social study as dependent on the plausibility of an objective understanding of an essentially subjective reality. While facing a relatively new adversary and a novel task, Weber could however draw from the findings of Marx and his 'sociological translation'. It was Weber who brought Marx's sociological theory, shaped in the argument with Hegel's historicism, into a direct relevance to hermeneutical debate.

A major proposition Dilthey firmly established in the methodology of humanities was that essential 'commensurability' of the two traditions who meet in the act of understanding is a necessary condition of the validity of interpretation. Accordingly, Weber's task consisted of the demonstration that our society (in its tendency, if not yet in its actuality) makes the fulfilment of this condition highly plausible. For the first time in history the subject and the object of understanding meet on the ground of rationality – this most prominent feature of the truth-seeking activity which we call science. Objective knowledge is rational knowledge; one can, therefore, objectively understand human actions as they are, and in as far as they can be viewed as, rational actions. But rational action does become the dominant mode of conduct in the modern society.

This last proposition, however, has been denied by Karl Mannheim. In his own analysis of the structural conditions of knowledge in modern society rationality did not emerge as a mode of thinking on the way to dominance and universality. On the contrary, having traced the divergence of meanings back to its source – to the very fact of social structure, the positional differentiation of society – Mannheim concluded that partiality, distortion and contention are and will remain a universal feature of social knowledge and stand in the way of understanding between various groups of society. History has brought nearer the chance of a truth-based consensus not because the conduct of society at large is becoming more rational, but because within the structure of the society a unique group, the intellectuals, has been brought into being which is determined by its structural location to think and act rationally. It is this group which can (or, rather, is bound to) merge the understanding into science. The intellectuals are to act as a sort of collective messiah, bringing the truth into human understanding.

The same role, albeit without reference to changing social structure or, indeed, to history – has been assigned by Edmund Husserl to the activity of philosophical analysis. Husserl sought to solve the problem of true understanding within the context of human knowledge as such, rather than as a question peculiar to the knowledge of the social. Husserl tended to merge science into the universal activity of understanding, rather than the other way round. Instead of showing how the understanding of human action can reach the precision of scientific knowledge, he demonstrated that all knowledge, science included, is ultimately founded on the activity of understanding, where its validity is, or ought to be, grounded.

In Husserl, hermeneutical discourse incorporates the French–Cartesian legacy of rationalism. The encounter has far-reaching consequences: the hope that meanings can be adequately grasped is now seen to reside in the possibility of freeing the meaning from its tradition-bound context, instead of meeting it there, in its 'natural' habitat. Historically and structurally determined tradition can only produce understanding inherently protean and contingent. Meanings can be grasped in their apodictic, absolute truth only outside that tradition, where they can be rooted in soil on which history and structural divisions have no impact. Husserl postulates 'transcendental subjectivity' as such a soil, as a sort of extra-historical 'community of meanings' which generates and sustains phenomena in the only relevant mode of existence – in the mode of 'being known'. True meanings can be glimpsed only if one gets access to this 'transcendental subjectivity'. This can be done by a phenomenological contemplation of 'pure meanings', as disclosed by the experience of phenomena laid bare of their historical–structural guise.

It will be shown that the sociology of Talcott Parsons is an attempt by applying Husserl's precepts to reach an understanding of human action which will be largely independent of the historical–structural contexts of meaning. Starting from the phenomenon of social action in its given state of 'being known', Parsons proceeds to disclose the action's transcendental, apodictically predicated features, which include the presence of society and a cultural system. With all its intrinsic meaning fully revealed and articulated, social action acquires an 'immanent' framework in which its meaning is founded and in which it can be objectively grasped. While admitting that human action is a meaningful entity which ought to be understood, one can now proceed to study it objectively – as it must be, rather than as it happens to be in this or that tradition-bound context.

Some of Husserl's major tenets, however, have been objected to and revised by Heidegger. Above all, the fundamental supposition that meanings, understanding and interpretation can be founded in a universe other than 'life-world', the world of existence, has been put in doubt. Meanings are constituted, and understanding is called for and accomplished, not in the act of pure, a-historical contemplation, which is always an activity within a tradition, and an activity which consists in recapitulating this tradition. Truth, though by no means dissolved in a mere communal consensus, becomes now a feature of existence-disclosing-itself, rather than a relation between existence and something (like a proposition turned out by a detached work of reason) which stands out outside existence. The demon of relativism is deprived of much of its terror by showing that the notion of truth cannot be sensibly grounded outside the tradition-bound context; therefore, the failure so to ground it should no longer haunt the conscience of men of science.

Schutz and ethnomethodology are discussed in this book as examples of the hermeneutically conscious sociology which operates within the Heideggerian framework of life-world as the ultimate foundation, and the only habitat, of meanings and of the activity of understanding. Here the community of interacting members is shown as a universe powerful enough, and the only universe able, to establish, to sustain in life, and to warrant interpretation of meanings. In a sense, the search for an adequate response to the challenge of hermeneutics has come full circle; ethnomethodology brings us back to the square one, to the realization that all meaning and understanding is essentially 'inside'.

The search did not stop with the advent of ethnomethodology and is not likely to stop. Our story is inconclusive, as no solution to the challenge of hermeneutics has yet succeeded in eliciting a consensus and escaped criticism of its own peculiar limitations.

Some recent suggestions as to how the relationship of consensus and truth could be satisfactorily posited and explored are surveyed in the last part of the book. It is the author's view that these suggestions indicate an interesting line of exploration, perhaps the most mature to date, and an exciting role for the social sciences to play. But this book is not a story with a beginning, complete plot and – above all – a conclusive (happy) end. It ought to be read as a progress-report of a debate still far from its end. The book has no ambition even to present a full history of the debate. Instead, major (and still influential) attitudes taken in the course of the debate are recalled and systematically presented, if possible each in its purest and most pronounced form. Leaving out of the story the many 'intermediate', compromise or eclectic solutions sharpens the distinct character and originality of the theories discussed. To an extent, chapters of the book are self-contained essays in their own right and can be consulted separately, if, for example, Weber's or Parsons's response to the challenge of hermeneutics is sought.

My debt to both the criticism and the encouragement of Anthony Giddens exceeds what the inevitably formal words of gratitude can express. I have been lucky as well in having Robert Shreeve as editor and publisher, and Gianfranco Poggi as attentive and critical reader of the manuscript. It would be impossible to overstate the help and inspiration I owe to Janet Wolff, Richard Kilminster, Robert Tristram, Joseph Bleicher, Kevin Dobson and other participants of the friendly though principled debate which constitutes and sustains the sociological community of Leeds.

Zygmunt Bauman

1 The rise of hermeneutics

It was the guiding idea of hermeneutics in Germany during the nineteenth century that – like the individual – every cultural system, every community, has a focal point within itself.[1] This focal point is constituted, above all, by a conception of reality and its evaluation.

This view of the community was a fair reflection of a century-long practice of historians, above all German historians, generated and sustained by the mood of Romanticism. This is how, indeed, historiography was performed – as a vivid insight into the mind of the nation viewed as a collective subject, complete with intuitive longings, emotions, a sense of unique destiny, distinctively individual colourings of world perception. Historical works of the era read like psychological treatises, so replete are they with terms either borrowed directly from psychology or otherwise calculated to send the reader's imagination into the unfathomable depths of the Spirit.

It is difficult to say whether the Romantic conception of the work of art inflamed the imagination of Romantic historians, or the other way round. But surely both fed, at least in part, on the rising German nationalism – an ideology all the more passionate and compelling for its role as an overture to, and a temporary substitute for, the national state, rather than its spiritual adornment. Unlike the enthusiastic preachers of the *Machtstaat* later in the century, the German patriots of the Romantic era had no political structure or state-generated symbolism to fall back on. For the lack of better-defined objects, they turned to the elusive, intangible *Volksseele* with the same natural ease with which their successors would turn to the all-too-tangible powers of the Prussian *Kaiserdom*; and they sought to ground their nationalist urge in a continuity of spiritual tradition with the same matter-of-factness with which their successors would ground it in the claims of the *Staaträson*. It was *'der deutsche Stamm'* which, in Schlegel's words, was *'alt und stark'*. It was, correspondingly, 'the original moral character of a people, its customs, its peculiarities', which 'must be regarded as sacred'.[2] The inscrutable and impenetrable, but stubborn and indomitable 'spirit of the people' was the only fount from which history could draw its meaning and human life its value. History in general, and the most imposing and memorable of its works in particular, had all been made of this sole creative stuff.

Herder called Germany the '*Reich* of ten peoples'. The Germans of the early nineteenth century did not face their nationhood as an aspect of nature, as a fact of life, the presence of which did not depend on reflection and active appropriation. On the contrary, Germans faced their nationhood as a fully spiritual phenomenon, to be intellectually grasped before it could be possessed. Herder called his contemporaries to search for the essence of their nationhood by digging deep into the rich lore of ancient songs as the earliest and the purest expression of the nation's creative spirit. Fichte sought the mystery of Germany's historical fate in the unique psychic traits of German people: *Charakter haben und deutsch sein* undoubtedly meant the same.[3] Spirit came to fill the empty centre of the stateless nation; lacking the kings whose chronicle could form the subject of historiography, 'the people' usurped naturally the vacant role as history's subject. Like all subjects, they were seen as spiritual beings, moved by thought and emotions, acting of their own decisions, bearers (at least potentially) of *poïein* (doing) rather than *paschein* (suffering). Unlike other subjects, however, the people were many and anonymous. The individual psyche still served as their prototype, but it could be accommodated to the new purpose only if subjected to a subtle transformation: what had been an individual's property became a supra-individual power; what had been the individual *Seele* turned into a collective *Geist*, and later *Kultur*; what had been a name for individual autonomy and freedom became the theoretical expression of the individual's submission to a larger community, the *Volks-* or *Zeit-geist* which no individual could transcend, as only inside it could he fulfil his individuality.

All the same, at least on the surface, the similarity between the two was striking. In the Romantics' view, the artist represented the human individual at his best, the human spirit at its highest reaches. And as for the substance of artistic work, 'all art begins with a state of mind and ends with a work of art', which was always an objectified residue of 'an attempt on the artist's part to discover the formal equivalent of a state of mind.[4] Artistic creation is, therefore, a struggle between the artist's vision and the medium, adamant to shrug off the form the artist wishes to impose. The work is a compromise between the two. But of the two elements who meet to beget it, only one carries the seed of life and meaning; the second is sheer stubbornness, pure negativity capable only of distortion, never of creation. If one wishes, therefore, to reach the original, pure meaning of the work of art, one has to go beyond the product, beyond the object itself, back into the 'state of mind' in which the artist's vision, this sole spring of all meaning, still enjoyed pristine purity. To understand a work of art, in other words, is to reconstruct the artist's intention which the artistic object, its end-product, could only deliver in a modified, mediated, and necessarily ambiguous form. The intention is always richer than its tangible traces, as these are invariably residues of its defeats.

If we now turn to the Romantic vision of artistic work (and remember, the artist is the fullest embodiment of human potency) projected at the large screen of history, we find strikingly similar patterns of thought anchored, however, in a 'collective artist' of creative nation. National institutions, law, literature, forms of government, modes of family life and all the rest are seen as residues of the age-long work of the national genius: they all are supreme works of art of sorts; there is an artist's intention standing at their cradle, though the artist this time is the people, *Volk*, this uniquely German 'collective singular'. Gustav Hugo, in the eighteenth century, had already taught that law is a product of national genius; the idea was taken over by his famous disciple, Karl Friedrich Eichhorn, and explored in full in the monumental *History of German Law and Institutions*, the work which set the pattern for the whole of the nineteenth-century historiography. Karl von Savigny and Jacob Grimm quickly joined forces with Eichhorn and used all their considerable skill and brilliance to help the idea of law as the product of *Volksgeist* to turn into a common-sense truth for at least a century. It would reach its most impressive in the work of Karl Lamprecht, already Dilthey's contemporary, who impressed the learned public with a sweeping generalization of the century of the Romantic historiographic experience: what governs the history of any age is a unique conjunction of dominant psychical traits, the *Zeitgeist*, which shines through all significant historic events and ought to be recovered from them.

It was this practice of historiography, propped by the twin pillars of makeshift spiritual nationhood of a nation-in-search-of-a-state, and the romantic vision of creative work, which constituted the discursive formation inside which the nineteenth-century hermeneutic was born and sustained.

The author of the most comprehensive study of this hermeneutics, Joachim Wach,[5] traced the beginnings of virtually all the significant topics of hermeneutical discourse to Friedrich Ast (1778–1841), pushing back the birth-date of the modern theory of understanding well beyond Schleiermacher, its widely acclaimed father. Following the final victory of the 'moderns' over the 'ancients', the ancient world, complete with its artistic, philosophical and legal accomplishments, was for the first time confronted by Europe as a stage in its history, rather than a paragon of timeless perfection. The ancient world had been present in European consciousness throughout most of the middle ages and certainly from the outset of the modern era; but it had appeared before either as a ready-made, timeless pattern of superior achievement, or as a self-enclosed entity with few, if any, contiguous points with current events. Only when Europe woke up to its own historicity could ancient Greece and Rome be disclosed as historic societies, as Europe's past, as a contribution to Europe's tradition. Ast stood in the long line of philologists who tried hard to take full stock of the consequences of the new situation, who tried, above all, to articulate the overall task of assimilating the ancient message into the emerging European tradition as a series of methodological postulates.

What was, in their view, at stake was the restoration of truth beclouded or downright distorted by centuries of scholastic treatment; or, as Ast would put it, the problem of *Verständnis* versus *Missverständnis* (understanding versus misunderstanding).

In confronting the task, Ast spelled out all the major problems which were to remain in the very centre of hermeneutic thought for many years. Above all, the very notion of understanding had been given the truly Romantic interpretation which came to be virtually identified with the idea of hermeneutics: '*die Erfassung des Geistes*',[6] the capture of the Spirit, which expresses itself in, and lives through, monuments of intellectual and artistic creation, as well as the ordinary forms of public life. The visible, tangible legacy of the past – texts, paintings, legal codes, recorded customs – had been thereby posited as *Äusserungen* – externalizations of the Spirit, sentient leftovers of Spirit's self-estrangement, documents of its expressive powers; the true object of understanding was however perceived as standing behind them, never exhausted by them, always fuller and richer than any of its expressions.

Ast, and several generations of hermeneuticians after him, hoped that the road could be traversed in both directions: since the objects of historical study emerge from the Spirit, where their untarnished prototype is stored, since they emanate from the inner depths of spiritual Being – there seems to be no reason why one could not, starting from the known objects, perform a return intellectual journey back to the starting-point, from the objects to their spiritual origins, from the blurred copies to the pristine clarity of the proto-type. Hermeneutics, at least at this early stage, was self-confident, not to say light-hearted, about the difficulties that venture might involve.

This self-confidence was grounded philosophically on the assump-tion of essential unity of the Spirit. It had been accepted that no understanding is possible between totally strange, unconnected worlds. (Wittgenstein would later say: if lions could speak, we would not understand them.) If there is any understanding, its very presence contains already the proof of a primeval unity and unifor-mity of the spiritual element hiding behind the messages. In Goethe's words, which Wach quotes as consonant with Ast's idea,

> *Wär' nicht das Auge sonnenhaft,*
> *Die Sonne könnt es nie erblicken,*
> *läg' nicht in uns des Gottes eigne Kraft,*
> *wie könnt uns Göttliches entzücken?*

> Were not the eye sunny,
> It would not descry the sun;
> Had not we divine power,
> How could the Divine enchant us?

A total strangeness would be totally numb. There is no under-standing without affinity of spirits. *Dem Verwandten erschliesst sich das Verwandte*[7] – any object can disclose its meaning only to a kindred spirit. We can reach in our effort to understand only such objects as have been begotten of essentially the same Spirit which saturates our own thought. If the opacity of objects strikes us as a disturbance of what should be a clear and unimpeded perception, if it urges us to bridge the gap between us and the object, to 'restore' true understanding – it is only because our estrangement is relative and temporary, one component being temporarily out of touch with the spiritual developments of the other.

All understanding, therefore, starts from the establishing of an affinity between its subject and object; or, rather, between two subjects, standing respectively at the beginning and at the end of communication. We can rescue the meaning of antiquity from oblivion in as far as our Spirit forms a unity with the Spirit of the ancient Greece or Rome; a unity perhaps temporarily disturbed, marred by a transient estrangement, but unity all the same, struggling against all odds for its own restoration. What applies to antiquity can in fact be extended to mankind as a whole. However insuperable the differentiation of the human species may seem from a short distance, a truly historical perspective will justly reduce it to a middle stage which separates the primeval from the future unity. Everything in human history has emanated from the common Spirit and everything will return to the common Spirit in the end.

The interpreter (a historian, a philologist, a theorist of art) has a crucial role in this journey of the human Spirit back to its original unity. He is, in a sense, a cultural broker, mediating between ages and nations, and bringing about the gradual re-unification of divided humanity. He becomes, therefore, a genuine agent of history: it is he who unwinds the knots tied up by the spontaneous and unsystematic action of the Spirit. If the Spirit, following its insatiable creative urge, externalizes itself in its own creations, and so hides its universality behind a multitude of its own particular incarnations, the hermeneutician unravels the concealed spiritual content of the Spirit's works, and thereby restores the totality lost in the particular. The hermeneutician is, in a way, forced to do this. It is not a matter of free choice in the method of action – even less a question of preferred cultural ideal. Understanding as such can be achieved only by 'universalizing' anew the Spirit hidden in the endless variety of human cultural creation. The famous 'hermeneutic circle' (another idea which Wach credits to Ast) is not a particularly ingenious and effective method of study; it is, in actual fact, the very logic of understanding as such. There is no understanding of history apart from the perpetual movement from the particular to the total and back to the particular, in order to render transparent what previously, in its uncompromised particularity, was impervious to our interpretation. One would rather speak of a hermeneutic spiral, to be sure: in our search of the lost affinity, in our urge to re-appropriate fully estranged creations of the kindred Spirit, we never really finish our job. But we move from the particular to the universal and back in ever-widening circles, ever closer to the ideal of the Spirit once again, but this time self-consciously, unified.

It was left to Schleiermacher, an active member of the Romantic movement, a personal friend of Schlegel, Novalis, Herz, and Mendelssohn, to bring these ideas into systematic order and thereby to lay the foundations of historical hermeneutics. Schleiermacher's contribution, above all, was to extend the notion of hermeneutics and hermeneutic circle beyond the confines of philology, exegesis, art criticism. Like Hegel, though naturally in a different way, he brought the problem of understanding and interpretation into the very centre of universal human experience; in Wach's words, he located them in the practice of living, in daily life, in lived experience.[8] With Schleiermacher, hermeneutics ceased to be a philologist's analysis of the texts left by other writers: it became the question of a member of one culture struggling to grasp the experience of another, a denizen of one historical era trying to embrace another era's practice of life, its 'quotidianity', the kind of experience which can be conveyed only by the German word '*Erlebnis*'. One can easily see the Romantic origin of this remarkable shift of attention. Romanticism's paramount legacy – the elusive, polysemic notions of '*Leben*' and '*Erlebnis*', have from then on haunted forever the self-reflection of humanities.

There was another innovation for which Schleiermacher was responsible – one of perhaps yet greater import. In Gadamer's words,[9]

Schleiermacher's particular contribution is psychological interpretation. It is ultimately a divinatory process, a placing of oneself within the mind of the author, an apprehension of the 'inner origin' of the composition of a work, a recreation of the creative act. Thus understanding is a reproduction related to an original production, a knowing of what has been known (Boeckh), a reconstruction that starts from the vital moment of conception, the 'germinal decision' as the composition's point of organization.

This means placing squarely the sought-for meaning of the act in its actor's project. To understand this meaning, one has to literally 'identify' oneself with the actor. Sympathy is his major tool of impersonation. The idea of 'losing oneself' in the course of cognition, to forget oneself in order to 'remember' other people's meanings, the strategy of bias-free investigation in terms of 'indigenous categories' – are all germinally contained in Schleiermacher's programme of '*psychologische Interpretation*'. Only germinally, to be sure. Schleiermacher's psychology was unaware of late-nineteenth-century introspective ambitions and did not define itself as the quest for 'inner' thought and feeling. It did not ask 'How did the intention look to its holder?' 'What did the actor feel when he experienced this or that?' Schleiermacher's psychology was akin rather to those 'humanistic' views of the human psyche which people like Maslow, Murray or Biswanger would develop, in their respective ways almost a century and a half later. Psychology meant to Schleiermacher the art of perceiving an act as an organic part of the totality of *Leben*.

The postulate of psychological interpretation means simply that hermeneutics is to accomplish, with sustained and methodical effort, what ordinary conversationalists achieve without noticing and as a matter of course. When two persons communicate by talking, their words are woven into the texture of life they share (since they talk and understand each other); their words, therefore, come to them not as isolated sounds, but as inseparable elements of the totality of their common life. The words' manifold entanglements and multiple references are known and therefore seldom give reason for inquiry. The speech solves the problem of its comprehensibility using its own resources, and does it in passing, in the course of its own development, seldom stopping to reflect upon its accomplishment. This is possible thanks to the immediacy of speech. The speech is normally coherent with the rest of life, in its 'natural habitat', allowing no mistake as to its correct location. Hence its transparency: life shows through the words. Words reveal life at the first hearing. Correct understanding is achieved without interpretation. The end and the means blend into one.

A written text, a work of art in the town square or in the museum, a code of law or a ritual – unlike direct speech – do present the problem of understanding-through-interpretation, because they have lost the original link with life which accorded them meaning. What appears to us as the opacity of phenomena whose meaning escapes us is our ignorance of their natural context, of the form of life which pumps blood into their veins and makes them throb with meaning. Incorporating the act in the totality of life, which in speech is achieved effortlessly, here demands special and purposeful action. It is this action which Schleiermacher defines as 'psychological interpretation'. His psychology, as we can see, means above all treating an act as an element in the totality of life; psychological interpretation, accordingly, means restoration of this lost, forgotten, or misconceived totality.

Leben therefore comes to replace the *Geist* as both the central ontological concept and the leading methodological principle. The postulate of hermeneutic circle undergoes a similar transformation:

it will consist now of a laborious construction of the totality of life, which is simultaneously unknown and not available to direct insight, out of the odds and bits of life which are sentiently accessible, but yet incomprehensible. The circle starts from the divination of the totality to which the confronted element belongs; if the guess is correct, the element in question reveals part of its meaning, which in turn gives us the lead toward a better, fuller, more specific reconstruction of totality. The process goes on, in ever wider circles, until we are satisfied that the residue of opacity still left in our object does not bar us from appropriating its meaning.

Interpretation, therefore, is considerably more laborious and difficult than the sort of understanding which speakers reach without resorting to reflection. On the other hand, however, the prospects of knowledge and understanding it opens are considerably broader. Since speech contains its own interpretation, or rather achieves understanding without its help, it seldom, if ever, faces the speakers with the task of consciously scanning the totality of the life-context in which their speech makes sense. The context is too trivially obvious to be noticeable, to congeal into an estranged object, to offer resistance. For the facility of their task the speakers pay a penalty in their ignorance concerning the full context of their action.

The modern reader easily recognizes in this idea Garfinkel's concept of those innumerable 'for granteds' which are ineradicably, though invisibly, present in the simplest act of conversation. To Schleiermacher, such 'for granteds' intertwine to weave the tissue of life, but neither weft nor woof can be sketched by those inside it. Only from the vantage point of an outside observer does the tissue become visible in its totality, so its exact plan can be drawn. Hence Schleiermacher's famous assertion of the cognitive superiority of the interpreter over the author. Inevitably, and in no relation to his own intellectual virtues, the interpreter knows more of the life texture of which the particular element under scrutiny is a part. He knows more not because his methods are better; not because he has been better trained in the special skills of the art of interpretation; not even for being 'wiser after the fact', or for having accumulated experience which the original author naturally lacked. He knows more purely and simply because he, unlike the author, confronts the object as an object, from the outside, as a strange phenomenon: this mode of confrontation sets the process of interpretation in motion and can, therefore, lead to the reconstruction of the totality of life. In principle nothing stops the author from embarking on such a journey of interpretation; but once he starts on the journey, he loses his specific relation of 'author' to his work, and joins the long line of fellow interpreters. As long as he clings to his original position of author, i.e. as long as he refuses to confront his work 'from the outside', he occupies no privileged position in the interpretive debate; his views are no better, no more reliable evidence than all the other data about the life-context in which his work has been located.

To Wilhelm Dilthey, the great codifier of the nineteenth-century hermeneutic, the Spirit – this, simultaneously, the subject and the object of historical understanding – was already fully identical with the Romantic notion of *Leben*: this indefinable, irreducible to any other factors, primeval mode of human existence, prominent for its capacity of having experiences (vivid experiences, inner experiences, 'seen-from-inside' experiences, *Erlebnis* in its opposition to *Erfahrung*; experiences which underline whatever in *poïein* is different from *paschein*), of expressing these experiences in momentary or lasting, but always objectified and observable, events, and of re-appropriating such events in their experiential meaning. What for Romantics, however, was to be a universal mode of existing-in-the-world, the full development of genuine human potential fettered and hamstrung by the scientific illusion of the modern era – was for Dilthey the matter of a critique of historical reason,[10] of a method of historical cognition, the peculiar tool which men can employ in order to comprehend their own – but only their own – action. As Makkreel recently put it, it was Dilthey's hope to show that[11]

Romantics were right in claiming that some human form of intellectual intuition is possible, but wrong in thinking that nature could be so grasped. Nature is not a text to be interpreted for its concrete meaning, in the way human actions may be said comparable to historical documents or poetic expressions and analyzed for their significance.

Kant would deny the validity of insight, intuition, 'feeling through' as a method of scientific cognition. To Kant objectivity of scientific knowledge was an undisputable ideal, and objectivity is thinkable only in so far as the self 'becomes mute before the factual existence of the natural object; here a definite object is to be known, the subject directs itself toward it, striving for objective validity.[12] Only the sphere of freedom, of moral judgement, is one in which the self asserts itself above nature; but then this is not a sphere of science or, for that matter, of objective knowledge. Dilthey's ambitious project of the fourth *Critique*, of historical reason, aims at correcting Kant on this point. It is true that inspired divination in relation to nature is not a possibility open to the humans. A direct, unmediated insight into nature can be predicated only on God, and never as an attribute of men. In as far as nature can be thought of as the *Äusserung* of God's will, the 'externalization' of His intent, God, the author of nature, may be trusted with the ability to penetrate His own creation intuitively, 'to understand it', to recognize in it the will and the intention He knows intimately and without any mediation of externalized objects. But not men, who bump against nature in all the frozen, numb strangeness of an object whose origin, and therefore purpose, are bound to remain unknown forever; objects of hopeful guesses and perhaps intense beliefs, but never of objective knowledge.

Is not man, however, the *Deus occasionatus* Nicholas of Cusa told us about many centuries ago? Is not man every once in a while, 'on occasion', like God whenever man makes his free choices and therefore behaves like the creator? And is not history the field in which occasions for free choice arise as a matter of rule? Is not therefore the case that the unique facility of insight, attributed to God alone in relation to the world as a whole, can be still ascribed to man in the more modest field of human history? If history is of man's making, men can recognize themselves in its externalized products just as much as God can recognize Himself in the world. God can understand the world, but men can understand history. The Romantic hope of grasping intuitively the hidden meaning of nature is philosophically preposterous and methodologically absurd. But human history can indeed be seen as Goethe's *gefühlte Welt* – the world 'given in feeling'. We can understand our history precisely because, like nature for God, it has for us no existence of its own. It exists only in us and through us.

Understanding, therefore, is a particular method which only 'sciences of the Spirit', the study of human history, can employ. Their recourse to this method is not the sign of their deprivation or, indeed, of their inferior position in relation to the sciences of nature. On the contrary, they enjoy a privilege inaccessible to natural sciences. Understanding is the pastime of gods; striving to understand history and hoping that their effort can be successful, men climb heights of truly divine knowledge, which the natural scientists cannot as much as dream of reaching. . . .

Obviously, one cannot understand a tree;[13] to say that one cannot understand the tree means that the tree has neither significance nor value. Only such objects can be significant which are, in principle,

open to understanding. Understanding and the discovery of significance, or value, are one. But understanding is, as well, the overcoming of resistance. One can think seriously of an understanding as
a planned and deliberate activity only in as far as resistance has been
encountered, as the significance of the object is not given matter-of-
factly, at first sight. The field in which understanding becomes the
subject-matter of a systematically constructed method is, therefore,
limited in two respects: understanding starts at the point where pre-
reflexive, spontaneous comprehension shows first signs of insuffi-
ciency; it ends where it comes across a wall of total strangeness,
impervious to sympathetic identification. Between these two extremes
extends the vast realm of *Lebensäusserungen*, expressions of life,
which constitute the proper object of methodical understanding, or
interpretation (*Auslegung*). Here, and here only, human cognitive
faculties are on a par with God's, and divination of meaning is both
possible and imperative.

Nature and the spiritual world are two methods of cognition. It is
the cognitive mind which constitutes objects of its cognition as,
respectively, nature or history. In the first case it sets upon exploring
the connections and dependencies between the objects as they are by
themselves. It formulates its task in the eleatic spirit, as the exploration of fixed, static, consistent beings which already are there,
immovable and inexorable, self-contained and complete, not dependent for their attributes on the cognitive mind. According to the
profound insight of Ortega y Gasset, this 'naturalist' cognitive mode
'is, at bottom, intellectualism, i.e. the projection on to the real of the
mode of being peculiar to concepts'[14]; or, we would add, the projection of scientific practices which endow their products, the concepts
of science, with a mode of being which reflects, mirror-like, the
self-image of scientists and their definition of their activities. In the
second case, however, the cognitive mind sets higher ends for itself;
it obviates the limitations imposed by naturalistic attitude; it does
not settle for the mere description of things as they are – it wants
nothing less than to grasp their meaning, the hidden sense which, if
the natural scientist were to search for it, would transform him into
a theologian. It is only the cognitive mode of the sciences of the
Spirit which allows us the luxury of obliterating the boundary line
between science and theology, explanation and the knowledge of
purpose.

Is the choice of the method (or, more generally, of the cognitive
mode) free, or is it predetermined by the nature of the cognized

object? This is not a simple yes or no question. On the one hand, treating objects as part of nature is a possibility which, unlike the Spirit sciences' mode, is unlimited. One is free to approach phenomena in the manner developed within the eleatic mode and set strict limits to one's own inquiry. One can decide not to expect reciprocal communication, not to allow the object under scrutiny to reveal itself as a subject, and an intentional, purposeful subject above all. One can resolve to interpret the object's conduct in terms of *poïein* alone, and therefore aim at a causal explanation: to refer what is seen back to the antecedent observations rather than to the invisible 'inside' of the object, something which can be only intuited by sympathetic identification. It is easy to see that the likelihood of such a resolution is greatly increased with the growing of the distance between the cognizing subject and cognized object. To give just one example: people far removed from the centres of state power, deprived of all direct experience of decision-making, of politics as an expression of wilful intention, naturally tend to see it as a quasi-natural phenomenon, and account for it in the language of causal links, determinations, inexorable tendencies. This view is probably hotly contested by the insiders, who view the same process as a contest of intentions, as an outgrowth of fellow politicians coming together, thrashing out contentious issues, bringing into the debate their respective intentions and purposes, bargaining, quarrelling, reaching a compromise, gaining an edge over their opponents, or failing to accomplish what they wished. Both accounts are, in a sense, viable and have their good reasons. There is nothing in human affairs which in principle renders the natural-scientific approach inapplicable. Its application can be contested, if at all, only on the ground of practical intentions and preferences. All argument coming (truly or allegedly) from the 'nature of the object' must be, however, ungrounded.

This universality does not apply, however, the other way. One can posit everything as nature, but only some parts of reality would allow themselves to be treated as history:[15]

To understand is to re-discover you in me; the Spirit retrieves itself on ever higher levels of the configuration; identity of Spirit in me, in you, in every subject of our community, in every system of culture, finally in the totality of spirits and in universal history, renders possible this collaboration of its diverse effects in humanities. The subject of knowledge is here one with its object, which – on all levels – is its objectification.

This is the point most crucial to Dilthey's theory and, indeed, to the whole issue of understanding as a particular method which constitutes human sciences and sets them apart from their 'naturalist' neighbours. Understanding is re-discovery of myself in thou; I cannot discover myself in a tree, much less can I re-discover myself there, as there was nothing to establish our kinship in the past. I can re-discover myself in thou, however, as both thou and me are particularizations of the same 'Spirit', ultimately identical with itself in all its manifold incarnations. In order to re-discover myself, i.e. in order to understand, I must be confronted with an object with whom my unity has been already established. If historical understanding, as a method, is a matter of choice, the range of objects to which it can be applied is not.

To sum up: understanding, in Dilthey's view, means a *choice* of the opportunity *determined* by the nature of some potential objects of cognition, but not of the others. By what, however, is this opportunity determined? What lies at the foundation of the momentous difference between these objects which can, in principle, be understood, and those which are doomed forever to be looked at only from outside? It is here that *der Geist* comes in: 'These data are always life-expressions. In the world of meaning, they are expressions of the spiritual; this enables us to cognize them.'[16]

The potential objects of our understanding are, therefore, expressions of the Spirit. It is *because* they are expressions of the Spirit that we *can* understand them. The sentence has the grammatical structure of a causal explanation. Does it, however, offer one? If we ask what *der Geist* is, how to know that what we see is indeed its manifetsation – the only answer we are likely to get is this: we know it when we feel that we can understand, and eventually grasp the meaning of, what we see. The seemingly causal explanation turns out to be a tautology; or, rather, a contraption to avoid or to hide the tautology. The circular reasoning never allows us to ask what the universality and the unity of the Spirit is ultimately founded on; our effort to understand, and our satisfaction with its results, obviates our concern with the question. We can understand whatever is a manifestation of the Spirit; whatever we can understand is a manifestation of the Spirit. Once we busily engage in the enterprise of understanding, the very concept which allegedly lent legitimacy to our project recedes in the background, much like the 'mandate of the people' in the course of the daily administrative bustle. Or, rather, the concept reveals its role as another 'metaphysical prop' – the role ascribed by Parsons to the 'invisible hand' allegedly guiding the market which could perfectly well sustain itself anyway with all the laws we have discovered or ascribed to it.

The rules meant to sustain the activity of understanding have indeed been articulated by Dilthey in a way which leaves to the Spirit no role except as 'metaphysical prop'. Understanding, so we learn from Dilthey, is grounded on the continuous operation of exchange (*Wechselwirkung*) with inner experience (*Erleben*); it is on the understanding of one's own inner experience, presumably given unproblematically and without recourse to a specially developed methodology, that the understanding of strange manifestations of life and of other persons gradually builds up.[17] The realm of inner experience is the training ground for this insight with which we can penetrate the otherwise impervious depths of the Spirit's creations.

Not all human-made objects require such an insight in order to be understood. Dilthey seems to suggest that at least two broad classes of human actions and their products can be grasped in a simpler manner. One is the class of concepts, judgements, or even larger thought-formations. Their thought-content can be grasped in its own context. This can be read as a statement of the context-independent nature of intellectual work, or as a refutation of the sociology or psychology of scientific knowledge: one can ignore the experiences and feelings of the author of a scientific theory. They are not relevant to the understanding of the theory itself. The 'pure reason' entails its own meaning, and is not dependent for meaning on anything which is not itself.

The other class consists of human conduct, presumably what we classify as observable human behaviour. This is related to its end (whatever the end may be) in a regular manner. The 'spiritual' constituent in behaviour boils down to this relation of the act to its end. To understand the meaning of an act would mean, therefore, to spell out the rule which governs the relation of ends to means. Unlike the first case, one has to step beyond the object in order to grasp its meaning, but in doing so one can use the vehicle of systematic scientific observation (presumably supported by statistical aids) rather than any particularly *Geisteswissenschaftliche* method. Our search of meaning stops when we name the end to which the observed activity has been subordinated. Not that the actor whose behaviour we observe has no 'inner experiences' while acting; he certainly has them all the time. But for the task of trying to understand behaviour *qua* behaviour, these inner experiences are irrelevant. While the objects of the first class contained all their discoverable meaning in themselves, the objects of this second class entail whatever elements are necessary for their understanding in the field of their relation to the end-product of action (as in Weber's famous illustration of this idea of Dilthey, in the field between the rhythmic swinging of the axe and the pile of chopped wood). Neither class sends us inside the mysterious, impenetrable depths of the actor's feelings and other inner experiences.

It is only the third class of 'life-manifestations' which presents problems of unique complexity. In order to convey the flavour of this complexity, Dilthey resorts to a curious mixture of lyrics and mysticism:[18]

> It is entirely different with an experiential expression! Such an expression . . . emerges from the depth unilluminated by consciousness. . . . It cannot be judged in terms of truth and falsity, only in terms of veracity and disingenuousness. It is so since disguise, lie, and deception break the continuity between expression and the expressed spiritual entity.

The depth, which knowledge cannot illuminate . . . something which cannot be judged as true or false, only as genuine or mendacious . . . feint, lie, deception conspiring to break the assumed connection between the Spirit and its manifestation. . . . No lie or false pretences can possibly seep into the connection between the act of swinging the axe and the pile of chopped wood; in so far as we agree to define the action in terms of its end results, our findings are either true or false. We can check and re-check which is the case by looking at things objectively, i.e. as things. If, however, we consider the same activity as a manifestation of 'inner experience', we open up a Pandora's box of ontological dangers and methodological traps. In our hesitation between truth and lies we cannot count on the assistance of objective observation. The unfathomable darkness of the Spirit will not be dispersed by the light of objective knowledge of statistical regularities. Each case is unique and cannot be subsumed under a general rule. 'Understanding has always the particular as its object.'[19]

This 'particular' is, above all, the individual. The business of understanding is to understand objects and events as 'life-manifestations' of other individuals. In doing this we are guided by admittedly weak and vague methodological rules. In the last reckoning such rules are set in the hope that the venture is in principle viable and can be improved. Once again the *Leben* supplies the prop: *Leben* is a shared activity, and there is a community (*Gemeinsamkeit*) which permeates all and every individual. One can imagine the community as a 'common substance' in which any individual *Leben* is carved and which simultaneously is the carrier of the activity called understanding. More appropriately, one could conceive of the community as a postulated similarity-cum-affinity, a sort of family resemblance, on which the sympathetic magic of understanding would be founded. The foundations of hope Dilthey never took care to clarify. The hope enters his consideration ready-made, supported by a century or more of Romantic faith. It is true that Dilthey is looking for a method of understanding; but the categories which he coins in order to construct the method in fact play the etiological function; their main role consists in accounting for the mystery of understanding between individuals, rather than in facilitating such an understanding.

There are three such allegedly methodological, while in fact etiological, categories: 'Putting oneself in somebody else's place' (*Sichhineinversetzen*), 'copying' (*Nachbilden*), 're-living' (*Nacherleben*). The first category is fundamental, as it provides the basis for the other two. It refers again to the idea of our essential community which unites individuals. Thanks to this community the individual can put himself in the place of another, 'transmit oneself into given contents of life-manifestations'.[20] Dilthey obviously assumes this activity, accomplished daily in each, however simple, act of communication, is trivial, common. It is because this activity is so common, effortless and unproblematic, that we can hope for the other two, more demanding achievements. Copying and re-living are activities of the 'highest kind'; only in the course of these activities is the 'totality of spiritual life' grasped. Copying and re-living is clearly considered a privileged domain of those persons endowed with faculties not commonly given. Re-living is an act of creation; in order to re-live, it is not therefore enough to participate in *Leben* as all people do. The 'community' which underlies the act of re-living is the community of creativity.

The higher forms of understanding are matters of art, skill, and special endowment. It is true that re-living requires in the first place sympathy (*Mitfühlen*), which intensifies the energy of the act.[21] But fantasy is one of the main pillars which support such sympathy; thanks to fantasy emotions and aspirations incarnated in a given manifestation of life can be sympathetically grasped and re-experienced, therefore be made alive again. The number of doors the fantasy can open depends, however, on what sort of a key a particular fantasy is. 'The more endowed one is, the richer are his possibilities [to understand].'[22] The re-living of great historical events or great works of art is a possibility open only to a selected few; to the persons who, owing to their talent, training and amassed knowledge, can lift themselves to the heights akin to those on which the original actors of events or authors of the works of art operated. The more sublime forms of understanding are, therefore, supported partly by a method and partly by a special talent; the nature of these supports precludes their universal accessibility and transforms them into art or into a historical accomplishment commensurable with their objects. In its more sublime forms, understanding becomes 'an intellectual process requiring a most extreme exertion'.[23]

It has been accepted since Schleiermacher, however, that re-living, defined narrowly as re-creating the individual experience which accompanied the act of historical creation, does not bring the act of understanding to its end. To engross oneself into the motives and emotions of long-deceased actors of historical drama would be in fact a misbegotten effort to dig up a corpse. Understanding is about grasping the meaning of an event or a work of art. As we remember, one can grasp the meaning of only such an object which in itself is meaningful (not a tree!). Now we are told that only such moments of the past are meaningful (i.e. we can grasp their meaning) as did not turn into corpses, i.e. as owe their significance to something more than the motives and aspirations which once led to their conception. 'A moment of the past is meaningful, in so far as it binds the future.'[24] In other words, a moment of history derives its meaning from its relation to a larger totality, from relating the past to the future, the individual existence to mankind. Obviously, the larger the totality to which we can and choose to refer the historical event, the more its otherwise concealed meaning is brought into relief. Understanding is therefore not only a personal process, but a historical process as well. We already know that it depends on the qualities of the historian as a person. We now learn that it depends as well on the qualities of the historian as a contemporary of an historical age. 'What we set as an end for the future, conditions our determination of the meaning of the past.'

If this is so, is not our understanding of historical creations bound to remain forever partial and protean? How can we know that our understanding today is better than yesterday and worse than tomorrow? Is not the idea of smoothly growing totality another version of uncritical belief in progress?

Dilthey is fully aware of the possibility of such conclusions. He knows that a full and conclusive understanding, one which is open to no more change, is conceivable only as a hope. Its possibility has been proved much like the existence of God was proved by St Anselm: the revealed totality of human history is constantly growing by piling up new events and new cultural creations – it must at some point reveal all of itself, and therefore supply a fully exposed and fixed frame in which the final meaning of everything will once and for all be ascertained. This hope is, however, as feebly grounded as was St Anselm's ontological proof. 'One has to wait till the end of history to grasp the material in its determined totality.' But why ought we to agree that history will ever come to its end? Why ought we to accept that its movement in time can indeed be described as a movement *towards* an end? This is a crucial question, since on the acceptance of an ideal 'end' of history hangs the possibility of viewing history as a uni-directional movement, as a process with a pointer, in the course of which some properties (in our case understanding of the past) gradually accrue.

The tenuousness of the assumption on which the 'processual objectivity' of historical understanding is grounded has been promptly exposed by radical critics of Dilthey's hesitant, half-measure solutions, above all by Benedetto Croce and his English follower, R. G. Collingwood. To Croce, the assumption of the 'directedness' of history is superfluous, and above all untenable: our belief in the veracity of the assumption is itself history, and naturally has no more ground than other historical events, every so often changing their meanings:[25]

All judgment is historical judgment, is, in fact, history. . . . The theory that genuine knowledge is historical knowledge is not . . . in any true sense in contrast with natural science, for this, like history, does its work in the world, the humble world. The theory is in contrast with that philosophy, or, more accurately, that traditional idea of philosophy which has its eyes turned to heaven and thence obtains – or awaits – the supreme truth.

And so it is only our 'waiting for the end of history', the elusive thought which can amuse and enthuse only philosophers, but otherwise bears no direct relation to our daily activity, which divides the Diltheyan trust in the ultimate objectivity of historical understanding from the 'absolute historicism', Croce's style. In the words of Croce's perceptive analyst Raffaello Franchini,[26]

According to Croce, history is never an abstract totality from which we could draw, from time to time, a part which we are interested in. On the contrary, history is born of our life interests. . . . There is no history in itself, history of facts – observes Croce – for the same reason for which there are no historiographic 'cases as such'. Facts are brought into focus solely by present life interests, and are constructed and reconstructed by them.

It is our present interest which gives birth to the so-called 'facts of history', which thrusts them to ever newer reconstruction. The possibility of 'absolute historicism' is organically contained in the very idea of understanding as the activity of relating the past to an ever-changing totality, and subdued only by the doubtful expedient of the 'unidirectionality' of this change; 'absolute historicism' means in practice the total merger of understanding of history and history itself. There is no history apart from an 'understood history', i.e. apart from the past as it is intellectually accessible to us. And what makes it intellectually accessible is our present-day interest. Prompted by our philosophical urge to the 'absolute truth', whatever that may mean, we resort to another metaphysical prop, in the form of an image of the past as a huge pool of 'facts' from which we draw more and more units leaving less and less in the container. In Croce's view the past is not such a container; above all, it would not matter even if it were, as we could never be sure of it. Our judgements of history are cut from the same rock as the history we 'judge', i.e. are themselves history. The hope that with the help of some wonderful methods (historical again!) we can escape our own and our judgements' historicity can be based only on either naïvety or conceit:[27]

> The past fact does not answer to a past interest, but to a present interest, in so far as it is unified with an interest of the present life. . . . It is in our breasts alone that is to be found that crucible in which the *certain* is converted into the *true*. . . .

The somewhat poetically expressed ideas of Croce found their systematic and cogent exposition in the works of Collingwood. The relativity of inescapable historicity of thought was contained already in the very act of an event becoming 'historical':[28]

> The peculiarity which makes [an object] historical is not the fact of its happening in time, but the fact of its becoming known to us by our re-thinking the same thought which created the situation we are investigating, and thus coming to understand that situation. . . . It is the historian himself who stands at the bar of judgement, and there reveals his own mind

in its strength and weakness, its virtues and its vices. . . . By understanding [an event] historically we incorporate it into our present thought. . . .

And so, whatever the hypothetical ontological status of an event, it becomes historical because of our effort to reach it, to grasp it, to understand it and thereby to incorporate it in our present. All these efforts are actuated by our present interests rather than by true or alleged intrinsic peculiarities of the event itself. Therefore, the changing shape of history as we know it, as it is given to us at any time we think of it, is to be traced back not so much to the logic of happenings 'in themselves', but to our present-day preoccupations. The hermeneutic circle includes, as its source of rotative energy, the present practice of which we, the historians, are irretrievably a part.

Where does it leave the 'absolute truth' in historical understanding, the idea of historical knowledge ever more closely approximating its objectivity? Whatever happens to pass for objectivity at any particular time is itself history, and so it is subject to the same rules which have been spelled out for historical events in general. The following statement by Collingwood comes, therefore, by no surprise:[29]

> How can we ever satisfy ourselves that the principles on which we think are true, except by going on thinking according to those principles, and seeing whether unanswerable criticisms of them emerge as we work? To criticize the conceptions of science is the work of science itself as it proceeds; to demand that such criticism should be anticipated by the theory of knowledge is to demand that such a theory should anticipate the history of thought.

In these words Collingwood reconciles himself, and invites us to reconcile ourselves, to the necessity of living, working and trying to understand with no certainty, and perhaps no hope, that the end of the road which inspires our efforts will ever be reached. Since we can never know whether we are on the right track, to plod on is the only sensible advice. It is highly probable that sooner or later the track, as so many others before, will be abandoned and we will be urged to enter another one by our new interests; but there is no guarantee that the next track will be in any measure 'better' or 'more final' than the previous one. 'Every new generation must rewrite history in its own way. . . . The historian himself, together with the here-and-now which forms the total body of evidence available to him, is a part of the process he is studying.'[30] One could object that this statement triggers off an infinite regression. One can refer the positivist complacent belief in historical truth anchored in the past 'as it once and for all took place' to the age of faith and certainty of which the positivist historians were a part; in the same way, one could refer Collingwood's serene scepticism to the age of uncertainty and the lack of faith of which he in turn was a part. The objection which Collingwood would take easily in his stride, with one rejoinder only: that infinite regression, another name for the ever-rotating hermeneutical circle, is a necessity which his concept of historical understanding accommodated to an extent the positivist idea of historical cognition could never dream of.

Deliberately or not, Croce's and Collingwood's radical criticisms exposed the inherent ambiguities of Dilthey's conception of historical understanding. What they showed is that the concepts of hermeneutic circle and of objective historical knowledge can only be reconciled by building up a feeble construction propped with unwarranted metaphysical assumptions. It is either this way or the other: either our historical knowledge is subject to the law of unilinear accretion and therefore historians let historical occurrences 'speak for themselves'; or historical facts are activated (indeed, brought into being) by the beams of light cast by our own historical practice, and then they are part and parcel of the current flow of history. Dilthey's frantic efforts to put a foot in each camp were doomed from the start.

The other aspect of Croce's and Collingwood's criticism is a perhaps unintended, but evident shift of emphasis. Dilthey's concept of understanding was subject, so to speak, to a 'double bind'; the psyche of historical actors (which the historian is called to re-live) on the one hand, and the totality as it is accessible to the historian (which conditions the forms and the limits of such re-living) on the other. Though both critics pay more than occasional tribute to the first factor, their attention is squarely on the second. With the current totality initiating the intent and the content of understanding, why do we need the dead actor's psyche, except as the name for what we are describing? 'What we set as an end for the future, conditions our determination of the meaning of the past. . . . ' This assertion is not easily reconcilable with Dilthey's idea of hermeneutic as a *method* of penetrating the spirit of bygone people and events. In Croce's and Collingwood's work, it looks more as the awareness of necessity. This is how the understanding of history operates, rather than: this is what you ought to do in order to understand it.

The inherent ambiguity of Dilthey's hermeneutic can be resolved, therefore, in two ways only: either by insisting that the mind of historical actors (prominent leaders, artists, etc.) contains the ultimate criterion of truthfulness of all understanding; or by conceding that the interpretive freedom of the historian is, for all practical purposes, unfettered, endlessly moving and never coming to a stop. The first solution brings little comfort, as no satisfactory rules of 'mind penetrating' have been invented which did not include the 'penetrator's' own experience (this crack in the dam enclosing the sea of subjectivity). The second solution is a downright surrender to the inevitability of historical relativism, which Dilthey tried so hard to ward off by positing understanding as a *method* in whose application historians are assisted by the unflagging progress of history towards its fulfilment.

It is, of course, a value-judgement to define the reconciliation to the historicity of historical understanding as a surrender. It is a surrender from the point of view of an ideal of science and scientists as full masters of their domain and sole dispensers of a truth to which they have a privileged access and exclusive rights, thanks to the tools only they can handle. It is a source of an infinite potential for development, and certainly not a surrender, from the point of view of recapitulation which clears the 'delivery' of the past (as in Heidegger) and by so doing is a paramount factor of further historical development. It is certainly not a surrender, but a source of optimism, for Johan Huizinga to declare that[31]

The historical interests of every sectional civilization are determined by the question: what are the things which 'matter' to it? . . . The past, without further particularization, means merely chaos. . . . *The* past is limited always in accordance with the kind of subject which seeks to understand it. Every civilization has a past *of its own*.

This is indeed a reason to be optimistic and to take comfort from our civilization's intense effort to understand all the past of mankind as a whole since 'it is the essence of a civilization that whatever its intellect conceives becomes a part of it'. It is therefore a source of joy for all of us who consider richness of culture as virtue that 'our civilization is the first to have for its past the past of the world, our history is the first to be world-history'. Here at long last we come across a foundation on which the belief in an essentially progressive character of historical understanding can be safely placed. But this foundation is not Dilthey's, not the methodical activity of historians which takes over the gradual 'piecing together' of an ever-growing totality of knowledge. It is a phenomenon reaching far beyond the limits of any professional historiographic activity. The foundation of belief is the civilization itself, ever transcending the limits it set for itself a moment before, gradually coming to identify the notion of 'we' with 'mankind', and finally reaching the old profession of faith: *Nihil humani a me alienum puto.* 'All knowledge of historical truth is limited by a capacity for assimilation which in its turn arises out of the study of history. History itself, and the historical consciousness, becomes an integral constituent of the civilization.' After all, 'history is the intellectual form in which a civilization renders account to itself of its past'.[32]

The richer is our own historically developed practice, the richer is the past which we consider a problem for, and are capable of, understanding. The richer the past which we treat in such a way, the richer becomes our civilization and its further absorptive capacity. The hermeneutic circle is not just a method to be appropriated by professional historians. The hermeneutic circle is the way in which history itself moves.

For the task Dilthey set for himself and the science of hermeneutics he proposed to codify, this conclusion means defeat. Dilthey hoped to devise a method which would ultimately lead us not just to comprehension of history, but to its *true* comprehension. But, having once admitted the crucial role of 'exchange' with the inner experience of the cognizing subject, and consequently the paramount importance of the subject's historically accessible horizon, Dilthey opened a gap between understanding and truth which later scores of thinkers would try to bridge with mixed success. We will see in later chapters that the whole history of the problem of understanding can be presented as a series of recurrent attempts to escape from the relativism of understanding which Dilthey revealed, perhaps contrary to his intentions.

These attempts took, as a rule, one of two alternative courses. These can be broadly described as, first, the search for a set of foolproof *methods* which would ultimately make the right understanding both possible and compelling; and, second, the developing of a *theory of history* which would present the history of knowledge as a progress towards true understanding. The crucial assumption underlying the first course is that understanding is a work of reason; the corollary of this assumption is that reason can reach this understanding only if it can emancipate itself from whatever comes from other sources (passions, historically limited interests, group loyalties, etc.). The crucial assumption of the second is that understanding is a work of history. Its corollary is the belief that true understanding cannot become universal until historical development paves the way to the rule of reason. For the sake of brevity we will call the two classes of solutions respectively 'rationalist' and 'historicist'.

The prominent feature of the rationalist solutions is their inattentiveness to the historically determined settings in which understanding is attempted. In their view, knowledge, as ignorance, is timeless. It can be reached at any time. Whether it is reached depends solely on the propriety of methods. If it has not been reached, wrong methods are to blame. People who fail to achieve true understanding obviously look in wrong directions or are misled by inappropriate assumptions. To correct their mistake they need the right methods. Together with their strikingly cogent results, the right methods, once invented or discovered, will be embraced without resistance; their 'fitness' will be the only argument needed to assure their triumph.

The historicist solutions differ in their refusal to believe that correct understanding is possible in all conditions, given the accessibility of effective methods. Knowledge, as ignorance, is historically determined. History must 'mature' to objective understanding. The range of improvement which may be accomplished by better methods in the self-consciousness of an age is and will remain limited until history 'transcends itself' and creates conditions in which understanding can be freed from historical limitations and rise to the level of objectivity. Right methods of understanding cannot arrive before their time; but even if they could, they would not be effective. No true propositions are 'compellingly obvious' without an appropriate historical setting.

As all typologies, this one overemphasizes differences between the types and plays down similarities. The two types are here presented as pure, though in practice specific theories mix the two tendencies in varying proportions. Nevertheless the typology seems to capture the major controversy which has always stood in the very centre of the debate about understanding. Most attitudes taken in the debate can be best understood within the logic of one or the other of the two types. Their presentation in this study is grounded on this assumption.

2   Understanding as the work of history: Karl Marx

It was not German hermeneutics, in the form portrayed in the last chapter, which furnished either impetus or direction to the social theory of Karl Marx. Nowhere in his work did Marx wrestle directly with recognizably hermeneutical problems, as defined by Dilthey or his predecessors; nor did he find the work of any of the thinkers we have discussed so far relevant to his own preoccupations. Yet Marx's contribution to the responses social science was later to give to the challenge of hermeneutics was formidable, and perhaps crucial. It was Marx who laid the solid foundation on which later the 'historicist' response was erected: he took the idea of history as the progress of reason toward self-understanding, as developed in its philosophical form by Hegel, and translated it into sociological terms.

Hegel gave historical dimension to the two revolutionary ideas of Kant: that the 'object of knowledge' is essentially distinct from the 'object of reality' (and not its passive reflection, copy or replica); and that the subject of cognition is and must remain an active agent, of whose impact no object of knowledge can be cleansed. The subject has been promoted from a distorting and unwanted factor of the cognitive act to a role as an indispensable condition of all knowledge. Subjectivity was shown to be inseparable from cognition; an objective knowledge, therefore, could be reached, if at all, only through this subjectivity.

Kant's 'subject' was, however, an a-historical entity; it came under analysis in its most universal aspect, as a transcendental condition of each act of cognition considered separately. Within the boundaries of a single cognitive act the subject and its real object seemed indeed to be sharply opposed to each other and autonomous, mediated only by the production of the object of knowledge. This opposition, however, dissolved when Hegel stepped beyond the confines of a single cognitive act on to the vast expanses of historical process. It then became transparent that subject and object – which confront each other within the act of cognition and can be abstracted from it as entities in their own right – are not so opposed when viewed in a historical perspective. They are no more than analytical abstractions from history, which is no more than a relentless progress towards a self-consciousness of the human spirit. The opacity, impermeability of whatever happens at a given state of history to be posited as an object for cognition, is a perverted appearance of a situation too young to be self-conscious. The effort to understand historical process will have to include an operation accomplished not only on its subject, but on its object as well: of the social and cultural products of the human spirit. The effort will reach its objective when the Spirit emerging at a truly revolutionary stage of history will be able, for the first time, to 'see through' itself; to understand its own meaning, since this meaning will be a direct correlate of its own conscious activity and full self-control.

It is this idea that Marx translated into the language of sociology.

Like Hegel, Karl Marx saw the problem of clear and true understanding as historically achieved conditions of self-awareness. He founded the hope that a full and unimpeded understanding of human existence and action might be reached on the view that history, in the course of its development, tends towards ever fuller universality and sheds, one after another, successive particularisms which hide the 'essence' of social phenomena behind an opaque screen of misleading appearances. It is not just that the owl of understanding spreads its wings at the end of the day (as with Dilthey); or, that history will lead to the triumph of a method of thinking which subsumes and subordinates all other methods (as with Weber); or, that history will hatch a special breed of eggheads enjoying a marginal position particularly propitious to the search for truth (as with Mannheim). According to Marx, history will obliterate the distinction between appearances and essences, will expose social relations and actions in their true human essence, and therefore will render it possible to understand them truly and objectively while applying the most trivial and common-sense tools of cognition. The very existence of an elaborate, sophisticated social science is the evidence that this stage has not yet been reached. Social science must mediate human understanding in so far as the true nature of human relations is mediated by distorting appearances. If, therefore, social science is genuinely committed to the task of true and objective understanding, the practical conclusion it should draw is to 'work itself out of the job', to facilitate the emergence of the 'transparency' of social life which will render social science redundant. If a method exists which can be geared to this task it cannot be just a set of rules to guide intellectual activity alone; it must be a set of rules which connect intellectual activity to the actual development of social relations, and therefore assure practical effectivity of science. In other words, the road to true understanding leads through a *social*, rather than a methodological, revolution.

From this perspective, the very opposition between individual and society appears as a manifestation of the essential 'unreadiness' of social relations for understanding. Both radically opposed solutions to the problem (explaining actions by causal reference to society as 'natural reality', or understanding them by teleological reference to individual thoughts and feelings) must remain partial and therefore unsatisfactory, as they wish to transcend in the field of ideas what is contradictory in reality. As in social science in general, the declared ends of hermeneutics can be achieved only in the social conditions which deprive hermeneutics of its problematics: conditions which in reality, and not only in intellect, make the consequences of social actions transparently linked to the intentions of actors, and their meaning reducible to actors' intentions. Until that stage is reached, the only way in which social science may bring closer the fulfilment of its task is to help the 'self-clarification of the struggles and wishes of the age'.[1]

Marx accused Hegel, as philosopher, of setting 'himself up as the yardstick of the estranged world'[2] by portraying historical process as a movement of thought, as the overcoming of the contradiction between abstract thought and sensuous reality which starts and ends inside thought itself. Hegel set himself a task entirely of this estranged world, hoping that the contradiction which gave the task its significance could be resolved without the world ceasing to be estranged. Were he instead trying to explore the conditions which gave rise to the task itself, he would probably discover that the same historical reality which created the task made its solution impossible; and that the only genuine solution to the task is to make it superfluous – together with the kind of reality which has given it birth and relevance. The Hegelian portrayal of history is tantamount to taking the distorting appearances at their face value; genuine and unresolvable contradictions of the world are assimilated into theory as its assumptions, instead of being brought into the focus of study; the illusion that the world's imperfection has its source in the flaws of intellect is thereby believed and elaborated into theory. The task is then articulated as a resolution of the contradictions of thought: a version which makes the task both unachievable and irrelevant to rectifying the very conditions which make the task both urgent and hopeless. Believing that 'mind alone is true essence of man', Hegel's *Phenomenology* had to be a 'concealed and mystifying criticism, criticism which has not attained self-clarity'. And so are all projects which, like Hegel's, are bent on rectifying the flaws of understanding while leaving unscathed the conditions of life in which the universal, objective understanding is unattainable.

In its distorted Hegelian form, Marx tells us, the transcendence of alienation presents itself as the 'supercession of objectivity'. This is to be expected, as Hegel conceived of alienation itself as the situation in which sensuous impressions, which are in essence nothing but chips hewn from the stem of originally undivided and thereby unself-conscious reason, assume the appearance of 'objective realities'. No wonder the apparent objectivity seems the main cause of 'unhappy consciousness' of divided reason. But blaming objectivity for alienated conditions means precisely that acceptance of appearances which Hegel intended to defy. The conflict-ridden, alienated social reality generates an illusion that man can get rid of his unhappy condition by 'looking through' the opacity of his thoughts alone and discovering their genuine structure; realizing, for instance, that apparently objective concepts like state, law, class, etc., are nothing but condensed subjective meanings. Hence in Marx's view Hegel's is only 'apparent' criticism: 'Man, who has realized that in law, politics, etc., he leads an alienated life, leads his true human life in this alienated life as such.'[3] To paraphrase Wittgenstein, one could say that Hegel's philosophical criticism of alienation of thought is an apparent criticism only, because it 'leaves the alienated world as it was'.

Marx considers the 'supercession of objectivity' as a misguided task. 'A non-objective being is a non-being,' Marx says; it is an empirical and logical impossibility. In a way Heidegger would applaud, Marx shows that 'being itself' is possible only by having an object outside oneself and by being an object for another being. In a way Husserl would deplore, Marx shows that outside such an 'objective' relation between at least two beings, each existing outside the other, only an unnatural condition of solitude is imaginable; and solitude, far from guaranteeing true knowledge and emancipation, means no knowledge, neither sensuous nor conceptual; there is not, and cannot be, a subject without an object outside him. But in a way which neither Husserl nor Heidegger could accommodate in their philosophies Marx shows that objectivity, as a 'natural' condition of human existence, is subject to history; neither objective nor subjective nature, those two sides of the coin called existence, 'is immediately present in a form adequate to *human* being'. Human subjectivity and objectivity of the human world, passion and suffering, the Aristotelian *po̍ein* and *paschein*, 'as everything natural, must come into being'. What is wrong with the human world is not that it is objective, as Hegel implied, but that it is objective in the wrong, historically immature, inhuman (or, rather, pre-human) way. Not objectivity itself, but its alienated form, is the major obstacle on the road to full and unconstrained self-consciousness. World is and will remain real and objective; at present, however, it is objective as 'something external' to human being, something which does not belong to its being 'and which overpowers it'. Hence the feeling of a chasm between opposing subject and object, which is but a necessarily perverted reflection of the fact that man has no control over his world, that the world is to him an alien, merciless, inhuman force. Before this strangeness of the world may be transcended intellectually, it has to be overcome in practice. Regaining control is a necessary prelude and condition of this transparency of the world, this 'subjectivity of the objective', which makes clear and true understanding and the self-understanding of the subject possible.

And so to achieve true understanding means to re-make the world. If men continue to see understanding as a problem, as a task not-yet-attained, it is not because they have yet to reach their own intellectual maturity; it is because the world has yet to reach its maturity, is not ripe to be understood as a human world. And this is because the world is indeed inhuman, estranged; a product of human practical activity which turned into shackles for that activity.

This is the major and decisive feature of Marx's approach to the problem of objective knowledge and understanding: the rejection of any contemplative way to objective knowledge; viewing the road to objective knowledge as involving transformation of *both* cognitive subject and the world, as history, leading to the annihilation of the very opposition between subject and object (the opposition which is not in the nature of existence, but an attribute of the alienated one).

Throughout Marx's study and writings one can distinguish a persistent structure of thought into which ever-new content has been successively poured as the Marxian analysis (and hope of emancipation) shifted from the political sphere to the economic. The structure is, in broad outline, as follows: what defies understanding of the true nature, of the reality of social phenomena, is the particularistic and therefore distorted form in which they appear in human history. On the whole, however, history is a drive to ever-fuller universality; in the process, the true, universal, 'just human' nature of the social world is maturing and being disclosed. As the shroud of particularism falls from reality, so the scales fall from the eyes of men. Men gain insight into the human nature of their own existence as this human nature is laid bare by the development of the existence itself.

This structure of thought was shaped in the earliest of Marx's works and never since abandoned. Perhaps for the first time it appeared in the 'Critique of Hegel's Doctrine of the State', written in March–April 1843. Then a radical democrat at war with Germany's illiberal monarchies, Marx focussed his attention on the particularistic distortion inherent in monarchy which defies all insight into the nature of political state. His main contention is that only democracy, i.e. transcendence of monarchy, can disclose the truth of monarchy, the truth which monarchy concealed. 'Democracy is the truth of monarchy; monarchy is not the truth of democracy.[4] 'Monarchy cannot be explained in its own terms; democracy can be so explained.' Both are just 'moments of the *demos*', but monarchy masks what democracy lays bare. Monarchy is the people whose will and sovereignty have been alienated and turned into an alien commanding force; in democracy the popular origin and foundation of this force is brought into the open. 'Democracy is the solution to the riddle of every constitution. In it we find the constitution founded on its true ground: real human beings and the real people; not merely implicitly and in essence, but in existence and in reality.' In democracy, therefore, the outer shape, the appearance, of the political constitution became finally identical with its essence. Here, 'the constitution is in appearance what it is in reality: the free creation of man'. Later, Marx changed his somewhat cloudless image of democracy; he discovered further distortions and appearances pretending to be essences in the practical embodiments of 'people's sovereignty'. Other phenomena took the place of the democracy-monarchy diad (very shortly afterwards, the dichotomy between civil society and political state as such; later that of social labour versus private property); but the structure of thought remained remarkably stable throughout.

The fundamental assumption of this structure is that whenever a social institution appears in an abstract form, as an entity in its own right, apparently leading its own existence and subject to autonomous laws, one can suspect that behind it stands the historical act of estrangement, of turning a part of human power into a force which opposes itself to its natural foundation. The solution of this mystery is always a practical one; far from being just an intellectual explanation of origins, it involves the transcendence of *both* the cause of effect and their abolition. In 1843 Marx believed, for instance, that 'electoral reform in the abstract political state is the equivalent to a demand for its dissolution and this in turn implies the dissolution of civil society'.[5] True understanding is possible only by creating the practical conditions in which the understanding becomes possible; and this means transcending the false oppositions and pseudo-abstractions which posited the problem of true, as against illusory, understanding in the first place. To understand the true social character of political society, one has to dissolve the autonomy of state in the democratic rule of the people, thereby abolishing both the separation of the state *and* the civil society, transformed into a separate entity by the opposition of the state. To understand the social character of labour, one has to dissolve private property in the sovereignty of producers, thereby abolishing both property as such and labour reduced to 'an economic factor' by the opposition of property:[6]

The resolution of the theoretical antitheses themselves is possible only in a practical way, only through the practical energy of man ... their resolution is for that reason by no means only a problem of knowledge, but a real problem of life, a problem which philosophy was unable to solve precisely because it treated it as a purely theoretical problem.

The resolution of problems posited by misapprehension, by mysteriousness of the setting in which human action takes place, is a practical problem, because errors of judgement and their consequences in misguiding action are not due to weaknesses of intellect, and therefore cannot be rectified by operations committed on intellect alone. In an alienated world it is not consciousness which is false (as many commentators and followers of Marx, particularly since Lukács, later maintained); it is reality itself which is falsified. Erroneous understanding, therefore, is the true reflection of false reality. To undo the error, one has to restore reality to its true form, i.e. the form attuned to its essence. There can be no transparency of consciousness in so far as reality remains opaque, wrapped in a thick shroud of false appearances. The more human consciousness strives to be correct and true to its object, the fuller and more implacable is its surrender to the falsity of alienated reality. To truly reflect the alienated world, is to present things as other than themselves:[7]

> Estrangement appears not only in the fact that the means of my life belong to another and that my desire is the inaccessible possession of another, but also in the fact that all things are other than themselves, that my activity is other than itself, and that finally . . . an inhuman power rules over everything.

What, in short, is wrong with our understanding, and what prevents our knowledge from becoming really objective, is the untruth contained in the alienated world, not the ineptness of our cognitive methods. Reaching the truth must be, therefore, an operation accomplished on the world of human life. Mystification is the truth of reality as long as reality is estranged.

Mystification consists of appearances and essences changing places. In the early phase, when he still tended to locate the source of estrangement in the political sphere, Marx exemplified this idea in the relationship between state bureaucracy and public consciousness, as it appears to be and as it truly is. The reality of an alienated state presents bureaucracy as the true form, as a full adequate representation of the essence of state; while 'the real, empirical state-mind, public consciousness' is 'a mere hotch-potch made up of the thoughts and opinions of the Many'. This faithful record of appearances 'credits the bureaucracy with an essence alien to it', while attributing 'to the true essence the inappropriate form of mere appearance'.[8] When criticizing Hegel for taking the separation between civil society and political state as his starting-point, Marx admits that 'this separation really does exist in the *modern* state', but comments that 'the mere fact that Hegel draws attention to the strangeness of this situation does not imply that he has eliminated the estrangement it entails'.[9] In another application of the same essential idea, Marx points out that dependence is the most common experience of a society in which man 'lives by the grace of another'; consciousness is 'incapable of comprehending the self-sustained existence (*Durchsichselbstsein*) of nature and of man, since such a being contradicts all the palpable evidence of practical life'. For the same reason, the creation is 'an idea which is very hard to exorcise from the popular consciousness'.[10] Again: consciousness does not distort the reality it reflects, but the other way round: consciousness errs because it faithfully reflects the only experience reality is able to offer. One does not need the heavy battery of 'State Ideological Apparatuses' or a sinister octopus of a Ministry of Truth to keep consciousness in a state of error and misapprehension; reality itself takes care of this, having created a mind-twisting world in which the more exact intellectual reflection is, the deeper it flounders in the quagmire of false appearances.

In the later phase, when Marx's attention shifted to the sphere of economic life – this 'true anatomy of civil society' – the same idea is still clearly discernible. Marx points out that twin illusions, individual freedom and the 'impersonal' nature of its restrictions, far from being mere blunders of a wayward or hypocritical intellect, are faithful records of the form in which modern society appears to its members. In the money relation, so we are told, when the ties of personal dependence in all forms have been cut, individuals seem independent of each other, free to collide or enter into contractual agreements. Hence:

> The definedness of individuals, which in the former case appears as a personal restriction of the individual by another, appears in the latter case as developed into an objective restriction of the individual by relations independent of him and sufficient unto themselves.

Since these relations can be expressed only in ideas, they tend to appear as the rule of ideas, values, principles of legitimation, etc. This error is 'all the more easily committed' as the reign exercised by relations does appear 'within the consciousness of individuals as the reign of ideas'.[11]

The theoretical image of social reality and the common sense entrenched in daily routine and daily reinforced are, therefore, in full agreement; neither can be accused of mere obtuseness, not even of technical faults which prevent them from seeing the truth. The falsehood they so faithfully reflect *is* the truth of reality which in practice had falsified the universal, human essence of social relation well before theoreticians started to theorize, or common sense forged daily practice into folk wisdom. They fall for the illusion not in spite of, but because of their honest effort to be objective and to submit themselves to the test of practice; the illusion must first dissipate (or at least cover itself with enough fissures to reveal the previously concealed essence) for them to undergo the 'crisis of consciousness' which leads eventually to a new image of social reality:[12]

The whole semblance, that the rule of a certain class is only the rule of certain ideas, ends of its own accord naturally, as soon as class domination ceases to be the form of social organization: that is to say, as soon as it is no longer necessary to represent a particular interest as general or the 'general interest' as ruling.

This is the crucial message, and the paramount distinctive feature, of Marx's theory: objective understanding is not attainable unless the criticism of science and common sense is developed into the criticism of the social reality which both science and common sense *truthfully* reflect. The method of attaining true and objective understanding must include practical activity to eliminate 'false reality'. Criticism of whatever is false in dominant consciousness, in order to be effective, must aim at the disclosure of such features of reality as lead cognitive reflection to untrue results; it cannot be effective if confined, as in so many cases, to witty or vituperous comments on inadequacies of the consciousness itself:[13]

Man's reflections on the forms of social life, and consequently, also, his scientific analysis of these forms, take a course directly opposite to that of their actual historical development. He begins, *post festum*, with the finished results of the process of development. The characteristics that stamp products as commodities, and whose establishment is a necessary preliminary to the circulation of commodities, have already acquired the stability of natural features of social life, before men try to give an account, not of their historical character, since they are already regarded immutable, but of their meaning. . . . [These forms] are socially accepted, and thus objective forms of thought which express the productive relations of a definite, historically determined mode of production, viz. the production of commodities. The whole mystery of commodities, all the magic and sorcery that surrounds the products of labour as long as they take the form of commodities, vanishes, therefore, as soon as we pass to other forms of production.

In this latter idea – that progress in understanding demands that history passes into another, 'higher' stage of its development – Marx thinks along lines not very distant from those of Dilthey, Weber, or Mannheim. He sharply differs from them and, for this matter, from literally all other theories of knowledge, in that he, and he alone, locates this 'historical movement' which underlies the progress of understanding not in the development of a wider cognitive perspective, or the introduction of more reliable forms of thought, or the setting of a selected group of people free from historical constraints, but in reality's own exposure of more and more of its universality which unmasks its own previous stages as particularistic distortions. Only Marx locates the roots of miscomprehension not in the mind of cognizing subject, but in the structure of the object of cognition; ultimately, within the structure of domination which constitutes the object.

That is to say: Marx transforms epistemology into sociology. Criticism of knowledge is never complete without criticism of the reality which made knowledge vulnerable to, and eligible for, criticism. And criticism of knowledge is the one road available which may lead to the criticism of reality: such contradictions of thought as intellectual analysis may discover offer an invaluable insight into the contradictions of the reality they reflect and while reflecting it get tangled in contradictions:[14]

A truly philosophical criticism of the present constitution does not content itself with showing that it contains contradictions: it explains them, comprehends their genesis, their necessity. It grasps their particular significance. This act of comprehension does not however consist, as Hegel thinks, in discovering the determinations of the concepts of logic at every point; it consists in the discovery of the particular logic of the particular object.

The programme of hermeneutics-turned-sociology is put to action throughout Marx's work. A famous example is Marx's analysis of religion. Its central idea is that religion 'is an inverted consciousness of the world, because [this state and this society] are an inverted world. Religion is the general theory of this world.' If one takes to unmasking religious erroneous images, one has to be aware of what is necessarily involved. 'To call on [people] to give up their illusions about their condition is to call on them to give up a condition that requires illusions. The criticism of religion is therefore in embryo the criticism of that vale of tears of which religion is the halo.' In short, 'the criticism of heaven turns into the criticism of earth, the criticism of religion into the criticism of law and the criticism of theology into the criticism of politics'.[15] Later Marx added social structure, as founded on productive relations, to his list and, with an unsurpassed mastery, turned his criticism of political economy into the criticism of the economy of capitalism.

It is a peculiar kind of sociology to which Marx is turning in order to solve the tasks of hermeneutics. A sociology which stops at registering the earthly roots of spiritual blunders will not do. Remember: 'Man, who has realized that in law, politics, etc., he leads an alienated life, leads his true human life in this alienated life as such'; a 'recording sociology' leaves everything as it is; mere awareness of the earthly sources of distortions is not yet, by itself, a truly radical criticism, as it stops short of attacking things 'at their roots'. A sociology truly geared to the task of historical understanding must not shy away from drawing practical conclusions from its discoveries and turning intellectual analysis into social practice:[16]

> If I know religion as alienated human self-consciousness, then what I know in it as religion is not my self-consciousness but my alienated self-consciousness confirmed in it. Thus I know that the self-consciousness which belongs to the essence of my own self is confirmed not in religion but in the destruction and supersession of religion.

But this destruction and supersession of religion, as we know already, can be accomplished only when the conditions of which religion is a mere reflection are destroyed and superseded.

Without practical re-shaping of reality, criticism of its theoretical reflection is incomplete and, moreover, ineffective. This theme is widely elaborated in the *German Ideology*. We are told that spiritual criticism is not enough to destroy forms of consciousness. It is not sufficient to dissolve these forms in 'self-awareness', or to present them as phantoms, mere appearances, or illusions. The practical abolition of real social relations which incessantly give birth to criticized forms of consciousness alone can bring the tasks of criticism to fulfilment. The idea that man can change his plight merely by acquiring the right consciousness, by an insight into the murkier aspects of his condition (and the very idea that such an insight is plausible on a truly social scale while the condition is still in full force), is itself a sample of perverted consciousness, i.e. a consciousness which takes perverted reality at its face value. Thus one cannot transcend 'commodity fetishism' by mere understanding that the apparent relations between things only hide and mask relations between people; one would need, in addition, to subject 'thing-like' forces to the power of human individuals and abolish this division of labour which transforms things into alleged masters of men.

One conclusion of particular interest and importance for contemporary sociology is related to the discovery, made practically by each successive generation of scholars for about two centuries, that the apparent opposition of society and individuals is illusory; the so-called 'common interest', the requirements of the society as a whole, is nothing but a product of the diffuse activities of dispersed human individuals. To know that the opposition is illusory, since in 'actual fact' there is no society only the society-generating actions of individuals, changes nothing in the real (however logically incorrect) contradiction between society and the individual, between human intentions and the constraints imposed on their fulfilment, between private needs and societally determined necessities. Discovering the unity, where daily experience and the common sense it feeds inform us of an opposition, means therefore little – unless what follows is the material annihilation of the mode of existence which generated this unity and this opposition; in other words, practical destruction of the opposition together with its unity. A century and a half ago, Marx already transcended the discovery which our generation of sociologists, as every other generation before, arrived at with so painstaking an effort and in such jubilant mood – 'at last we know the truth'.

Thus indispensable to progress towards objective understanding is the re-making of reality. What, however, about the intellectual moment of the process? Mere spiritual 'putting on its feet again' of reality turned upside-down is just a beginning of the process; but does this beginning at least depend solely on the power of insight, perspicacity, methodological prowess of professional analysts? And, providing that the genius of a single scholar has already discovered the truth, can his vision (it is only a vision at this stage, as it contradicts all the material evidence of common-sense routine) be actualized, become the practical truth of human existence?

Marx's answer to this crucial question is contained in a statement frequently quoted, but not so frequently accepted in all its consequence: 'It is not enough that thought should strive to realize itself; reality must itself strive towards thought.'[17] That is to say, the revolution which completes the effort of understanding may come to pass only when reality matures to accepting the truth about itself ('Theory is realized in a people only in so far as it is a realization of the people's needs'). Hence another equally famous assertion of Marx: 'Mankind always sets itself only such problems as it can solve; since, on closer examination, it will always be found that the problem itself arises only when the material conditions necessary for its solution already exist or are at least in the process of formation.'[18] The conditions of transcending historically determined miscomprehensions are themselves historically determined.

Let us consider, for example, Marx's analysis of conditions in which the universality of labour as the source of all value, 'abstract labour', could be discovered, and the truth of discovery could be appreciated. We are told in the *Grundrisse* that only the advent of capitalism, with its total domination of the market and the ensuing universal exchangeability of the products of human labour, exposed the 'abstract', universal aspect of labour:[19]

Indifference towards specific labours corresponds to a form of society in which individuals can with ease transfer from one labour to another, and where the specific kind is a matter of chance for them, hence of indifference. Not only the category, labour, but labour in reality has here become the means of creating wealth in general.

Only here, therefore, does the universal essence of labour as the source of all values become evident for everybody to see. In a fashion similar to Weber in form but sharply distinct in substance, Marx concludes that even the most abstract categories, which because of their generality are valid (though applied only in retrospect) for all epochs, are nevertheless 'discoverable' as products of specific historic relations. This is how reality 'strives towards thought'. In *Capital* Marx ponders why it was impossible for Aristotle, all his indubitable genius notwithstanding, to discover that 'in the form of commodity values all labour is expressed as equivalent human labour'. The answer is that Aristotle's society was a slave society, while[20]

the secret of the expression of value, namely, that all kinds of labour are equal and equivalent because and so far as they are human labour in general, cannot be deciphered until the notion of human equality has already acquired the fixity of a popular prejudice. This, however, is possible only in a society in which the great mass of the products of labour take the form of commodities, and in which, consequently, the dominant social relation is that between men as owners of commodities.

It took Aristotle's genius to sense in such a society an equality which expressed itself in commodity values; but even Aristotle's genius could not make up for the immaturity of his era, and he stopped short of a real understanding of this equality.

This means that in some historical conditions the contemporary mind, even if armed with unequalled analytical skill, cannot perceive universality of a level higher than that already disclosed in the existing web of human relations. Universality is already there; it remains, however, invisible to the contemporary perspective. Hence 'human anatomy contains a key to the anatomy of the ape. . . . The bourgeois economy thus supplies the key to the ancient, etc.'[21] Like the unsurpassed rationality of the modern epoch in Weber, so the unmatched universality of capitalist social relations in Marx legitimate the application, in retrospect, of the laws suggested by the modern economy to the analysis of past societies. As in Weber, this 'forcing' of categories forged in one society on the theoretical image of another is not considered relativistic. The opposite is the case: the belief that logic of a 'higher epoch' can be legitimately applied to 'less developed epochs' allows both Marx and Weber to reconcile consistent historicism with unshakeable trust in the possibility of objective knowledge.

In the light of this vision the kind of historicism (as represented particularly in the historiography which inspired the methodological work of Dilthey) which demands that each era ought to be analysed and 'understood' in its own terms becomes unacceptable. Not because we, members of another society, are unable to 'feel' alien values and concepts; Marx never considered this a serious constraint. This kind of historicism is unacceptable because of its neglect of the things revealed by later epochs, and its refusal to accept them as categories reflecting the reality of the past more fully, more deeply than the necessarily limited ideas of past thinkers. The demand to apply only 'contemporary', 'local', 'indigenous', 'emic' (or under whatever names they appear) categories in the search for the true meaning of a historically given setting, Marx sees as equivalent to the demand that historians[22]

share in each historical epoch the illusion of that epoch. For instance, if an epoch imagines itself to be actuated by purely 'political' or 'religious' motives, although 'religion' and 'politics' are only forms of its true motives, the historian accepts this opinion.

Having accepted it, our historian becomes a party to the misrepresentation of times he admittedly wants to understand. The ideas of contemporaries, which he clings to in hope of penetrating the true essence of the epoch, have been exposed by later developments for what they really are: images of immature relations which, far from revealing the truth, prevented it from being revealed.

Thus students of India or ancient Egypt tend to believe that the ideas of caste, purity, hierarchy, etc., are keys to the understanding of these peculiar social systems. They would shun interpretations reaching beyond the cognitive horizons of members of those societies; the idea that caste hierarchy was just a primitive form of an inchoate

division of labour would strike them as a major distortion of historical truth, at odds with the task of understanding historical forma-
tions as they truly were. To Marx, the development of history – or
rather the development of that human material practice which is
called history – consists in exposing the falsity of every successive
illusion which has to inform human action in a formation 'not ripe'
for full and uncurbed intellectual control. If that is so, then to turn
one's back to the truth revealed by later stages of history, and to
cling instead to already discredited beliefs, is an unforgivable error,
which can be explained only by new illusions which the historian's
own era still supports. We know already what Indians or ancient
Egyptians did not and could not know – that the mundane, banausic
routine of the multitude in producing conditions of their own life is
the force responsible for the way in which people can live and do
live their lives. To discover this simple truth, millennia of tortuous
historical development have been necessary: several awe-inspiring
masks (religious, political, legal) had to be peeled from the face of
historical necessity; artificial limbs of church, hereditary monarchy,
estate system had to be broken and taken away for this necessity's
own material legs to become visible. And, last but not least, to be
revealed as the unanticipated outcome of human conscious activity,
this necessity (called 'society' or 'history') must have reached a form
in which it can be subjected to the conscious control of its producers.
All this has now happened, and at last we have the chance of looking
into the true foundations of past societies with an eye as sharp as
never before. We can understand now what the lives of our predecessors were really about.

We can, but our predecessors could not. Their own practice still
far from completing the full circle, they could only reflect upon an
immature, opaque reality; unable to gain control over the conditions
of their life (their era could hardly posit control as a task, as 'the
material conditions for its solution' were still lacking), they could
not see them as their own product; instead they had to invent imaginary powers (idols, gods, sacred rights of dynasty, nobility of birth,
laws of history – many names, one referent: a power which must be
obeyed because it cannot be subdued) to account for the narrowness
of their sphere of choice. Their theories of social life had to be as
immature as their object. These theories served them as explanation
of their life, but a scholar bent on objective understanding can hardly
assign to them a privileged role. They were as inferior to our own
theories as the social conditions (and hence cognitive chances)

reflected in these theories were inferior to ours. For this reason, Marx – unlike the idealist historians he castigated – was never particularly excited by the 'immanent' analysis of past beliefs. He considered them singularly unattractive as a potential source of illumination. Though he never used such terms, he would not believe that these 'native theories' (as Lévi-Strauss called them later) contain a peculiar 'kerygmatic message' (as Paul Ricoeur insisted in his polemics with Lévi-Strauss) which gives them some lasting intrinsic value beyond their transient role of vicarious understanding of a specific type of historical practice. 'Native theories' were of interest to Marx in one capacity only: as illusions which testify to the immaturity and contradictory nature of conditions which could reflect themselves only in a distorted, illusionary form. The meaning of native theories which our understanding is to grasp is not inside them, but outside: the falsity of native theories, so clearly visible when floodlit by our own historical practice, is an important clue for the understanding of the true mechanism of those practices in which they had been embedded. One would vainly search the content of native theories for reliable information about this mechanism. The information we need is not there. But once we have accepted that a theory which stops short of acknowledging the human, practical essence of society is an offshoot of a society which has broken loose of conscious human practice, then the theory can offer invaluable assistance to our search for understanding. We would know, that properly to understand and assess the way of life we study, we have to turn our attention to the historically specific form in which 'outer necessity' established its autonomy and its power over the only active subjects of history. The falsity of native theory, rather than its content, guides our investigation. The importance of a native theory is as a clue without which our theory of society cannot operate, rather than in what it actually says and how it articulates its message.

So it was the question 'why', rather than 'what' or 'how', which Marx's theory of society posited as central to historical understanding. To understand a belief is to find out why it took the shape it did; or, rather, why it fell short of reaching that clarity of sight which has been hard won by our own consciousness. The answer is to be sought in the network of social relations which a given historical practice laid out. And to grasp this network is to elucidate the conditions in which various people of the era had to work through their lives: the range of options open to them, the resources available and those which were inaccessible (though physically present), the costs of gaining access to resources – all those uncontrollable, external conditions in which the human effort to remain alive had to take place.

The identity and uniqueness of an era, which Dilthey saw in the unrepeatable constellation of beliefs, Marx located in 'one specific kind of production which predominates over the rest'. Students of history have been always after something which could account for the particularity of an era, a society, a culture; a decisive link in a chain of cultural traits, a hub around which the whole wheel of life rotates, an invisible substance which 'saturates' every sector of life and marks it unmistakably as a part of this, and not that totality. Those who viewed history as above all cultural history, the work of human spirit, reflecting the historically specific form of self-consciousness, tended to define this 'something' as a central idea, a superior consummatory value, or – as cultural anthropologists following Boas, Sapir or Kluckhohn would say – the 'ethos' which colours every single cultural trait and draws the borderline between the 'inside' and the 'outside' of a culture. Marx, to be sure, describes the 'specific kind of production' in terms very similar to those used by, say, Kluckhohn, in his description of 'ethos': 'It is a general illumination which bathes all the other colours and modifies their particularity. It is a particular ether which determines the specific gravity of every being which has materialized within it.'[23]

To understand an epoch, one has to find out the epoch's specific kind of production: how people made their living. This kind of production circumscribed the field which their historically constrained freedom could roam. Whatever denizens of the era did, whatever they believed in, whatever illusions they held to make their life intelligible, would disclose its significance and meaning when looked upon as one of the limited number of ways in which life could be lived in this, and not another, field. Rather than determining life-style and beliefs, the 'specific kind of production' sets the outer limits to the freedom of randomness of choice, and therefore marks all forms 'within the boundaries' with some common features which no form 'outside' could possess.

Marx's idea of understanding is, therefore, 'representational' rather than 'immanent'. To understand historical forms and actions is to approach them as representations, clues, hints, perverted reflections of something else which they hide rather than reveal. This somewhat denigrating view of historically held beliefs, this blunt refusal to take them for the face value, was to Marx, however, a matter of necessity rather than virtue. As in so many other cases, it is history which must endow immanent understanding with value and transform it into the right method of grasping the significance of human action. In as far as the rupture between subjective intentions and objective effects, subjective beliefs and objective realities, persists, immanent understanding can only mean condoning deception and self-deception; in no case could it lead to objective understanding. Society must first acquire the transparency which makes the subjective and the objective blend, for immanent understanding to become the way to grasp the truth. Society must first in practice be reduced to the conscious activity of individuals (transformed into 'real community'),[24] for the consciousness of individuals to become the truth of their social life. Thus the possibility and the validity of immanent understanding is, again, a matter of revolution. Human life must become 'true to itself' for human consciousness, this object of immanent understanding, to become true to the real life of humans. And this can be accomplished only by restoring to humans practical control over their activity and its consequences; by submitting the 'objective reality' of their condition to the control of their consciousness.

For the time being, with the historical development toward immanent consciousness still short of its final stage, interpretation (representational understanding) must occupy the place not yet ready for the analysis of consciousness-becoming-one-with-history. This is exactly what has been done in history all along. Forms of self-consciousness, uncritically embraced in one era, were discredited as illusions by the next. Their criticism always took the form of condemning their particularity, the narrow-mindedness or selfish interests behind them, from a position relatively more universal; the universality of the receding era was presented as particularity, as a distortion of 'true universality'. Such criticism always had as its bearers a group (class) whose characteristic way of being could not develop fully in the previous era. For this reason the class experienced their condition as a constraint, an artificial limit imposed on their 'natural' opportunities, as a crime against the true nature of man. Their struggle, therefore, was one of universality against particularism. Each revolution appears to its participants as a sacred war of mankind against one selfish class, of the 'rights of man' against the usurped privileges of the few. On the aftermath of all previous revolutions, however, the victorious 'universality' invariably revealed its true nature as a new class particularism, if only founded on a broader basis.

This appearance as the embodiment of universal interests of man is, according to Marx, an indispensable characteristic of each revolutionary class – in so far as this class has not yet passed the peak of its revolutionary potential. Himself he considers the harbinger of the most radical and decisive of all revolutions: the only one in which the appearance of universality will not be limited to the fleeting moment between the challenge and the victory; the only one which will do away with all limits to the true universality of man, and will leave species characteristics as the only outer limits of human conscious action.

He writes about his own theoretical work:[25]

My *universal* consciousness is only the *theoretical* form of that whose *living* form is the *real* community, society, whereas at present *universal* consciousness is an abstraction from real life and as such in hostile opposition to it.

A theory which discovers universality denied by real life is a revolutionary theory. It can 'actualize' itself only in the act of revolution. A consciousness of universality which is not yet present in real society is by the same token critical to the society, 'in hostile opposition to it'. Such a consciousness has become possible since the universality it reflects is covered with only a thinnest film of appearances. The market brought into relief the universal nature of labour as the source of all values, and only the estranged status of conditions in which labour 'actualizes' its potential prevents labour from controlling its own activity, from achieving universality in practice. But consciousness cannot actualize itself on its own. As all theoretical criticism, it needs a carrier powerful enough to reorganize the conditions of social life.

Marx believed that the proletariat will turn into the executor of theoretical criticism. This was because the proletariat, in Marx's view, was the only part of the society which already reached that level of universality on which the society as a whole has yet to climb. Private property, which stands in the way of the final triumph of human universality, has been already abolished for the proletariat. So have other obstacles been abolished – like nationality or the family. Or, rather, the more consistent and radical is such a destruction, the more likely is the class in which the destruction took place to become the carrier of the universal revolution.

Both the selection of proletariat as the revolutionary force and the view of the revolution itself as, above all, radical annihilation of *les pouvoirs intermédiaires* have since been widely discussed and criti-cized. Their evaluation is, however, of a relatively minor interest to our topic. For us two points are important: first, Marx's insistence on the correspondence between the degree of universality in the socially determined position of a group and the measure of univer-sality which this group can assimilate in its self-consciousness and, above all, its historical practice; secondly, Marx's assertion that analysis of the subjective aspect of human action can lead to objec-tive understanding only in conditions in which the still-persisting opposition between the subjective and the objective, between living labour and its estranged products, is finally transcended.

In this is the major distinctive feature of Marx's approach to the problem of understanding. This is why, for Marx, to say that 'natural science will in time subsume the science of man just as the science of man will subsume natural science'[26] is not a methodological statement, but a *theoretical* statement about the tendency and the logic of the totality of *human history*. The chance of true under-standing of human activity is, in Marx's view, at one with the historical tendency towards supersession of the alienation which made the results of human action diverge from the actors' intentions. The identity of the two, if achieved, will render obsolete the task of understanding as a special problem distinct of human knowledge in general.

3 Understanding as the work of history: Max Weber

Max Weber, as Marx before him, vested his hope of objective understanding of history with the historical developments taking place in
the western world. Not, however, with the change 'round the corner',
with the imminent demise of the capitalist structure of domination,
responsible – in Marx's view – for producing a meaningless 'social
reality' out of meaningful, intentional human acts. Max Weber saw
the chance of objective understanding in the very changes already
brought about by the advent of capitalism: in the crucial role
capitalism assigns, to an ever-growing degree, to rational-
instrumental action. In its capitalist stage, western civilization has
shed its particularistic commitments to arbitrarily chosen consummatory values, which elude rational discourse, and replaced them
with an instrumental reason able to neutralize the impact of constraints arising from time and place. Rational-instrumental behaviour
can be grasped objectively, as it is rule-governed and self-conscious,
and above all, because of its structural affinity to rational science, to
'objective reason' itself. Modern rational science, which self-
consciously limits itself to the pursuit of instrumental sequences of
action and forgoes the discussion of end-values, finds in the modern
bases of human behaviour an object cut to the measure of its ends
and means.

Unlike Marx, Weber faced the task of 'objective understanding' in
the form used by the German *Geisteswissenschaften* debate, and
above all by Dilthey and Rickert. Only at a relatively late stage,
when he had singled out economics as inspiration, and sociology as
the answer to the problems of historical hermeneutics, did he turn to
a sociological method patterned on economics as the way to resolve
the tasks posited by historical understanding. Weber's methodology
can be, therefore, interpreted as an answer to the challenge of
hermeneutics in a much more direct sense than Marx's.

The life-long methodological preoccupations of Weber, centred
around the categories of understanding and interpretation, had been

animated by the essential divergence of 'natural science' and 'cultural science' projects, as asserted by Dilthey and later variously elaborated by Windelband, Rickert, and an entire generation of German historians and social scientists.

Suppose that somehow an empirical-statistical demonstration of the strictest sense is produced, showing that all men everywhere who have ever been placed in a certain situation have invariably reacted in the same way and to the same extent. Suppose that whenever this situation is experimentally reproduced, the same reaction invariably follows. Which is to say: suppose that this reaction is, in the most literal sense of the word, 'calculable'. Such a demonstration would not bring us a single step closer to the 'interpretation' of this reaction. By itself, such a demonstration would contribute nothing to the project of 'understanding' 'why' this reaction ever occurred and, moreover, 'why' it invariably occurs in the same way. As long as the 'inner', imaginative *reproduction* of the motivation responsible for the reaction remains impossible, we will be unable to acquire that understanding. *As long as* this is not possible, it follows that even an ideally comprehensive empirical-statistical demonstration of the regular recurrence of a reaction will still *fail* to satisfy the criteria concerning the *kind* of knowledge which we expect from history and those 'sociocultural sciences' which are related in this respect to history.

Again in strict accordance with hermeneutical tradition, this essential distinction between two types of knowledge is ultimately rooted in their respective purposes as posited by analysts; if a cultural analysis can attain its completeness only when it accommodates understandable human action – it is 'because the "historical" *interest* is anchored in this theoretical purpose'. In a truly Diltheyan fashion, Weber had initially defined this specifically 'historical' interest as one that has its goal in 'empathy', 'reproduction in immediate experience', in short, 'interpretive understanding'.

Interpretive understanding, however, was for Weber not the end of historical exploration; methodologically, it was conceived as a means which could 'serve the purpose of "objectifying" knowledge'.[1] One could say that Weber dedicated the rest of his life to working out the methodology of such an 'objective' knowledge of history, founded on interpretive understanding and using as its major tool a theory of interpretation.

The impact of the original discourse in Weber's work has never been completely expurgated. In his fullest statement of the sociological project (*Wirtschaft und Gesellschaft*) understanding is, true to Diltheyan spirit, still considered as the great chance, rather than a limitation, of the human sciences. It is not something to apologize for; on the contrary, thanks to the possibility of understanding, one can study human action much further than a natural scientist ever can in his description and explanation of inanimate phenomena. There are no more references to the 'universal unity of the human spirit'. This metaphysical prop, still felt necessary by Dilthey, is dropped; the foundation for the understanding effort has once and for all been established. But the essential distinction between the situation of the natural and the human sciences is upheld, though now on methodological, rather than ontological, terms. Weber says of phenomena that 'the more precisely they are formulated from a point of view of natural science, the less they are accessible to subjective understanding'.[2] Once embarked on the exploration of causal relationships in the way typical of the natural sciences, one will be carried away from, rather than towards, understanding: 'This road will never lead toward interpretation of the intended meaning.' Again, this disjunction is the privilege, rather than the handicap of the human sciences: 'We can accomplish something which is never attainable in the natural sciences.'[3] The jubilant mood and self-confidence of Dilthey is gone. To avail oneself of the opportunity offered by the study of human action means sacrificing other values, a loss more serious than Dilthey would admit. What is at stake is not only the particularly acute problem of objectivity (this worry Dilthey fully shared), but the precision and conclusiveness of findings, criteria of accomplishment which, in scientists' self-consciousness, were slowly becoming the defining features of scientific activity as such. It is, therefore, with regret that Weber admits: 'This additional achievement of explanation by interpretive understanding, as distinguished from external observation, is of course attained only at a price – the more hypothetical and fragmentary character of its results.'[4]

The intense preoccupation with reconciling the unquestioned advantages of such knowledge as can employ the facility of understanding, with the uncompromising demands of scientific code of action, as institutionalized in the academic science, distinguishes Weber's work from Dilthey's and can be seen as responsible for most of Weber's departures from Diltheyan solutions.

While accepting that sociology, together with other studies concerned with social action, will never produce interpretations and explanations like those of the natural sciences, Weber insisted that sociology ought to be exactly like the natural sciences, or at least as similar to them as diligence and skill of its practitioners can allow, with regard to the degree of exactitude and acceptability of its findings. The major contributions to social-scientific methodology commonly associated with Weber can be seen to stem from his continuous efforts to grapple with this antinomy. Weber's life-work, at least in its methodological aspect, derived its dynamics and purpose from a tension between his view of social reality, the subject-matter of sociology, as irretrievably subjective, and his determination to find a way of knowing it objectively. The task Weber set himself with unprecedented determination was nothing less than an objective science of the subjective.

The two methodological innovations which contemporary socio-logical folklore most readily associates with the name of Weber bear direct relation to this over-arching task. The first is the need to eliminate value-judgements from sociological discourse (though not necessarily from the speech of the sociologist as a person). The second is the method of ideal types, as a means of grasping subjec-tively held meanings in an objective way. It will be seen later that the two allegedly separate postulates have common roots in Weber's global view of the origin, unique spirit, historical tendency and mission of western civilization with western capitalism as its crowning stage. It was this view which made the objective–subjective problem particularly acute to Weber and transformed the problem into the major tension and source of his intellectual energy.

The most notorious highlight of Weber's uphill struggle for 'value-free' social sciences was the *Werturteilsdiskussion*, which took place on 5 January 1914 at the plenary meeting of the 'Social Policy Association', in the presence of fifty-two of the most prominent social scientists of Germany. There Weber launched his assault against value-judgements in a most determined and comprehensive fashion. The text of impassioned speech delivered by Weber is now an essential reading in sociology, and its major assertions, whether accepted or not, have become indispensable to sociological thinking. Not so when the speech was first delivered. According to Franz Boese, the Association's historian, not only the older generation but the youngest members present would not accept, if they did not downright reject, Weber's plea.[5] They perceived Weber's demands as an assault upon the established rights of academics to advise decision-makers either directly, or via public opinion, on matters of policy and administration. Their academic expertise and know-how was the only justification professors could claim for such an elevated role. Weber's opponents unmistakably spotted the danger: to say that science has nothing to tell us about superiority or inferiority of alternative policies, that science must remain silent about the relative virtues of conflicting values, meant expropriation of this justification and, indeed, a radical change in the status of social and political scientists. Weber, to be sure, made no bones about the inevitable outcome if his plea were to succeed: he castigated university professors for pretending to carry marshals' batons of statesmen or cultural reformers in their knapsacks.[6] 'To take a practical political stand', he would say four years later, talking to the audience at the University of Munich, 'is one thing, and to analyse political structures and party positions is another.'[7] It was the duty of academics to stick to the second task and never to abuse their scientific authority by interfering with the first: certainly not in their capacity as scientists.

To avoid value-judgements in the works of science does not mean that values are irrelevant to scientific activity. While *Werturteil* (value-judgement) is an alien and cancerous body in the organism of social science, *Wertbeziehung* (value-relevance) is its flesh and blood; here Weber draws heavily, and explicitly, on the concepts developed by Heinrich Rickert.[8] In fact, the value-abstinence Weber called social scientists to accept was in his view the only way in which their activity can become and remain relevant to the values of their own times. Moral convictions, which 'installed themselves in the saddle through the distortions incurred by psychological understanding', have no more worth than the religious beliefs which science has destroyed.[9] If ours is the scientific age, there is no place in it for a science, presumably a rational activity, infused with explicitly professed or surreptitiously smuggled-in value-judgements which can claim no ground but moral convictions. A science free of these value-judgements is the only knowledge up to the standards set by our times: the only 'value-relevant' kind of cognitive activity.

This point about the essential harmony between value-free science and the historical tendency of our time is pressed most poignantly and forcefully in the Munich speech (though it remained perhaps a most obsessively harped-on motif of Weber's work, as I shall try to show later). 'The fate of our times is characterized by rationalization and intellectualization and, above all, by the "disenchantment of the world".' If that is so, then whoever 'tries intellectually to construe new religions ... will create only fanatical sects but never a genuine community'. For a scientist who cannot face the demands of our sober, rational times, who longs for a value-committed activity in the walls of the Academia, who prefers prophesy to the diligent study of reality, Weber has advice: 'The arms of the old churches are opened widely and compassionately for him. . . . In my eyes, such religious return stands higher than the academic prophecy.' As to those who can resist their temptations and keep their value-sympathies clear of the gates of the House of Science, they will 'set to work and meet the "demands of the day", in human relations as well as in our vocation'.[10]

Let us make this point as clearly as possible, since it is crucial to Weber's idea of understanding, and indeed to the strategy of social science: value-freedom, defined as self-limitation of analysis to rational, instrumental statements, is considered, on the one hand, as the only intellectual activity in tune with our time and our part of the world, but on the other hand, as a cognitive attitude which has universal validity, i.e. which can be applied to phenomena of other times and other parts of the world and still lead to objectively valid results. Parsons defined this idea as a 'basic universalism of values involved in [rational] social science' and saw it as akin to Karl Mannheim's selection of the 'free intelligentsia', bound to no particular cultural system, as the carriers of objective knowledge.[11] Parsons interprets Weber's postulate of value-free social science as the demand of, and belief in the possibility of, detachment of scientific activity from the historically limited culture of which it is a part: 'Value-freedom ... implies that a science need not be bound to the values of any particular historic culture.'[12] This is a very essential distortion of Weber's view. Nowhere in Weber can one find the view that social science owes its chance of reaching objectivity to its possible independence from history: on the contrary, the gist of Weber's idea is that social science can reach this ideal only because a culture has historically emerged within western civilization which can offer a science attuned to its values, a true universality genuinely superior to any other alternative interpretation of all cultural reality. Let us repeat: Weber's intellectual formation came from the German debate about historical understanding, and his sociological methodology emerged as a transposition of concepts forged in the smithy of historical hermeneutics.

First, Weber was acutely aware that he, as any other student of history, was himself a product of history; to be precise, of one historically created formation: modern European civilization. Secondly, he believed that whatever chance of objective, universal knowledge he may possess is due to this rather than in spite of it. In the major study which marked the turning-point from Weber the historian to Weber the sociologist, he made this point as clear as anyone could:[13]

A product of modern European civilization, studying any problem of universal history, is bound to ask himself to what combination of circumstances the fact should be attributed that in Western civilization, and in Western civilization only, cultural phenomena have appeared which (as we like to think) lie in a line of development having *universal* significance and value. Only in the West does science exist at a stage of development which we recognize today as valid.

Weber remained true to the paramount idea of the German classical tradition: freedom from historical limitation may be only a result of history. In this there was no contention between him and Hegel, Marx, or Dilthey, however distinct the specifically Weberian variation on the common theme.

The specifically Weberian treatment expressed itself above all in the selection of technically oriented, instrumental, rational activity as the product of historical development which endowed our own civilization with a degree of universality unmatched elsewhere and at any other time in the past. The prevalence of this unique type of human action has made an objective social science a realistic possibility. The numerous historical studies to which Weber dedicated a a better part of his life (and the comparative studies of historically significant religions in particular) were not separated from his methodological concerns. On the contrary, the clarification of the conditions which made a universally valid social science possible, and thereby the clarification of the rules of conduct which can bring this possibility to pass, supplied Weber with the rationale for his historical explorations.

The decisive turning-point in the history of civilization was, therefore,[14]

the emergence of a rational, antitraditional spirit in the human agents involved. The two main aspects of this are the evolution of modern science and its comparatively modern relationship to economics, and the growth of the modern organization of individual life [*Lebensführung*].

Modern, universally valid science has become possible as one element of the whole complex of historical developments which can be summarized as the emergence of modern capitalism. 'Inner-worldly asceticism' was, in Weber's view, the cultural adhesive which welded together the apparently diverse constituents of modern western civilization: the readiness to delay the immediate satisfaction of wants in the name of more remote ends, the willingness to subordinate one's life today to the distant rewards of the future, the propensity to assess one's own action in terms of its instrumental efficiency, and to give this efficiency precedence, in terms of loyalty and normative authority for action, over consummatory ends it is expected to serve. In Wolfgang Mommsen's words, Weber[15]

embarked upon the study of the great world religions primarily in order to corroborate his findings *ex negativo*. In the end Max Weber was convinced he had found an exhaustive answer to the universal historians' question why 'modern capitalism', 'modern science', the 'bourgeoisie' as a social class with its own peculiar ideological outlook, the rational organization of the political order by means of the modern administrative state, a 'rational law', and, last but not least, a 'rational type of music', had been developed only in the West. The *Vorbemerkung* to Weber's essay on the Sociology of World Religions can well be called a (however brief) substantive outline of universal history.

Rational science, so Weber tells us, appeared nowhere in the world and at no time in history except in the western world when it was already advanced on the road to capitalism. The coincidence hints on a deeper bond between the two which transcends a mere contemporaneity. The conduct typical of rational science and the life-style of a capitalist society are specialized applications of the same pattern. 'Continuous, rational, capitalist enterprise', 'rationality of capitalistic acquisition', 'actual adaptation of economic action to a comparison of money income with money expenses',[16] are all expressions of the same instrumental rationality which is the decisive resource of scientific objectivity. The progress in objectivity is broadly speaking synonymous with the increasing dominance of instrumental rationality over all other criteria of action. The reduction of alternative criteria to a subordinate and marginal position (when 'the ultimate and most sublime values have retreated from public life either into the transcendental realm of mystic life or into the brotherliness of direct and personal human relations')[17] makes possible this unequivocality of judgement, this objectively controlled comparability of contentious solution, which makes the agreement called 'objectivity' achievable. Objectivity is not simply a derivative of the suspension of evaluations; objectivity can come to pass only when *objective* evaluations become possible; to wit, only when a given civilization (like ours) offers a way to render such evaluations universally acceptable and, therefore, univocal:[18]

> The evaluations are unambiguous *only* when the economic end and the social context are definitely given and all that remains is to choose between several economic means, when these differ only with respect to their certainty, rapidity, and quantitative productiveness, and are completely identical in every other value-relevant aspect. . . . The use of the term 'progress' is legitimate in our disciplines when it refers to 'technical' problems, i.e., to the means of attaining an unambiguously given end. ['Technique', Weber emphasized elsewhere, 'is used here in its broadest sense, as rational action in general.'] It can never elevate itself into the sphere of 'ultimate' evaluations.

One could almost say that in such conditions, which become dominant with the advent of the capitalist market, value-judgements merge with objective interpretations. This, however, relates only to those value-judgements which are value-relevant, i.e. accept the dominant ultimate values of the era and, therefore, limit themselves to purely instrumental questions, and take the means as their sole object. Here lies the secret of the unsurpassed achievement of the civilization which, by securing an unchallenged domination of instrumentally rational conduct, took the sting of relativism out of evaluation. It is in this way that the practical utility of social science has become possible for the first time *without* sacrificing the principle of non-partisanship and value-neutrality of science. To be more precise, the one battle science can fight legitimately (i.e. whilst remaining true to its nature) is the one aimed at facilitating and prompting the tendency of our civilization towards reason, efficiency, instrumental perfection, and rationality.

Rationality being genuine (at least in the light of our civilization) only when confined to the consideration of technical-instrumental problems, it can serve as a basis for universal agreement, and hence 'objective validity', only if science similarly concedes that ultimate, consummatory values are beyond its bounds:[19]

> Only positive religions – or more precisely expressed: dogmatically bound *sects* – are able to confer on the content of *cultural values* the status of unconditionally valid *ethical* imperatives. Outside these sects, cultural ideals which the individual wishes to realize and ethical obligations which

he *should* fulfil do not, in principle, share the same status. The fate of an epoch which has eaten of the tree of knowledge is that it must know that we cannot learn the *meaning* of the world from the results of its analysis, be it ever so perfect; it must rather be in position to create this meaning itself. It must recognize that general views of life and the universe can never be the products of increasing empirical knowledge, and that the highest ideals, which move us more forcefully, are always formed only in the struggle with other ideals which are just as sacred to others as ours are to us.

The kingdom of ultimate values belongs forever to religion and religiously based ethical imperatives. Fortunately for science, one religion at least – the *innerweltliche Askese* preaching puritanism – proclaimed instrumentality and efficiency as the major command-ment and test of religious precepts, and thereby legitimized an instrumentally organized life-style and, simultaneously, instrumen-tally focussed knowledge. The society to which this unique religion has given birth favours action which is planned, decided upon, carried through and retrospectively assessed solely from the technical-instrumental point of view. Hence science, as an activity rational by definition, is tuned to the main current of social life; the kind of things science is best equipped to deal with have now become dominant in social reality. Society has come to be amenable to objective understanding:[20]

The question of the appropriateness of the means for achieving a given end is undoubtedly accessible to scientific analysis. Inasmuch as we are able to determine (within the present limits of our knowledge) which means for the achievement of a proposed end are appropriate or in-appropriate, we can in this way estimate the chances of attaining a certain end by certain available means.

Being tuned to the basis of social action that our civilization sus-tains, science is, by the same token, tuned to our common experience. All of us necessarily have an 'inside', introspective knowledge of the intentionally rational, teleologically (purposefully) organized action. Weber evidently agrees with the German hermeneutical tradition (Dilthey in particular) that 'sympathetic magic' is a powerful factor of understanding. But he confines its role to the non-universal types of conduct. In principle, so Weber asserts, one need not have been Caesar in order to understand Caesar. Unlike his predecessors, Weber emphasizes the operative role played in understanding by 'mutual tuning' of experiences, and hence by the personal endowment of the individual engaged in the effort to understand, only in relation to non-rational behaviour:[21]

> The more we ourselves are susceptible to them the more readily can we imaginatively participate in such emotional reactions as anxiety, anger, ambition, envy, jealousy, love, enthusiasm, pride, vengefulness, loyalty, devotion, and appetites of all sorts, and thereby understand the irrational conduct which grows out of them.

The obverse of this is that the subject can understand only those acts which may be portrayed as pursuing a motive which the subject himself could (even if he would not) adopt.

But the most common propensity of the members of a society which 'ate of the tree of knowledge' is, of course, to consider their own action as instrumental, i.e. as aimed at something other than the action itself; for instance, at achieving in practice some specific state of affairs which at the beginning of action existed only as an ideal. For such people 'to understand' would mean, above all, to envisage an end to which the observed act could lead – in the light of its consequences or in the intention of the actor. Hence in order to understand events they observe, these people will tend to organize their knowledge of them in a means–end sequence: to portray the visible behaviour as subordinated to, and explicable by, an end which has been 'on the actor's mind'. If this is a 'natural' tendency determined by the character of our 'rationalized' era, the method of understanding which Weber suggested and which will be explained below is nothing but a clarification of conditions in which, at our times, understanding is possible. 'How to make human action intelligible' and 'on what conditions human actions are intelligible to us, born in the epoch of rational market and science', merge into one question. Meaning, Weber tells us,

> may derive from a relation to exceedingly various purposes. Without reference to this meaning such an object remains wholly unintelligible. That which is intelligible or understandable about it is thus its relation to human action in the role either of means or of end; a relation of which the actor or actors can be said to have been aware and to which their action has been oriented. Only in terms of such categories is it possible to 'understand' objects of this kind [in the German original: understanding of such objects takes place – *findet ein Verstehen solcher Objekte statt*].

Events are 'devoid of meaning if they cannot be related to action in the role of means or ends but constitute only the stimulus, the favouring or hindering circumstances'.[22]

What follows from the above propositions is that we can understand only such actors as intend to act rationally, i.e. attempt to
relate whatever they do to an end they wish to attain. Or, rather, we
can understand only such actions as we are able to portray as being
of that nature (notice that the awareness of the actor of the purposeful nature of his action is not the condition of understanding; the
condition is only the possibility of such an awareness, i.e. finding a
purpose of a kind one can be, in principle, aware of). This conclusion
finds its further corroboration in another crucial definition, that of
the motive in terms of which the action can be understood: 'A motive
is a complex of subjective meaning which seems to the actor himself
or to the observer an adequate ground for the conduct in question';
later on Weber further clarifies the point, singling out 'our habitual
modes of thought and feeling' as the paramount factor in deciding
whether a given motive is, or is not, the 'adequate ground' for
action.[23]

The very concept of social action, which, in Weber's view, is for
sociology 'its central subject matter, that which may be said to be
decisive for its status as science',[24] is defined in a way which incorporates the connection between 'what is socially regulated in our
type of society' and 'what is intelligible sociologically for members
of such a society'. Social action is only that action which is oriented
towards other human beings, i.e. a part of social intercourse; but it
must be a part of normatively regulated intercourse (e.g., economic
activity is only social if, and then only in so far as, 'the actor's
actual control over economic goods is respected by others'[25]). And
it must be motivationally oriented towards relations with other
people, and hence be amenable to understanding. Thus the mass fury
of a crowd, in which thoughtful control of behaviour is for a time
suspended, is not a social action. Neither is the mere thoughtless
imitation of others social. Or, rather, both types of behaviour stand
'on the indefinite borderline of social action'. Somebody can, just,
make imitation the conscious and deliberate principle of his conduct;
for instance, a *nouveau riche* may wish to be accepted by the aristocracy of inherited wealth, and for this purpose to imitate their style
of life slavishly. Somebody else may consciously seek in the anonymity of the crowd an escape from the responsibility which otherwise
he would have to take individually and which he finds unbearable.
Thus the specific cases of crowd behaviour and imitation can cross
the boundary between social and non-social action in both directions.
Their doing so presents a serious empirical ambiguity which ought

not, however, to be confused with a lack of conceptual clarity. Though it is difficult to determine on which side a given act is to be located, the borderline itself can be drawn unequivocally. What distinguishes a 'non-social' imitation from imitation as a social action (i.e. as the 'central subject-matter' of sociology as an 'understanding' science) is the difference between the causal and the purposeful determination of behaviour.

In the light of these central ideas of Weberian sociology the widely quoted and uncritically accepted fourfold typology of social action seems strangely out of place and, indeed, the one part of Weberian sociology at odds with its central idea. On the one hand, the instrumentality, or purposefulness of conduct (and therefore the possibility of viewing it as a quasi-rational behaviour), is taken by Weber as the defining feature of action as distinct from mere behaviour. On the other hand – in his notorious typology – such an action is presented as one type only alongside three others; the other three, presumably, do not bear the characteristics which elsewhere have been singled out as its indispensable conditions. This is particularly striking in the case of acting out overwhelming affection or internalized habit; in these cases either powerful emotions or habituation reduce or subdue the powers of judgement and calculation which render an actor a free agent capable of setting a purpose and selecting the means appropriate to it. A person is fully in the grip of his emotions, or his traditional upbringing, and therefore does what he or she is forced to do rather than what he or she wants; his or her conduct obviously does not fall into the category of action as defined by Weber. Or, on the contrary, a person acts in a specific way because he or she is conscious of unbearably strong emotions which must be released for the sake of sanity or affectual balance, or because he or she is fond of tradition and considers it right to uphold the legacy of the past; the actions are straightforward instances of the class of 'instrumental rationality' and can be portrayed and evaluated as all other actions of the class are. The third of the 'odd' types of social action, '*wertrational*', which admittedly troubled more than anything else the numerous interpreters of Weber's ideas, seems to have been separated according to different logical criteria. Indeed, if seen as deliberate pursuit of a chosen end (to the detriment of all alternative ends), the so-called *wertrational* action is in no way distinct from the *zweckrational*, the one which limits the choice to the means only and never puts the ends in question. What distinguished the *wertrational* from the action which Weber would classify as *zweckrational* is, presumably, the end itself, which is at odds with the ends which ordinary *zweckrational* actors aim at in our *zweckrational* society; perhaps an end which comes into conflict with the pursuit of gain, the moving force of the capitalist market. The social nature of action has been defined, however, irrespective of the specific ends to which it might be oriented: it was the orientation to an end as such, rather than the orientation to one specific end, which has been proclaimed its distinctive feature. The criteria used to separate the *wertrational* as a distinct type of action have been, therefore, illegitimate according to Weber's own methodological rules. If these rules are applied consistently, the *wertrational* cannot but be subsumed under the category of *zweckrational*; it is indeed an instrumentally rational action, only aimed at a somewhat unusual, i.e. not universally accepted, end. (What seems to underlie Weber's amazing inconsistency is his unease in the face of 'dissident' values in a society which in his view has left the value-discussion behind and is well on the way to fully 'instrumental' rationality.)

All this having been said and considered, the structure of the instrumental–rational action emerges as the only framework in which sociological study as an activity aimed at the objective understanding of human behaviour can take place. Human behaviour can be the subject-matter of sociology in so far as, and to the extent in which, it can be considered or portrayed as having such a structure. In this, sociology is at one with the dominant tendency of modern society, which renders only instrumental–rational action socially relevant and therefore subject to normative regulation. Thus the stage has been set for a methodical analysis of the process of understanding itself.

Weber starts from the tripartite division of understanding borrowed from Dilthey. The first two types differ from their Dilthey's version in little but the dropping of the 'metaphysical prop'. They are cases of *'aktuelle'* (current; 'direct' in Parsons's translation) understanding. In this fashion we grasp the sense of a sentence, a thought, a mathematical formula, and other 'manifestations' of human thinking; or, for that matter, manifestations of human emotions as couched in naturally determined symptoms. In the same matter-of-fact way we grasp the relation between overt behaviour that we observe and its end-result, thereby perceiving the 'outer rationality' of action (for instance, the relation between opening a jar of preserves and eating up its contents). The choice of the term *'aktuelle'* to denote this kind of understanding suggests an underlining of the matter-of-fact, common, unmediated character of the understanding universally practised by ordinary people in ordinary circumstances. The *aktuelle* understanding, indeed, proceeds as a 'current activity' which takes place in the course of observation, reading, talking, listening. No knowledge of a wider framework in which the texts or the observed acts appear is necessary in order to 'make sense' of them.

Sometimes, however, we set ourselves more demanding goals. We want to go beyond the mere grasping of the sense of what we see; we want to understand as well the reasons which led to the actual creation of the text or performing of the observed activity. We ask the question 'why' in addition to the matter-of-fact 'what'. To Dilthey, the question 'why' means naturally referring the observable traces of action to the *Geist* whose expressions they are; to picture them as *Lebensaüsserungen*. To Weber, the question 'why', which represents the search for 'explanatory understanding', is naturally tantamount to referring the action back to the motives, i.e. the 'adequate ground' of action in the form of a subjectively adoptable purpose. This is an explanatory understanding. It goes beyond what we actually and 'currently' see and experience; it is an intellectual operation, which requires bringing together bits of knowledge obtained at other times and occasions than the reading of the text or the observation of the act. In order to attain explanatory understanding, we have to follow Dilthey's recipe of 'tying together' the past and the future – above all, of locating the act in question inside a larger totality (in Weber's words, 'in an intelligible and more inclusive context of meaning', or in 'an understandable sequence of motivation').[26] Unlike *aktuelle* understanding, explanatory understanding is itself a rational action, subordinate to the observer's consciously chosen purpose, monitored throughout and amenable to the same efforts of improvement and criteria of evaluation as rational action in general.

Weber never explicitly breaks clean with Dilthey's confusing demand to reconstruct the actual motive which guided the actor whose action we wish to understand: to penetrate the actual 'psychical event' in the head of the actor at the time of, or prior to, the action. At the time he wrote his monumental *Grundriss der Verstehenden Soziologie*, Weber was still willing to concede that the actually intended meaning, this elusive, never directly observable entity, is the object sought by explanatory understanding in the historical approach. It looks as if at this late stage Weber was prepared to take the historians' word for what is and what is not the legitimate business of their scholarship; himself, he considered his own field was socio-logy; his original enthusiasm for legislating for history was all but gone. By now Weber had his grand vision of 'rationalizing' society and science, akin to the nature of society it serves, and historic scholarship, an activity not of the same stock, interested Weber less. All his attention was now focussed on such explanatory understand-ing as can be furnished by science and by the application of scientific methods – a character which historians' quest for intended meanings did not possess. It seems that Weber considered the final emancipa-tion from pre-scientific preoccupations of historians as the major message of the *Grundriss*. After all, the only substantive declaration he made in the preface to his *magnum opus* is that it draws 'a sharp distinction between subjectively intended and objectively valid meanings'. Weber's attention, fully and indivisibly, was by then on the latter.

True, among the contexts in which explanatory understanding may arise as a problem and a task, historians' interest in intended meaning is followed by the case of 'sociological mass phenomena' when 'the average of, or an approximation to, the actually intended meaning' is sought; this is possibly a tribute to the long rule of the *Zeitgeist* as the central explanatory category of historical trends, and particularly of the traits by which mass behaviour in various epochs and parts of the world differ. Whether the supposition is true or not, the crucial fact is that Weber, this one brief sentence apart, never returns to the topic and nowhere attempts to furnish it with more methodological flesh. Such neglect would indeed be odd if Weber viewed this unspecified 'approximation to actually intended meaning' as an important and widely applicable tool which sociologists ought to use.

Instead, a full and detailed treatment is given to what are called in the preface 'objectively valid meanings', meanings which are 'appropriate' to a scientifically formulated type of phenomenon; note that only in the context of this kind of 'explanatory understanding' is the adjective 'scientific' used. What objectively valid, scientifically formulated meanings in sociology could be like, one can learn from the economic theory, which has taken the place of historiography as the source of methodological inspiration:[27]

They state what course a given type of human action would take if it were strictly rational, unaffected by errors or emotional factors and if, furthermore, it were completely and unequivocally directed to a single end, the maximization of economic advantage.

The objectively valid meaning of social action, which the science of society ought to declare its main concern, is therefore distinguished by two crucial characteristics: (1) there is no diversity of ends; on the contrary, alternative ends have been eliminated and the field of action is indisputably open to the pursuit of one, universally coveted, value; and (2) the action is thoroughly cleansed of all and any deterministic element, and therefore fully explicable by reference to the purpose and the relative cost and efficiency of available means. This is, as we know already, the pattern of rational conduct, modelled after idealized market behaviour, and representing, in Weber's view, the type of action ascending to the level of true universality.

This is the decisive step on the road to the final and irreversible rupture between the methodology of an 'understanding sociology', i.e. a sociology committed to approaching social facts as subjectively motivated and as oriented towards subjectively held values, and the hopeless and discredited effort to 'transfer oneself' into the actor's mind and to re-live his reasonings and feelings. Weber offers nothing less than a way in which subjective phenomena can be grasped and described objectively, while their uniqueness, admittedly defying any scientific treatment, can be raised to the level of 'generalized individuality' (Rickert's notion of the task of cultural sciences). The elegance of Weber's solution is that it does not entail, much less depend on, a denial of the inescapable historicity of cognition and the cognizing subject: on the contrary, the assumption of historicity is indispensable for validating the method in its Weberian form. The historically produced ascendance of rationality has supplied the missing foundation for universal agreement as to the interpretation of human action. Rational sequences are value-related, but the values they are oriented to are no longer disputed; given the universal agreement concerning the ends of action (universal for the western civilization as a whole), the rest is determined in purely technical terms, fully comparable and therefore value-free. Hence it is one stage in the development of historical relativity which has brought, at long last, its own demise.

Weber goes out of his way to make the distinction he promised in the preface as strict as possible. He tells us that 'the ideal type of meaningful action where the meaning is fully conscious and explicit is a marginal case'. Indeed, 'in the great majority of cases actual action goes on in a state of inarticulate half-consciousness of its subjective meaning'. As it were, 'the "conscious motives" may well, even to the actor himself, conceal the various "motives" and "repressions" which constitute the real driving force of action'. Hence the sociologist ought to be prepared, as a matter of principle, to describe and analyse the motivational situation 'even though it has not actually been concretely part of the conscious "intention" of the actor'.[28] This attitude is valid, let us repeat, for the twin reasons of its harmony with the historical tendency and its methodological superiority over all alternative attitudes. On the one hand, an interpretation of action as rationally purposeful has 'the highest degree of verifiable certainty'. On the other, the ever-increasing universality of legal–rational behaviour in our western world will gradually render theoretical, excessively rationalized ideal types ever closer approximations of empirical reality, and narrow the gap between theoretical concepts and empirical descriptions.

For the time being, before the hypothetical merger is attained by history, the decisive factors of strategic choice are methodological. For the purposes of scientific analysis 'it is convenient to treat all irrational, affectually determined elements of behaviour as factors of deviation from a conceptually pure type of rational action'. 'The construction of a purely rational course of action in such cases serves the sociologist as a type ["ideal type"] which has the merit of clear understandability and lack of ambiguity.'[29]

We have arrived, therefore, at a conclusion which has been tersely expressed by Arun Sahay: 'Understanding, for Weber, is not the subtle intuitive sympathy which philosophers favour – but intellectual, analytical, and predictive explanation of action.'[30] Understanding, as it finally emerges from the concept of ideal types, becomes a rational, codifiable, technically evaluable activity of men of science – people specially trained in the art of thinking rationally, in cost-and-effect analysis, and therefore exemplifying most fully the historical tendency of our times at a stage when this tendency has not yet succeeded in drawing the numerical majority of individuals into its orbit and re-moulding their behaviour. Born within the discursive formation of the German historical hermeneutics, Weber's discussion of understanding gradually disengaged itself from its original involvement and turned into the legitimation (though couched still in traditional hermeneutical vocabulary) of structural concepts and categories of a general nature,[31] fully controlled and administered by professional sociologists.

The circumstances in which Weber's work was discovered by the then-dominant American sociology facilitated a different reading of its actual intent. When seen against social science employing de-personalized and de-psychologized 'objective' variables and categories, Weber's significance seemed to consist in restoring unjustly neglected subjective meanings to their due prominence. Weber seemed to make a plea for a 'return to subjectivity', to the individual understood as the carrier of subjective intention to understanding interpreted as 'empathy', a sympathetic identification with the author. But the dominant style of American sociology in the 1940s and 1950s was not the discursive formation in which Weber's work developed, and which determined the significance and meaning of his sociology. Weber's struggle was not about forcing a sociology thoroughly dedicated to objectivism to pay a little more attention to subjectivity and subjectively held values. On the contrary, his was the long and exhausting battle for the emancipation of social science from the relativism in which it floundered, burdened as it was with its idealist and German-hermeneutical legacy. 'Granted that meanings are subjective; granted that historical categories, to make sense, must be relevant to these meanings; we can still have objective social science' – this, it seems, was the central portent of Weber's sociology. Weber spelled out the conditions under which social science can indeed become objective. Transforming the activity of understanding into construction of rational models was, alongside the acceptance of value-neutrality, the most crucial of them.

The possibility of objectively understanding a subjectively oriented action rests, as we remember, on the analyst's assent to refrain from the discussion of ends and therefore to evaluate the action solely in terms of its instrumental rationality. In Horkheimer's rendition, 'value-judgement should be justified by the setting of the task, not by its execution'.[32] The one value-judgement that sociologists bent on objectivity are allowed to make is concerned with their own task. As the value-judgement is a prerogative of authority, the right to decide which values their own activity is to serve amounts to setting up sociology as an autonomous profession with full sovereignty inside its own field. In choosing their consummatory values, however, sociologists are not entirely free. All authority in our modern, rationalizing society can be only cut of the same rock; sociologists' self-government rests safely on legitimate authority only if the end-value of their activity is akin to the end-values dominant in their society. The choice they face is, therefore, between the loss of scientific status and the self-proclaimed limitation of their project to the construction of models of rational action. Sociology can become a vocation only by surrendering the right to dispute the dominant values of its society, and by rendering this surrender the central value of its own activity. Of which Horkheimer caustically remarked that, 'if by value-freedom is not meant the obvious platitude that the scientist wears neither pink nor black glasses, and is not misled by his followers or by hate, then it means inhibition of thought';[33] while Habermas tried to decode its sociological meaning: 'So far as the postulate of value-freedom aims at restricting the social sciences to the production of technically utilizable knowledge, it is analogous to the political claim for protection of the decision-making authority from the competent expert's arrogance.'[34]

One could easily imagine Weber agreeing with Horkheimer and Habermas that these, indeed, are consequences of the model for the social sciences he sketched. But having frankly admitted that, Weber would undoubtedly retort that the courage to accept the consequences is precisely the act which divides objective understanding, the objective science of the subjective world, from romantic dalliance with inscrutable depths of human soul: the more confident are pronouncements on the subject of human nature and calling, the less warranted they are. One has the right to feel unhappy about the soulless, disenchanted, dehumanized world. But if one wishes to participate in the activity called science, one can as well embrace the chance this world, and this world alone, has to offer.

4 Understanding as the work of history: Karl Mannheim

In a sense the work of Karl Mannheim can be described as a consistent attempt to build a sociological foundation under Max Weber's methodology of understanding. Objective understanding, as we remember, was to Max Weber a unique chance created by the modern era of rationality. Two questions, however, remained curiously unattended in Weber's work: is the 'rationalist trend' of the modern era something more than just a historical coincidence, a lasting sediment of charismatic giants of the recent and not-so-recent past? And why ought we to trust that the chance these trends created will be taken up? Who is likely to do the job and why? Through most of his creative life Mannheim struggled to take a full stock of the problems these two questions entail, and to solve them in a systematic way.

Mannheim's work bears all the significant imprints of the discursive formation of *Geisteswissenschaften*. He takes it for granted that one needs to explain nature, but to understand culture; that to 'cognitively assimilate' natural phenomena one has to arrange them in causal chains, but to know cultural phenomena one has to grasp their meaning. And like Dilthey and Weber before him, he is not at all apologetic about the preoccupation of cultural study with meanings and understanding, entities so alien to the spirit of scholarly activity as natural scientists see and practice it. Like Dilthey or Weber, Mannheim ascribes the difference to the richness of cultural exploration which natural science is deprived of. The 'objective meaning' of phenomena, visible 'at a glance', carved all over the experiential 'surface' of the phenomenon, is a matter of concern for both natural and cultural scientists. But here, where natural scientists end their journey, students of culture begin the most important part of their cognitive task: to go beyond the observable object, into the wider realm of the 'spirit' of which it is an offshoot and a part, in order really to 'exhaust' its significance. Natural scientists, however, have nowhere further to go. If, for instance, they attempted to conceive of nature as a documentation of God's work on earth, they would 'merely shift to nature the mode of analysis properly suitable to culture'.[1]

There is, therefore, a wide area of investigation in which the cognitive tasks and methods of natural and cultural study do not significantly differ. This 'objective interpretation' is broadly equivalent to the '*aktuelle*' understanding in Dilthey or Weber. Mannheim has in mind the possibility of knowing the object by merely looking at it, and of constructing its full description while exploring it alone, in no relation to 'something different'. All the information to be incorporated in the knowledge of an object is derivable from the object itself. Since no intentional action is presupposed as its cause, no questions about intention need to be asked.

The question of intention leads us to the second level of understanding, which natural scientists need not, and could not, bother themselves with: expressive understanding. Here again the affinity between Mannheim, Weber and Dilthey is close: the object is seen as a 'manifestation' of a psychic event not directly visible. What we are after is accessible only in a mediated way; conclusions about what we do not see are made from what we do see, conclusions about the intention from its manifestation. The task is notoriously troublesome. The risk of error is considerable, and no hard and fast rules could stave it off. The success of expressive understanding hinges on the admittedly ill-defined factor of the subject's 'spiritual affinity' with the other human being whose actions or creations he wishes to understand. Affinity may extend the full range from the intimate sharing of life to mere membership of the same species; it never reaches the analytical extreme of full identity, and hence 'expressive understanding' never reaches the finality of the absolute. To make the task even more difficult, one cannot rely on 'stereotyped meanings' of human acts, on a fully institutionalized 'universal grammar of expression', as in the case of objective understanding; the essential assumption of expressive understanding is that the connections between acts and their intentional meanings are not codified or depersonalized, but on the contrary, in each case are essentially unique.[2]

Mannheim, however, seems to confine his interest in 'expressive understanding' to determining its distinctive features and listing the pitfalls one has to beware of when treading on the treacherous ground of intention analysis. His own interests seem to lie elsewhere. Like Weber, Mannheim was above all preoccupied with reaching an understanding which could legitimately discard invisible and inaccessible personal motives and thereby acquire the degree of methodological systematism which brings it closer to the ideal of objectivity. He clearly wishes to attune the kind of understanding he seeks to the essential spirit of the age of rationalism, which is to 'exclude from knowledge everything that is bound up with particular personalities and that can be proved only to narrow social groups with common experiences, and to confine oneself to statements which are generally communicable and demonstrable'.[3] Whereas, however, the dominant form of science tends to reach this end by the shortcut of simply declaring off limits all statements which, in principle, are not immediately demonstrable or communicable, Mannheim's project is more ambitious: without surrendering any of the stern requirements of universality, to extend the concept of legitimate rational knowledge in a way which includes assertions arrived at through understanding. But then, he tells us, only one understanding meets such stern criteria of legitimacy: 'documentary' understanding.

The first step one has to take in order to make his understanding demonstrable, i.e. objective, leads, according to Mannheim, towards disengagement from all intentional meanings invested in the analysed fact either 'objectively' (through deliberate employment of common, unequivocal and uncontentiously codified signs) or 'expressively' (through establishing a unique configuration of experiences and their manifestations, geared to personal feelings). In Mannheim's 'epoche' the murky realm of subjective intentions is suspended, put permanently in brackets: of course people have intentions, of course their action is intentional, of course the actors put their subjective meanings in what they do; but this is not the only clue to our understanding their action. More important still, it is not the best one. Documentary understanding can disregard the intentional meanings of the actor and still grasp his action as a cultural, spiritual, meaningful phenomenon. Documentary meaning is at no point intentional; it is, in fact, an analytical model of the subject's activity.[4] Documentary meaning, in other words, is not present spatio-temporally 'in the act'; it is not a psychic event which took place in the head of the actor (like expressive meaning), nor the significance brought into the act together with certain culturally established means of expression. Documentary meaning cannot be grasped by being 'dug up', 'read out', 'uncovered', etc. Documentary meaning must be construed. This is an analytical concept; an 'extraneous' meaning imputed to the action not by its subject, but by an objective observer who remains permanently 'outside' (does not attempt to 're-live' subject's experience, to spark off his feelings in himself, etc.). Through documentary understanding, the student of culture can grasp meanings of which actors of cultural drama are unaware; thereby it can rise above the level of routine cultural activity and achieve the degree of objectivity which in daily life is unattainable. This is possible because documentary understanding employs rational means only, and sternly refuses to resort to vehicles of empathy, co-feeling, and similar Romantic favourites:[5]

The best way to get this difference clear is to imagine oneself sharing the life of an artist, spending every living minute with him, taking part in all his moods and every wish of his, constantly occupied with all the things that occupy him – all this without ever bothering about documentation. In such a case, one would understand the artist's work in the 'expressive' dimension and one would have a more or less adequate picture of the latter's stream of experience in which one would be a partner – and yet one would lack insight into the artist's personality, his *Weltanschauung*, his ethos. And conversely, another analyst with scant familiarity with the artist's work and actions, but with an acute documentary sense, could build upon the little factual material at his disposal a complete characterization of the artist's personality and outlook, not in the psychological but in the cultural sense.

Documentary meaning is the work of the analyst. It is the end-product of a long and laborious gathering together of hints and clues scattered all over the wide range of cultural phenomena, and synthesizing from this disparate evidence a totality, anchored in a person, or in a group, or in a historical age. Categories employed by sociologists are all, in the last account, of this kind. The 'Classical' or 'Romantic' spirit, the ethos of knighthood, proletarian consciousness, middle-class life-style, and so many other similar concepts all belong to the same category: they all are documentary meanings constructed in the process of documentary understanding.

All of them are suggestive of a collective subject, be it the diffuse community of Romantic artists, the stratum of medieval knights, or the modern industrial proletariat. One has to remember, however, that as much as the documentary meaning itself, the collective subject postulated as its bearer is by no means an objective, spatio-temporal being. The subject of a documentary meaning is an analytical construct and exists nowhere but in the scholar's discourse. It is a grave error to expect that every proletarian identified by sociological criteria of occupation, class membership, etc., must be, as a person, the bearer of 'proletarian consciousness' (in its documentary sense), an error arising from a confusion of sharply distinct fields of discourse: expressive and documentary meanings. One commits another serious mistake if no clear distinction is made between the collective subject of expressive meaning and the collective subject of a documentary one. Expressive meaning refers to real, empirical individuals, and to the experiences they went through at a definable point of time and an empirically determinable occasion. If we treat this collection of individuals as a collectivity, it can be only in the sense of an aggregate; what we articulate as a 'collective expressive meaning' has, accordingly, a similarly aggregate nature – it may mean, for instance, 'the average intention', or the 'common denominator' of all individual experiences. The correspondence between the collective subject as a collection of individuals and the collective expressive meaning as a statistical derivative of their actual experiences is, therefore, assured 'objectively', by the very logic of empirical investigation. Not so in the case of documentary meaning. Since meaning in this case has been consciously and consistently detached from the subjects' thoughts, feelings, or intention, the overlap between its postulated collective subject and the collective subject of expressive meanings is not guaranteed by the logic of analytical method. The presence or absence and the extent of such overlapping is an empirical problem. Having worked out the documentary meaning and related 'collective subject', one must empirically establish the group of actual individuals whose characteristics fit the analytically postulated features of this subject. In this respect, we find a striking similarity between the status Mannheim ascribed to his 'documentary meanings' and one assigned by Max Weber to 'ideal types'.

There is, therefore, a rupture between the sociological notion of consciousness and the concept of consciousness as implied by documentary method. If in its methodological status the latter is akin to Weber's 'ideal type', in its ontological premises it goes well beyond Weber, straight to the central idea of the German idealist tradition. In this tradition, a nation, class, or any other group of a similar category is viewed as an entity constituted by the very function of 'bearing' a particular variety of consciousness. It has no empirically ascertainable characteristics which precede the onset of consciousness-bearing; something of the sort of 'documentary understanding' is in fact the only, and therefore unchallengeable, empirical anchoring of the 'group'. It is therefore wrong to describe the group as a collection of members, and its collective features as derivatives of members' properties and activities. Individuals do not collectively produce the 'spirit' of the group; rather, they 'partake' of it. The group itself exists on the authority of its 'spirit'; it is, for all we know, the incarnation of 'spirit', rather than its carrier. This philosophical notion of the group is therefore immune to argument from empirical evidence; it does not really challenge the notion of, say, proletarian consciousness, if it is discovered that almost all people sociologically classified as 'proletarians' have only a vague idea of it, or even actively resent its essential tenets.

This empirical immunity of the 'spirit' is by no means a minor irritant, particularly to an age which has assigned high authority to empirical evidence. Max Weber, as we remember, hoped that the hiatus between the ideal-typical meanings and those actually held would eventually shrink or disappear altogether in the advancing rationalization of modern society; ideal-typical meanings were, in a sense, anticipations of what the real consciousness would be like when the subjects acted according to the rules of rationality. Mannheim, however, has nothing to buttress the hope that the hiatus will turn transient. He has not taken up Weber's offer of a historiosophy of rationalization as a solution of the difficulty.

Having neglected Weber's solution, Mannheim reopens the whole question of the compatibility between sociological description and the task of understanding as posited by historical hermeneutics. This question, never satisfactorily answered, was to become the major tension of Mannheim's project:[6]

Between these two kinds of subject – the subject of collective spirit, derived from the interpretation of cultural objectifications, and the anthropological and sociological subject – the discrepancy due to their heterogeneous origin is so great that it seems absolutely imperative to interpolate an intermediate field of concepts capable of mediating between these two extremes.

While one of the boundaries of the intermediate field is, thanks to empirical sociology, tolerably clear-cut, the other is notoriously ill-defined. It is not easy to show the validity of a 'documentary meaning' with the same compelling cogency as is attained by describing the meanings actually held by 'sociological subjects'. The latter has achieved findings 'everybody must accept' by deliberately turning a blind eye to all the problems whose image is bound to be coloured by non-codifiable properties of cognizing subjects: the one act of cognitive austerity which the search of documentary meanings could not commit. In tying together the separate threads of cultural evidence, the perceptiveness and ingenuity of the observer admittedly plays a crucial role. And not all his insight is his personal achievement, to wit, something which can be acquired by proper training and mastering of standardized method. A good part of the perceptiveness by which the success of 'documentary understanding' stands or falls is determined by factors on which the researcher himself has little or no influence.

These are the personal or group faculties with which the cognizing spirit has been endowed in the course of its history or biography; among them, affinity with the cognized counterpart plays the crucial role. Mannheim has never succeeded in cutting the umbilical cord linking his methodological tools to the 'sympathetic magic' of Dilthey's empathy. Even when discussing documentary meanings (nearest as they are to his idea of objective understanding) Mannheim insists on the decisive role of similarity of experience, biography-sharing, etc., in the successful construction of documentary models:[7]

To understand the 'spirit' of an age, we have to fall back on the 'spirit' of our own – it is only substance which comprehends substance. One age may be nearer in essence than another to a particular era, and the one with the closer affinity will be the one whose interpretation will prevail. In historical understanding, the nature of the subject has an essential bearing on the content of knowledge, and some aspects of the object to be interpreted are accessible only to certain types of mind.

Mannheim uses the example of inter-generational understanding: 'The characterization which has the best chance of being recognized as most "comprehensive" (rather than "objectively correct") is the one arrived at when the interpreter is of the same age as the person characterized.' For Mannheim, it helps to be a Caesar after all, to understand Caesar. Documentary meanings stop short of the ideal of 'objective understanding'. It is rather their richness, and the elusive quality of 'substantial affinity with the object', which distinguishes a better documentary meaning from an inferior one, even when both claim to be 'correct', i.e. in agreement with the known documentary evidence. This richness is not a product of gradual accretion of information. Unlike the natural sciences, the construction of documentary meanings is not cumulative: one 'does not add one item of knowledge to another but reorganizes the entire image around a new centre in each epoch.[8] Interpretation means discovering unity among apparently disparate expressions of meaning. This unity, however, is founded on an entity outside the interpreter. There is – Mannheim emphasizes repeatedly – a genuine personality of the artist, a real 'spirit' of an era, an actual religious outlook; documentary understanding, however large its 'modelling' element, is in its essence reconstruction rather than building from scratch. In order, for instance, to understand the curious and apparently haphazard alternation of asceticism and mysticism as expressions of religious selection, 'we must re-enact genuine religious experience'.[9] Documentary meanings are, therefore, subject to a double bind (again Dilthey's legacy): on the one hand, an objective totality unites various expressive meanings; on the other, the activity of the interpreter is propelled by another totality of which he in turn is a part. This double bind renders 'valid knowledge' problematic. Accordingly, Mannheim dedicated his most arduous efforts to elucidating the criteria and conditions of that validity.

First, one has to look closer at the totality which can become the object of valid knowledge. It is here that sociology is expected to help. Mannheim means sociology in its rather trivial, Durkheimian sense: for his task, sociology boils down to the 'assumption that individuals do not *create* the patterns of thought in terms of which they conceive the world but take them over from their groups'.[10] Then the 'unity' or 'totality' which is to become the object of documentary understanding is to be bought in the meaningful activity of a group, rather than of individuals; it can be grasped by sociological rather than psychological methods. The 'systemic whole' of real interest is, therefore, the 'style of thought' rather than the personality. Documentary meaning is a reconstruction of the style of thought. In order causally to explain a work of art, one has to place it inside a succession of events organized as the biography of the artist; in order, however, to grasp its meaning, one has to find first its location within the 'style of thought' in which the given artist, consciously or without knowing, partakes.

How are we to understand this? Mannheim coined the concept, or so it seems, to connote the somewhat obfuscate space which extends between Kantian transcendental, and therefore analytically universal, 'tuning' of the human mind, and the truly individual features of its products. The first are by definition universal conditions of any thought, and therefore present no problem, however powerful their impact on the final form of the 'object of knowledge'

as distinct from the 'object of reality'; the second, again by definition, can be dealt with by psychology alone and explained (causally),
rather than interpreted as a part of sociological totality. Between the
two, however, lies a fertile field waiting to be tilled by sociology: of
factors neither universal nor unremediably private, but social. If
Kant's 'transcendental pre-conditions' of all cognition spare us
from idle dreams of an eventual identity of objects of knowledge
with their real prototypes (or corresponding objects of reality), they
still do not account for the notorious variety of 'objects of knowledge' claiming to correspond to the same objects of reality. They
show convincingly that whatever is known must remain forever in
its specifically human form. They do not show why there ought to be
not just one but the whole variety of such 'human forms' of knowledge. Why, for example, medieval thought should differ from
Renaissance, liberal, or Romantic thought. Why 'bourgeois' thought
should insist on an account of the same reality different from
'proletarian' thought. Mannheim's project is, in a sense, an extension
of Kant's. Mannheim wants to reveal the factors responsible for the
fact that objects of knowledge do not just differ from real ones, but
that they differ in a variety of ways. Mannheim's idea of the variety
of thought as a manifestation of variety of social being is, in the last
instance, no more than a proposed procedure for an intelligible
systematization of thought. As such, it belongs to the category
Ernst Grünwald called 'external views' – which, in his opinion,[11]

are equally true – and each is true only if its basic thesis is assumed. None
of the external views has the character of absolute, unconditional truth –
each is only hypothetically valid. . . . The different external views can be
no more confronted than the dispute among metaphysical systems can be
settled by scientific means.

This seems the major weakness of Mannheim's implementation of
his own project. It can be accepted or rejected, equally inconclu-
sively, following the acceptance or rejection of its essential assumptions.

Mannheim himself unhesitatingly opts for sociology, in opposition
to psychology, as an approach whose results everybody will be
inclined to accept; as, in other words, a point of view which renders
possible the closest approximation to 'objective understanding'. His
choice is determined by the purpose of his project; otherwise – he
knows and makes it clear – psychological and sociological alternatives are equally valid and legitimate:[12]

Any human attitude or activity can be considered from both angles, and accordingly reveals its double meaning. One can observe and define any human action:

(*a*) in terms of the psychological, purely subjective intentions or motivations which are implied in it, or

(*b*) one can define its meaning in terms of the social functions it consciously or unconsciously fulfils.

On the one hand, therefore, Mannheim admits that there is a choice, dictated by the project at hand, between psychological explanation in terms of motives, and sociological understanding in terms of functions and institutions. On the other hand, however, Mannheim seems to suggest in places that the sociological interpretation of attitudes and actions is objectively sounder than the psychological; that, in other words, the assumptions on which psychological interpretation is founded are ultimately based on an erroneous view of individual psyche as a self-sustained world. The sociological approach, unlike the psychological, has etiological value. Motives and allegedly individual values are originally properties of the group. Groups hold to them because some patterns of acting, unlike others, perform a definite and important function for the group. The paramount function (a Durkheimian motif) is the promotion of group integration. This, according to Mannheim, becomes particularly evident in cases of action related to the 'public sphere', i.e. regimented by social institutions:[13]

You may start with subjective motivations or personal intentions of a quite peculiar kind, but as soon as you take over a function in a given system of division of labour, or you act as a member of a family or a club, you will probably tend to act according to certain traditional patterns or rationally established rules.

The above reasoning suggests a trivial sense of a group standing over and above individual members and instilling in their minds and actions the values and attitudes which have a survival value to the group as a whole (survival consisting, in the first place, of maintaining group integration). The 'style of thought' may be interpreted in this context as just another version of a group culture to which members of the group, by education, example and control, are being socialized.

But Mannheim's treatment of styles of thought as discovered by 'documentary understanding' is not consistent enough to warrant only one interpretation. The main tension of Mannheim's sociology of knowledge – between understanding as defined by historical hermeneutics, and sociological description – shows itself again. Mannheim seems to hesitate between interpreting the social origin of thought-styles in terms of the diffuse or wilful action of a supra-individual entity, or in terms of the inescapable correspondence between *Erlebnisformen* and *Lebensformen*, forms of consciousness and forms of life (*Wissensoziologie* style). In the latter case, the distinctive attributes of a style of thought are seen to stem from a selective approach to reality (and, therefore, its biassed cognition) conditioned by the group's particular way of life. All styles of thought reflect reality, but each reflects only some aspects of reality, brought to light or made relevant by the practice of a given group. As we will see, it is to this interpretation that Mannheim resorts when struggling with the prospects of agreement between the contentious 'thought-styles' of the modern era, and attempting to prove the possibility of 'scientific politics'.

It is mostly in *Ideology and Utopia* that Mannheim posits the social connections of knowledge as a difficulty, and their severance as a task which ought to be performed before true knowledge of social life can be attained. Right understanding is now merged with 'scientific control' and criticism, without which human activity 'tends to get out of hand'.[14] Socially influenced knowledge turns now into 'pre-scientific inexact mode of thought'; social influence itself becomes a socially induced prejudice or bias, which for the sake of truth ought to be exposed and eradicated. The change is formidable. Mannheim evidently acquired – or has chosen – a new audience. In the new context the reference to truth and objectively valid knowledge has become imperative, small as the previous role was in Mannheim's thought. In his previous writings, Mannheim did not seem particularly worried by the fact that some kind of group anchorage is an indispensable and determining feature of all thought. Now this universal phenomenon grows into a major irritant. For *Wissensoziologie* the socio-historical determination of knowledge was a fact of life to be explored, if possible neutralized in the effort of understanding, but otherwise lived with; for the sociology of knowledge it is a problem, in the same sense as, say, juvenile delinquency or alcoholism are problems for public administration. Significantly, Mannheim defines the principal thesis of the sociology of knowledge he wishes to introduce to his Anglo-Saxon audience as the admission 'that there are modes of thought which cannot be adequately understood as long as their social origins are obscured'. It is easy to conclude that there are also modes of thought which can be adequately understood without reference to social origin. The issue of social determination of knowledge has been thereby reduced to the problem of ideological perversions of truth.

To change faith is, however, less difficult than to change a mode of thinking. When Mannheim tries to spell out just what the 'social origins' consist of and why they are so important for correct understanding, nothing in his inventory of factors could not be applied universally to all thinking and to all categories of thinking creatures. 'He speaks the language of his group'; 'he thinks in the manner in which his group thinks'; 'he participates in thinking further what other men have thought before him'; 'they act with and against one another in diversely organized groups, and while doing so they think with and against one another' – all these features can with little hesitation be attributed to social beings of any era or class. We are still in the discursive formation in which reality is given to the human subject only as one of the socio-historically generated and sustained *Lebensformen*, and there is no compelling reason to exclude some people from this general rule. With all his conversion to the positivistically defined objectivity of social science, Mannheim cannot believe that one can shrug off one's group-induced outlook or thought-style by a sheer act of will. But he now hopes that in some critical situations such an emancipation may become possible. Moreover, he is inclined to accept that the emancipation is already round the corner. Imperceptibly, he shifts from Dilthey's historiosophical serenity to Weber's business-like determination – though he chooses a shortcut different from Weber's. Discovering conditions in which the 'severance from the social situation and context of activity' may become realizable turns now, in Mannheim's view, into the central task of the sociology of knowledge.

History, understood as a man-made, but superhuman in its compelling force, trend towards self-purification of thought, once again comes to the rescue of the thinker seeking a foundation for his hope. It is not, however, a history which brings up a new dominant mode of thought applicable to the understanding of all and any action (as in Weber); nor is it a history which makes transparent the world previously opaque and shrouded in false appearances (as in Marx). It is a history which finally generates a peculiar category of people whose social determination consists of the lack of social determination. In a world of partisan passions and parochial myopia this category alone climbs to the heights of generalized humanity. As Mannheim tells us,[15]

the crux and turning point in Western history is the gradual dissolution of the compact caste-like strata. The scholar was the first to be affected by this shift. . . . The modern intellectual has a dynamic bent and is perenially prepared to revise his views and make a new beginning, for he has little behind him and everything before him.

And, more forcibly still:[16]

The rise of intelligentsia marks the last phase of the growth of social consciousness.

Modern intellectuals, according to Mannheim, are the first (and, as one would conclude, the last) social category in history capable of seeing through the blinkers which impeded the vision of all the others. This unique gift, however, is due neither to their superior logic nor to their unprecedented disposition to scepticism. History, so to speak, spawned perspicacious intellectuals and revealed its secrets to their perspicacity at the same time; both remarkable occurrences resulted, in fact, from the same process. The advent of the first historical category capable of learning the truth was the consequence of modern pluralism.

The world determination of collective thought would never reach the level of consciousness if people were not given the chance of viewing their own world-view as just one of many plausible alternatives. According to Mannheim, this chance was absent for most of western history. Not that people of the past were unaware of the variety of co-existing views; the more intelligent among them were in all probability alive to the mosaics of ideas. But they hardly ever confronted the differences between views as oppositions. One never perceives views as irreconcilable until one faces the task of reconciling them.

Members of a society 'organized along the lines of closed castes or ranks' did not see things this way. There was no puzzle in the diversity of ideas as long as one had no need to choose between them. It was, in Mannheim's view, the beginning of modern social mobility – the human traffic between social positions, spanning of the social mosaic by an individual biography – which put the question of 'reconcilability' on the agenda. Our age, perhaps, is not unique in its degree and intensity of disagreement. But there is no doubt that the disagreements it harbours are more conspicuous to contemporaries than was the case before. The breath-taking pace of geographical, social and intellectual mobility brings face to face world-views which in other conditions would never become aware of each other's existence (or, if they did, would observe rules of territorial or social separation). For the first time, therefore, issues of communication, understanding, reconciliation and agreement pressed themselves with such a formidable urgency upon the society.

In the context of these new, characteristically modern tasks, the chance has been created of transforming the 'collective-unconscious' into a 'collective-conscious', to draw the hidden springs of human action from the depth of the unconscious where they remained for ages, right into the limelight of intellectual analysis. History, so to speak, has brought them already to the surface; 'the decisive change takes place when the stage of historical development is reached in which the previously isolated strata begin to communicate with one another and a certain social circulation sets in'; it is then that the question 'how it is possible that identical human thought-processes concerned with the same world produce divergent conceptions of that world'[17] almost asks itself. What is still needed is a kind of people capable of taking up the challenge and finding the right way to the right answer.

Now each society has a group of people who specialize in answering, for the society, all sorts of questions related to the interpretation of the ways of life in which the society is engaged – 'to provide an interpretation of the world for that society'. Mannheim calls this group the 'intelligentsia'. In a stable society, the intelligentsia is stable, with well-defined and rule-governed status. In a caste society, the intelligentsia is itself a caste. The new intelligentsia, however, is as unstable and as un-caste-like as our modern society. Again we learn that 'the decisive fact of modern times' is that 'in place of a closed and thoroughly organized stratum of intellectuals, a free intelligentsia has arisen'.[18]

Several features have hand-picked the modern intelligentsia for the task of seeing through the deceptions and distortions of the 'social determination of knowledge'. To start with, the new intellectuals, true to the openness of modern society, come from all strata and all walks of life. They bring into their intellectual activities traditions and experiences of most groups of the society, including such whose subconscious, diffuse longings and grievances never before reached the level of systematic articulation. More important still, 'the intellectual is now no longer, as formerly, a member of a caste or rank',[19] and is therefore free from the blinkers imposed by the sectarian discipline of a corporation, or the equally blinding *esprit de corps* of a caste. Intellectuals are now free to choose their own affiliations; there is no one world-view they are bound to voice, no one group interest they are forced, or trained, to preach. They have, at least as far as their external social constraints are concerned, a new ability to 'choose their affiliation', to 'attach themselves to classes to which they originally did not belong'.[20] Thus they have both rich material of which to mould true knowledge, and the freedom to do so if that is their wish.

Why ought access to various experiences and interests facilitate the production and acquisition of objective knowledge?

The central category of the traditional historical hermeneutics was, as we remember, that of *Zeitgeist*; the changeability of human consciousness expressed itself, according to this view, mostly in the changing spirits of successive eras. Each historical stage had a form of consciousness which was geared to its unique conditions and, simultaneously, determined the totality of its peculiar life-style. It was a tacit assumption of all hermeneutics that to this type of consciousness-differentiation (along the axis of historical time), the notions of truth and falsity are not applicable, or at least are irrelevant. A *Zeitgeist* can be sensibly judged only in the context of its historical setting; even if a later perspective can facilitate a better understanding of its contents, it could hardly expose it as a 'distortion' of truth. As Mannheim aptly emphasizes, this was not the attitude of relativism: relativism assumes one, indivisible truth as an ideal pattern which allows us to see all other forms of consciousness as departures from the 'right' form; only when such a norm-truth has been taken as a premise can one adopt a relativist attitude by declaring that in practice the truth is unknowable (because, for example, no man can step beyond the limits of his social upbringing, his culturally determined values, or his language). The relativist attitude is, therefore, a kind of 'negation of negation'; first one tries to criticize historical forms of consciousness in the light of an a-historical standard of truth, and then one concludes, rightly or wrongly, that the endeavour is futile and, consequently, the 'emic' (rather than 'etic') approach, the approach from 'indigenous categories', is the only way in which various forms of knowledge could be judged. In this sense, hermeneutics' approach to *Zeitgeist* was not relativist; no a-historical standard of truth had been assumed in the first place, and therefore no denial of its existence or 'knowability' was possible. Instead, the treatment of *Zeitgeist* was, in Mannheim's vocabulary, 'relationist'. To take a relational attitude means simply to assert that 'what is intelligible in history can be formulated only with reference to problems and conceptual constructions which themselves arise in the flux of historical experience'.[21] The relational attitude, one would say, does not go beyond the modest demands of applying what Florian Znaniecki calls the 'humanistic coefficient', i.e. that the student of cultural phenomena ought to try 'to discover not what this datum is to him, but what it has been and perhaps still is to those others'.[22] In this sense Mannheim concedes that the investigator who undertakes historical study as delineated by the concept of *Zeitgeist* 'need not be concerned with the problem of what is ultimate truth'.[23]

It has been our modern experience, the recent opening of our eyes to the coexistence of widely divergent interests and views in the *same* historical period, which has extended our view of history beyond the category of *Zeitgeist* – as an exclusive ethos of the era as a whole. The problem of truth, dormant as long as the task of historical understanding is confined to the study of *Zeitgeist*, enters historical investigation the moment we become alive to the variety of 'norms, modes of thought, and patterns of behaviour that exist alongside of one another in a given historical period'.[24] One ought not to be unduly disturbed by the succession of historical forms of human consciousness as long as one can assume a strict correspondence between changing forms of consciousness and changing historical conditions; validity to given conditions offers a criterion of judgement which makes the other criterion, that of a-temporal truth, redundant. But what about a whole series of forms which 'exist alongside of one another'? Surely they cannot be all valid 'in a given situation', if a given situation is interpreted as one and the same for all contemporaries. A person trained in the tradition of historical hermeneutics is likely to respond to this caveat by attempting an articulation of the new problem in old terms: to articulate the horizontal, co-temporal variety of outlooks in terms of the changeability of outlooks as a function of historical time. Indeed, this is the response given, at least initially, by Mannheim. Introducing the concept of 'false consciousness', absent in the earlier vocabulary of historical hermeneutics, he still attempts to accommodate the new notion (and the new experience) in the universe of discourse organized around the idea of *Zeitgeist*:[25]

Viewed from this standpoint, knowledge is distorted and ideological when it fails to take account of the new realities applying to a situation, and when it attempts to conceal them by thinking of them in categories which are inappropriate. . . .

In the same historical epoch and in the same society there may be several distorted types of inner mental structure, some because they have not yet grown up to the present, and others because they are already beyond the present.

Hence Mannheim's notorious distinction between ideology and utopia, two types of 'distortion of truth', two types of consciousness at odds with their time; one because it clings to too distant a past, the second because it looks too far into the future; both disregard the present and are disloyal to the *Zeitgeist*, which alone has the authority of setting the current standards of validity.

Mannheim's treatment of 'false consciousness' of partisan interests not just as conditions of thought, but as the source of truth-distortion, becomes intelligible when seen against the major tension of his work: between, let us recall, the discursive formation of the historical hermeneutics from which his work originated, and the universe of empirical sociology, with which he wished to communicate. Mannheim's concept of ideology seems to derive from his effort to master intellectually the concept of 'objective truth' as advanced by empirical sociology, while rescuing the basic categories of hermeneutical 'relationism' centred around the notion of historical time. The tasks of sociology, as Mannheim sees them, have been subordinated to those of historical hermeneutics: to determine 'which of all the ideas current are really valid in a given situation'. But in order to perform this central task, sociology ought to 'analyse without regard for party biases all the factors in the actually existing social situation which may influence thought'.[26]

I have mentioned already the difficulty of interpreting unambiguously the exact meaning ascribed by Mannheim to this 'social influence upon thought' – a difficulty again associated with the crucial antinomy of his work. On the one hand, numerous statements allow us to conclude that Mannheim's 'social influence' denotes the empirical limitations imposed upon individual or group experience by the place occupied within the social structure. Thus we read that the products of cognitive process are differentiated 'because not every possible aspect of the world comes within the purview of the members of a group, but only those out of which difficulties and problems for the group arise'.[27] The 'social influence' appears here to arise from technical conditions of cognition; if only the group were given access to an experience it has been denied, it would acquire a different kind of knowledge. An ardent follower of Mannheim, Ichheiser, used once the following simile to visualize this: suppose there is a windowless room with three doors *A*, *B*, and *C*; there is a switch by each door; the switch by door *A* puts on green lights, the switch by door *B* red lights, and the switch by door *C* blue lights; suppose that three men, *P*, *Q*, and *R*, enter the room often, each always through the same door, but never through the same door as either of the other two. *P*, who constantly uses door *A*, will firmly believe (and have unshakable empirical evidence to defend his belief) that the room is green; *Q*, who uses door *B*, will be as strongly convinced that the room is red; and *R*, of course, will have no reason to doubt that the room is blue. All three reason rationally and on the ground of reliable empirical evidence. However, as each is spatially situated in his peculiar way, they arrive at irreconcilable conclusions.

In some parts (though not all) of his famous list of the ideal types of modern thought-styles, Mannheim seems to apply the notion of 'social influence'. It is particularly conspicuous in his discussion of 'bureaucratic conservatism'. He asserts in this case, that[28]

the attempt to hide all problems of politics under the cover of administration (the defining feature of this style of thought) may be explained by the fact that the sphere of activity of the official exists only within the limits of laws already formulated. Hence the genesis of the development of law falls outside the scope of his activity. As a result of his socially limited horizon, the functionary fails to see that behind every law that has been made there lie the socially fashioned interests and the *Weltanschauungen* of a specific social group.

But not all ideal types lend themselves as easily to the interpretation suggested by Ichheiser's simile and inspired by sociological empiricism.

Of the so-called 'proletarian outlook', for instance, Mannheim says things reminiscent less of empirical sociology and more of imaginative constructs of hermeneutics. Thus we read that

the individual members of the working-class, for instance, do not experience *all* the elements of an outlook which could be called the proletarian *Weltanschauung*. Every individual participates only in certain fragments of this thought-system. . . .

Where, therefore, does this outlook come from, if not from the collective experience of the individuals? The answer is: the class outlook, which is not the outlook of the group, arises from the need (visible to the analyst) for such an outlook:[29]

Viewed sociologically this extreme need for theory is the expression of a class society in which persons must be held together not by local proximity but by similar circumstances of life in an extensive social sphere. . . . Hence a rationalized conception of history [which, according to Mannheim, is the distinctive feature of the proletarian outlook] serves as a socially unifying factor for groups dispersed in space. . . .

Note that in this case the 'social situation' urges the group in some not very clear way to 'have an outlook', but is hardly accountable for the actual form which the outlook may take. The 'proletarian consciousness' is, therefore, an entirely different notion from, say, 'bureaucratic conservatism', though both appear in the same typology as application of the principle of 'social influence on thought'.

However equivocal the sense in which Mannheim uses his major heuristic rule (to understand thought in conjunction with its social origins), he is consistent in his view that all knowledge bears the imprint of its origin and, therefore, that no knowledge can reach a really universal standpoint unless it dissociates itself first from its own social roots:[30]

It is clearly impossible to obtain an inclusive insight into problems if the observer or thinker is confined to a given place in society. . . . It seems inherent in the historical process itself that the narrowness and the limitations which restrict one point of view tend to be corrected by clashing with the opposite points of view.

Let us attend to the full import of this statement: the possibility that a standpoint inside the social system can be found which offers its incumbents a direct insight into objective truth is out of question. This, presumably, applies as well to modern intellectuals. One can reach the truth only through forcing various distortions of the truth to confront each other and clash. The truth may be extracted, as a precious nugget from worthless dross, from the debris of ideologies which called each other's bluff. 'Only when we are thoroughly aware of the limited scope of every point of view are we on the road to the sought-for comprehension of the whole.'[31]

Where, therefore, is this 'point of view' which is not like all the other points of view, when the human eye may acquire the equanimity or omniscience of the divine one? Only when it resembles a divine eye, i.e. when it jettisons itself beyond the bounds of society. Since this is impossible, the nearest substitute is intellectual detachment: an obdurate refusal to commit oneself to any point of view in particular, and an equally stubborn insistence on viewing all the outlooks as derivatives of particularistic points of view.

This is precisely the chance which history has offered modern intellectuals:

> Although situated between classes [this stratum] does not form a middle class. Nor, of course, is it suspended in a vacuum into which social interests do not penetrate; on the contrary, it subsumes in itself all these interests with which social life is permeated.

Unlike other social groups, intellectuals' group attachment is a matter of intellectual decision; hence their point of view, and their point of view alone, is mediated by activity subject to conscious control. Their determination 'by matter' is mediated by the activity of the spirit. Hence in their case, and in their case alone, the width of vistas and the depth of insights depend on the method of intellectual activity, which can be purposefully designed and willingly applied. On the top of all the usual social determinations, the intellectuals 'are also determined in their outlook by this intellectual medium which contains all those contradictory points of view'.[32] Even if they wished to submerge themselves completely in the ideology and practice of a particular class, they would never fully succeed; their own psychic characteristics will stick out. 'Over and above these affiliations [the intellectual] is motivated by the fact that his training has equipped him to face the problems of the day in several perspectives and not only in one, as most participants in the controversies of their time do',[33] because of the heterogeneous origin of modern intellectuals, their lack of organization and ensuing loose structure, lack of unified or monopolistic patronage, etc.

Unlike Weber's value-neutral social scientists, Mannheim's intellectuals cannot derive any comfort from the thought that society is with them, that they themselves merely reflect the major tendency of the society as a whole. On the contrary, they must be haunted by the unbearable knowledge of their own solitude. What they do goes against the grain of social life in its most essential features. They will remain forever strangers in the familiar world. Despairing of the impossibility of objective understanding ever becoming socially determined, they challenge in their practices social determination as such and, with it, society itself. They dedicate their life to a task which, as they know only too well, they cannot accomplish.

'Should the capacity to acquire a broader point of view be considered merely as a liability? Does it not rather present a mission?'[34] But *lasciate ogni speranza*; there is nothing to assist you, even to console you, if, propelled by your will alone, you undertake to fulfil this mission. What you know is 'merely that certain types of intellectuals have a maximum opportunity to test and employ the socially available vistas and to experience their inconsistencies'.[35] Indeed not much spiritual comfort, considering that your mission is a *bellum contra omnes*.

The unenviable task which Mannheim assigns to his intellectuals is his own last ditch of hope. His theory, aimed at getting the best of both hermeneutical and sociological worlds, petered out in its own contradictions. Most conspicuously, it failed to offer a ground for its demand of a truly scientific social science based on a truly objective understanding. Having done so, it left the intellectuals it conceived to bear on their shoulders the burden of a mission it could not accomplish in its analysis of social reality.

However theoretically ineffective, Mannheim's concerns – and above all those expressed most fully in the *Ideology and Utopia* – provided a major stimulus to the 'scientistic' tendencies in post-war sociology. For twenty years or so, Mannheim was quoted mostly, if not solely, as an authority behind the view that social determination of knowledge is essentially the matter of ideological distortion, and that sociology is called to transcend such social determination through the severance of all its social commitments. Mannheim was used – clearly against the testimony of his own, mainly early, work – to support the strange self-blindness of 'scientistic' sociology, oblivious to the *positive* role necessarily played by the recapitulated sociohistorical tradition in *all* knowledge. In short, for twenty years or so Mannheim served as a justification for the putative 'disengagement' of sociology from hermeneutics, simply a neglect and misunderstanding of the genuine questions posited by the hermeneutical tradition.

This 'social reception' of Mannheim, however grossly distorting the balance of his total work, was not entirely unwarranted; we have seen that the possibility of this interpretation was indeed contained in Mannheim's writings. Even if, however, more blatant distortions are disposed of (as has recently been the case), Mannheim's confrontation with the challenge of hermeneutics still remains wanting, for reasons deeply entrenched in the most fundamental structures of his theory.

Mannheim does not share Weber's view of the growing rationality of our world. For all he knows, the world may forever be torn between warring and narrow-minded factions. A logic geared to universal communication may never gain enough power to facilitate understanding through or above the frontiers of hatred and parochialism. Mannheim's 'transcendental sociological determinism' is articulated in too universal terms to make true understanding conceivable for matter-of-fact *hoi poloi*. Only in the case of intellectuals, this genuine collective Prometheus, has sociological determinism neutralized its own more cancerous aspects. The Prometheus gives the world a chance of true understanding. Otherwise it shows no traits which could make the task of understanding easier. In Mannheim's scenario of true understanding no role is assigned to the social world as the *object* of understanding. The possibility that some types of social world might be more amenable to the revelation of truth than other types is not seriously considered. In this he differs from both Marx and Weber, and because of that, brings into sharp focus the task of grounding the hope of objective understanding in something other than logic of history. True understanding as the function of the profession of intellectuals requires a deeper insight into the ways and means which could furnish their professional interpretations with a privileged and binding authority.

5 Understanding as the work of reason: Edmund Husserl

Husserl is perhaps the most radical and formidable proponent of the 'rationalistic' solution to the problem of meaning. His work, which revolutionized the twentieth century's approach to the task of hermeneutics, spans the highest claims ever made in the name of truth-seeking reason, and the revelation of limits which the pursuit of apodictic interpretation can never surpass. The method of phenomenological reduction, which was Husserl's answer to the historical relativity of understanding, required (in Paul Ricoeur's description) that consciousness cuts itself off from its historical and social entanglements, and constitutes itself as an absolute; when consciousness becomes the sole world left at the end of reduction, all beings will become meanings for consciousness; they will have no predicates but those which are relative to consciousness. Then – and then only – consciousness liberated from the world will be capable of grasping the true meaning; not the contingent meaning, meaning as it happens to be seen – but meaning in its true, necessary essence.

As in the case of every great work, there are many sides from which Husserl's contribution may be approached, and many contexts in which its significance reveals itself. We will concentrate here on one context only: Husserl's most radical attempt to purify the process of understanding from those germs of relativism which are brought into it by its contact with history and the psychic worlds of historically limited actors. This attempt founded the truth on more solid ground than the shifting sands of historically changing human psyche. Husserl accepts that thoughts as historical phenomena – as events in the heads of real individuals in specific moments of time – are incurably relative and no idea of 'absolute truth' can be possibly grounded in them. He therefore sets about the excruciating task of cleansing psychological connotations from the process of understanding. Whoever asserts that something is true because people happen to think it is, in fact destroys the notion of truth. Whoever asserts, for example, that the rules of logic are valid and lead to true conclusions because this is how human thinking is organized – deprives logic of its necessary, apodictic validity.

In Husserl's work the search of meaning is, therefore, dissociated from the world of psychical events. Meaning is not any more the 'property' of the empirical actor or a product of negotiation between two autonomous subjects, the actor and his interpreter. Either we find a way to grasp the meaning independently of such empirical beings 'soaked in history', or we have to abandon the very hope of ever capturing the true meanings – meanings so apodictic that every-body must accept them. Since no meanings of the apodictic kind can be grounded in the historical fact of 'being thought' by these or those historical individuals, the borderline carefully drawn by Dilthey between 'knowledge of nature' and 'knowledge of the spiritual' disappears in Husserl. The theory of understanding, in Husserl's view, can be solved only as a general theory of knowledge and truth.

That our knowledge is but a hypothesis which may well be false, is a common truth, though perhaps not a truth we enjoy and like to be reminded of. It dawns upon us in the moment of reflection, and when it does, the effect may be terrifying. I write 'may be', because some people manage not to be shocked. Karl R. Popper is one. He admits:[1]

It turns out that our knowledge always consists merely of suggestions for tentative solutions. Thus the very idea of knowledge involves, in prin-ciple, the possibility that it will turn out to have been a mistake, and therefore a case of ignorance.

Having admitted that, he still feels himself right to quote, approvingly, Xenophanes:[2]

'The gods did not reveal from the beginning
all things to us; but in the course of time,
Through seeking we may learn, and know things better. . . . '

By dint of this ungrounded hope Popper contrives not to be terri-fied by the possibility his own admission discloses. Indeed, if every single assertion we believe to be true is never to be fully confirmed and can only be endlessly, but never conclusively, defended against successive attempts of refutation; if, therefore, every single assertion we believe to be true may, in principle, hide its falsity behind our ignorance – how can we be sure that an assertion which we substitute for a discredited one is any *better*, 'truer', than the one replaced? If we can never know things *for sure*, how can we believe that we are able to know things *better*? Is not Leszek Kolakowski right when saying that for someone who has taken Popper's position 'it makes no sense to talk about the development of science as a movement closer and closer to the truth'; that person 'is bound to reject not only the "absolute truth" but the truth *tout court*, not only the certitude as something already gained but the certitude as hope as well'?[3]

Popper's equanimity is astounding because he retains it while seeing through the shaky foundations of his – and our – knowledge. But the attitude which in Popper must be viewed as Olympian serenity is assumed matter-of-factly and without effort by those who do not ask questions of the sort, 'How do I know what I know?', or, 'How can I be sure that what I know is true?' – by those, so to speak, who just know, without worrying about the legitimacy of their knowledge. And most people, through most of their life, fall into this category. Husserl's terror, Popper's quiescence, Kolakowski's sombre ruling are all a cut or two above the level of daily life and the questions it may generate on its own. The fragility of our knowledge, so disturbing when revealed to the philosopher's eye, somehow does not stand in the way of daily life. Somehow we go on with what we know. For our daily tasks, we do not need to ask questions about foundations of our knowledge. We hardly ever perceive the odds and ends of information we possess as parts of a totality called knowledge, with an identity of its own and with a need of its own foundation. Once in a while we wake up to the falsity of one or another of our beliefs; however painful some of these awakenings may be, they seldom add up to disbelief in the essential soundness of our judgement. From within our life-work, we can only view the philosophers' concern as a leisure-time occupation.

This unperturbed placidity, with which we wade through our respective lives, enraged Husserl; it was not our questions, but our silence which prompted him into action; it was not our fear of void he wished to placate, but our inattentiveness to danger he wanted to rectify. Husserl set out not to help us with the difficulties of our understanding, but to convince us that what we think we understand has our wrong beliefs as its only foundation. 'We' means here ordinary people in ordinary situations; complete with scientists who share their complacency.

In his famous metaphor of the cave, Plato articulated the problem which almost two and a half millennia later was to spark off

Husserl's inquiry. His cave dwellers, fettered for life to their seats, with their eyes fixed at the wall in front of them and thereby condemned to see only shadows of 'real things' paraded behind their backs – would they ever discover that they see only pale traces cast by true beings? It is hard to imagine that they could. 'Suppose the prisoners were able to talk together, don't you think that when they named the shadows which they saw passing they would believe they were naming things?' Indeed, 'such persons would certainly believe that there were no realities except those shadows of handmade things'. Worse than that, they would soon add dignity to necessity and invent a game with prizes and honours – the game they would eventually call science – which would enable them to be witty and critical about each shadow taken one by one, while never raising doubt about the unreliability of 'shadowness' as such: there would be honours and praise, and prizes 'for the one who saw the passing things most sharply and remembered best which of them used to come before and which after and which together, and from these was best able to prophesy accordingly what was going to come'. Little hope that a 'cave scientist' so honoured and praised will ever put his cherished prize to risk by casting doubt on the validity of his pastime. Even if he did, other cave dwellers would hardly listen to his revelations. Imagine that a restless spirit among them, for reasons inscrutable, left the cave in search of the true sunlight; imagine that he found out that things were but shadows, and wished to improve his fellows' lot by bringing them the good tidings. Would they indeed be any happier with the truth than without it? And would they, for that matter, acknowledge the verity of the message? To start with, they would see no reason to join the odd discoverer of truth on his sunshine trip; to make his point, he would have to drag his fellows out of the cave, probably against their wish. But now suppose he has succeeded, and one of his fellows has been forced out, to be 'shown each of the passing things, and compelled by questions to answer what each one was. Don't you think he would be puzzled, and believe what he saw before was more true than what was shown to him now?' Instead of being grateful, he would be 'distressed and furious at being dragged'. After a lifetime of shadows dancing on the murky cave wall, daylight could only 'hurt his eyes, and he would escape by turning them away to the things which he was able to look at, and these he would believe to be clearer than what was being shown to him'. Having failed to share his newly discovered knowledge with his fellows, the hapless harbinger of truth may now expect only ridicule, if not worse. He would be challenged to compete with 'cave scientists', but he would be hardly able to play their game again, as his eyes got used to a different light; so 'wouldn't they all laugh at him and say he had spoiled his eyesight by going up there, and it was not worth-while so much as to try to go up? And would they not kill anyone who tried to release them and take them up if they could somehow lay hands on him, and kill him?'[4]

All Husserl's worries are already here, in Plato's perplexing parable. First, the terrifying possibility that all we can see and all we believe may be just a dance of shadows. Second, that if it were so, we would have no way of knowing it. Third, that nothing in our daily life prompts us to find out. Fourth, that even if somebody has accomplished the impossible and looked beyond the shadows, at the things themselves – he would have found it exceedingly difficult to communicate his discovery to his fellows.

These worries are as old as human reflection itself. Descartes' God was a replica of Plato's anonymous carriers of shadow-casting things: 'How do I know that He has not brought it to pass that there is no earth, no heaven, no extended body, no magnitude, no place, and that nevertheless they seem to me to exist just exactly as I now see them?' For all I know (and 'all that up to the present time I have accepted as most true and certain I have learned either from the senses or through the senses') God may be deceitful and impress upon me an illusion passing for knowledge. After all, the only ground for the reliability of the evidence of my senses is my supposition that the nameless Manager did make them reliable. But when I suppose that, I allow the possibility that He could do otherwise. It is enough to engage in such cogitations to open my knowledge to doubt. Yet in normal circumstances we would stop short of abandoning the cosy security of belief in the solidity of the world disclosed in sensual impressions. The task of doubting[5]

is a laborious one, and insensibly a certain lassitude leads me into the course of my ordinary life. And just as a captive who in sleep enjoys an imaginary liberty, when he begins to suspect that his liberty is but a dream, fears to awaken, and conspires with these agreeable illusions that the deception may be prolonged, so insensibly of my own accord I fall back into my former opinions, and I dread awakening from this slumber, lest the laborious wakefulness which would follow the tranquility of this repose should have to be spent not in daylight, but in the excessive darkness of the difficulties which have just been discussed.

Without doubting, however, we will never reach certainty.

Doubt is the first stage of liberation; the very fact that we can doubt – indeed, we can question everything, there is virtually nothing we cannot doubt – is proof that liberation is possible. Against this possibility, the fact that we nevertheless seem to enjoy unreflexive, naïve credulity in our daily experience is particularly astounding. It is still more bewildering to the mind which has refused to stop at the first stage and goes on to a better knowledge which could replace the questioned one. To such a mind the second stage seems to follow the first with compelling clarity. How can he explain the fact that, the further he moves, the less people follow him? Only two explanations come ready to hand. The first: that even more powerful forces collude to prevent doubt from running its natural course. And the second: that our daily life is constructed in a way which staves off the very possibility of doubt.

Selbstverständlichkeit (self-evidence, self-obviousness, self-explica-tion) is, for Husserl, the essential quality of this life-world in which we are naïvely immersed. This world is intellectually self-sufficient. We can live our life in it without once being given a single reason to question its reality. In so far as I refrain from questioning (note: my abstention does not result from any decision I make; it is merely a correlate of my failure ever to consider questioning as a possibility), I remain in what Husserl calls the 'natural attitude'. The choice of words is significant. Refraining from doubt, naïvety, complacency, unwillingness to make use of one's freedom to question – all are *natural* proclivities of humans. It takes an extra-ordinary effort to overcome or suppress them.

While remaining in (rather than taking) the natural attitude, I find 'reality' as existing, and accept it, as it presents itself to me here and now (*ein Dies da!*). This general and exceptionless acceptance sets outer limits to all my minor and specific doubts. My attitude to every single evidence and every interpretation of it may be, and often is, suspicious and critical. Often I revise beliefs I previously held. Often I reject as untrue assertions which I was yesterday eager to defend. Yesterday's realities pile up on a dust heap of 'illusions', 'false appearances', 'superstitions'. One could almost say that reality, this postulated foundation of natural attitude, is in constant retreat; it is constantly forced to abandon new lines of trenches which yesterday's knowledge, today already disqualified, allowed it to dig. Constantly on the move, the reality of the natural attitude always lingers, however, as the ultimate horizon of all knowledge;

its right to authoritatively judge and correct our beliefs is never denied. Criticism of reality does not entail criticism of the natural attitude itself.[6] No evil intention, not even mental tardiness, has to be invoked to account for the astonishing tenacity of the natural attitude. To explain it, it is enough to realize that criticism *from* the natural attitude and criticism *of* the natural attitude are not conti-guous. There is no 'natural' passage from one to the other. As long as they remain within the natural attitude, people do not even define their position as such. When they accept the philosophical judgement and agree that it is only the attitude they have taken which grounds their life-world, they are already one step beyond, they look at their life-world from outside, as merely one of alternatives. While it is precisely the incapacity to be otherwise which is not even considered in the life-world.[7]

And so criticism of the natural attitude is impossible. The road to secure knowledge is hopelessly blocked. Nothing in the ordinary world of ordinary people can bring salvation from the abominable state in which deception and self-deception are constant possibilities. What one needs is a saviour, a charismatic hero, with enough power to break through the thick veil of illusions. He can still appeal to the natural instincts of those whom he asks to rescue. After all, their instinctive urge to certainty led ordinary people into the quagmire of allegedly self-evident truths from which they cannot lift themselves on their own. Since they have been, however, amazingly successful in their misguided efforts and manage to move with ease inside their limited horizon, and since stepping over this horizon is as painful as Descartes described it – how can the would-be saviour solicit assent of those who are to be saved?

Husserl's idea of certain knowledge is therefore, in Blumenberg's words, one of the theories of 'endogenous readiness for illusion'. Like so many other thinkers, and – much worse – men of practice before and after, Husserl assumed that ordinary people, while occupied with the ordinary tasks of life, do not know that their true interest is in truth. Given this assumption, his project has to be, inescapably,[8]

subject to the weakness of all such theories, which consists first of all in representing the endogenous mechanism as almost insuperable and then still claiming that the theory itself is the breakthrough to this overcoming. The life-world defined as the dense 'universe of self-evidences' simply renders impossible what must then be accepted as an innocuous 'conver-sion' of attitudes. The point in the Platonic allegory at which the anonymous intervention into the prison and the violent abduction out of the cave is presumed with poetic ease cannot be described with equal nonchalance for the move out of the life-world. No exogenous questioner helps the endogenous unquestionability on its way. It is characteristic that at such points in the history of philosophy, as now with Husserl, voluntaristic formulas take over the role of *deus ex machina*.

Whatever the weakness of such reasoning, it is not Husserl's alone. We encounter it often enough to suppose that this weakness is an incurable malady of practically all 'final recipes' for true and reliable understanding. There are, however, many forms in which the weakness manifests itself; above all, many forms in which thinkers propose to cure or, at least, to bypass it. Husserl's is his belief in the absolute, irreducible, axiomatic being of consciousness as the foundation of the world. One has only to immerse himself in its cleansing waters to wash out the polluting self-evidences. But Husserl would expect only philosophers to risk this heroic act. Or, rather, committing such an act is an act of philosophy. Obviously it is not an act of life moved by the natural attitude, but is prompted by an intrinsically unnatural attitude. Philosophy is an exception. Philosophers are exceptional people. Understanding is a feat only a chosen few can accomplish.

What is involved here is nothing less than a 'completely new beginning and a science of a completely new sort', not a critique of some specific sort of practice but a 'radical critique of life'.[9] This uncannily radical critique can be brought about by the method of 'phenomenological reduction'.

Phenomenological reduction is different from all previous attempts to extricate the kernel of certain knowledge from the husk of appearances. It is, in a sense, akin to the Cartesian universal doubt; like Descartes, Husserl puts his hopes into 'pure consciousness' and such ideas as can be conceived by pure consciousness. But his criteria of purity are more demanding than Descartes'. Descartes' doubt was scattered, aimed indiscriminately at any content of thinking, at everything that can be put in doubt, except for the act of doubt itself, i.e. except for the fact of thinking as such. Husserl's doubt is sharply focussed: it is aimed at eliminating all ideas related to the *existence* of objects our consciousness tells us about; to be exact – the existence of objects apart from, and independently of, their presence in our consciousness. Descartes, following concerns traditional to philosophy since ancient times, wished to ground in clear and indubitable ideas of our consciousness a convincing proof that the world exists and that our knowledge of it can be in principle reliable. Husserl wishes to emancipate us from his long-standing but abortive concern, which misdirected our search: our convulsive efforts to go *beyond* consciousness, into the world existing 'over there', allowed ourselves to be enslaved by the natural attitude and are bound to build our knowledge out of dancing shadows. What we need, therefore, is nothing less than transcendental *epoche* (suspension): let us suspend the essential thesis of natural attitude, let us put in brackets absolutely everything which such attitude exhorts us to assume. Above all, let us put in brackets, i.e. make irrelevant to any subsequent quest for secure understanding, all the 'natural world', that is such a world as may exist by itself, as reality which is 'out there'. The act of *epoche*, so Husserl tells us, differs essentially from supposedly similar operations accomplished by philosophers of the past. It does not mean denying the world in the style of sophist, nor questioning its existence in the style of sceptics. *Epoche* means simply a methodological limitation which allows us to make only such judgements as do not depend for their validity on a spatio-temporal world.[10]

So far, one does not see much difference between Husserl's *epoche* and Berkeley's or Fichte's retreat to consciousness as the only accessible ground of knowledge. On the other hand, the similarity with Descartes' cogito remains striking. But then follows the decisive turning-point: Berkeley, Fichte or Descartes, each in his own way, sought a secure harbour for the stranded ship of knowledge in the individual's existence: my own existence, my perceptions, my feelings, my thinking – the very fact of their presence to me – are beyond doubt. This 'myself' whom I so intimately know and whom I so trust has not, however, escaped the cleansing operation of Husserlian *epoche*. What emerges from the operation is, in Husserl's words, transcendental subjectivism; it differs radically from Berkeley's or Fichte's results by being transcendental; it differs from Descartes' 'absurd transcendental realism' by being subjectivism.[11] Descartes' mistake, Husserl tells us, was to assume that from the obviousness of the act of doubt I can safely derive the conclusion that I, the subject of doubt, exist. The very act of doubt Descartes perceives (or at least does not make it clear that he does not) as a psychological event; as a happening which can be located in space and time, which can be described as taking place inside the head of a tangible, material individual. Berkeley and Fichte, each in his own way, invite us to accept a sort of 'private ownership' of consciousness:

perceptions which I call phenomena, and which are given to me with dazzling clarity, belong to me, are my perceptions. Husserl would not accept either suggestion. Neither is radical enough. Husserl would not tolerate the individual himself, left by others either in the capacity of a material object or a 'pure', but still individual (and therefore not pure enough) subjectivity. If we only leave the individual outside the brackets of *epoche*, all the shadows to which we have turned our backs will come dancing back into our vision. The subjectivity Husserl would allow to escape bracketing has little in common with the 'subject of consciousness' of other philosophers. The 'ego' and 'ego-life' which remain after the *epoche* 'is not a piece of the world, and if it says, "I am, *ego cogito*" that no longer means, "I, this man, am"'.[12] 'We do not presuppose ourselves *qua* "persons" living in the world.'[13] The man, as an entity which belongs to nature and as a person related to other persons, to a 'society', is swept away by the broom of *epoche* together with other 'impurities'.[14] The impression one cannot resist while trying to follow Husserl's thought is that such a man is the *main* impurity to be removed. Or, rather, that such a man is precisely this 'crack in the dam' through which all other polluting substances pour into our knowledge, and sedimenting make up the natural attitude.

Let us consider briefly what exactly 'bracketing away' such a man would mean. It would mean a great deal. Much is intentional; i.e. has been indeed intended by Husserl as the means to true and secure understanding. But the other part, which follows the first with necessity, has not. Yet his other part cancels whatever benefit might have been gained by the first.

What is intended is the elimination of historical, cultural, social factors as operators of understanding. Following a long line of thinkers starting with Plato, Plotinus, Augustine, Husserl was deeply impressed by the essential eternality and 'exterritoriality' of truth; or, rather, by the idea that whatever is genuinely true must be so eternally and exterritorially. Anchoring truth, tying it down to a specific time, place, rigours of concrete practice – all this may only result in distortions. Whatever is handed in by history is transient and incomplete; whatever is offered by culture is almost by definition prejudiced and pre-selected; whatever is subject to societal pressures is interest-bound and therefore dishonest and partially blind; consequently, whatever is simply a spatio-temporal experience of an empirical individual, this combined product of history, culture, and society, must be burdened with all these liabilities. To bracket away the world but to leave unaffected the empirical individual would be like installing burglar alarms on the door but leaving the thief inside the house. If one wishes to grasp the truth in its eternal purity and radically cleanse it of all and any corruption, one has to get rid of history, culture, society. But one cannot do it radically enough unless one gets rid first of their creation, the empirical individual.

What is not intended is the sickly emaciation of whatever would be left when – and if – the empirical individual were 'bracketed away'. Is anything left at all? And if something is, is it dense and resourceful enough to support true knowledge and true understanding? Indeed, any understanding at all?

What is left after the operation of *epoche* has been carried out on the empirical individual is, in Husserl's view, pure consciousness: consciousness which is not anybody's, consciousness free of all earthly attachments. To speak of such consciousness 'is not to speak of the activity whereby a subject is conscious; rather it is to speak of a mode of being, the mode of being which things have when we are conscious of them'.[15] Well, to speak of such consciousness is above all to believe that the two named meanings of consciousness are indeed alternatives, that the second mode is conceivable without the first. But it is easy to see that the second concept of consciousness can be thought of in the negative way only. Indeed, it can be defined only in what it lacks of the rich content of ordinary 'natural' thinking: tradition, history, culturally pre-defined patterns of cognition, social practice. The negativity of the type of consciousness in which Husserl hopes to root his true understanding is strengthened by the method which Husserl calls us to apply to reach it. What is *epoche*, what is the whole series of phenomenological reductions, if not an effort to peel away successive layers of content, to arrive at the end at the tough nucleus which is explicable only from itself, and not reducible any more to either tradition, or culture, or society? But how do we know that such a nucleus exists? What kind of evidence can we ever get that it does? Is not our belief in its existence grounded on precisely those 'self-evidences' which Husserl wants us to get rid of?

Even more spectacularly, the Husserlian 'pure consciousness' allegedly produced by the operation of *epoche* is separated from the natural context in which formation and developments of meanings and rules of thinking takes place: the context of communication, of discourse, of sociation among people. From numerous psychological studies we know that the formation of the essential most general patterns of thinking is intimately interwoven with practical interaction with other people; we know nothing of these patterns being built into a mind existing entirely by itself, disengaged from the world populated by other people, and developing from its endogenous propensities alone. We have never seen such a mind, we can only imagine it; but then we can imagine it only in a negative way, as emptiness, as nothingness. . . .

To sum up: in Husserl's view, all knowledge consists of understanding; since things exist for consciousness (are 'given') only in the mode of *Bewusstsein* ('being known'), they may be only captured as meanings, and not as objects 'out there' which in themselves contain the ultimate pattern of true knowledge. These meanings, however, are not bestowed on things by individuals who perceive them. These meanings are not 'thoughts' in the sense accepted in psychology. They are not 'psychological events'. They are cut of an entirely different rock – infinitely more solid and immune to distortions induced by the endless play of cultural, class or historical factors and the transient passions they generate. Unlike ideas entertained by human individuals, true meanings are immutable and apodictic; it is hoped that, once discovered, they would sweep aside, once for all, the protean, inept substitutes pieced together from illusions of natural attitude.

If, however, meanings are not bestowed by the psyche of concrete, empirical individuals, by whom are they bestowed? By transcendental subjectivity. By the intentional effort of a subjectivity which is nobody's subjectivity, which precedes and underlies all concrete, individual subjectivities. It is subjectivity, like yours or mine, in the sense that it produces meaning (*Meinung*) through the activity of intending (*meinen*). Still, it is not a subjectivity like yours or mine in that it produces things themselves – these clots of transcendental intentions which later confront our individual subjectivities as objects which we keenly, though unsuccessfully, attempt to re-grasp in the course of our individual cognition. To comprehend the complex relation between transcendental and individual subjectivity, one could recall the scholastic image of God as the intentional source of all meaning: this meaning of the world which the imperfect human mind tries to capture in vain; the meaning which the imperfect human mind can grasp only by the act of Divine grace, through a mystical communion with God, once it has purified itself of bodily pollutions and earthly sins. This is not the analogy Husserl would use; but it is the structure of thought in which the hope of transcendental subjectivity as the seat of all meaning, and of the possibility of reaching it through purification of 'life-world' passions, can be best comprehended.

Husserl insists that things are, from the outset, meanings; and that knowing them is, therefore, to understand their meanings. But in order to do that one has to find the way to exercise direct insight into the work of transcendental subjectivity, where these meanings are forged and sustained. *Epoche* and transcendental reduction, the 'suspension' of everything empirical, historically transient and culture-bound, are the operations which have to be performed for this direct insight to become possible. As all the 'empirically given' data are to be disposed of on the way, they cannot be employed as steps leading to the final accomplishment: the capture of meaning. The 'worldly' knowledge they found is not the stuff out of which 'pure consciousness' can be sifted.

It seems, therefore, that 'pure consciousness', in which Husserl's last hope for certainty has been anchored, is in the last account an act of faith. Its foundation is no stronger than that of naïve realism. It is doomed to remain forever a hypothesis which no amount of 'tough evidence' will ever fully bear out. If the status of 'being unfounded' were a matter of degree, the phenomenologist belief would have to be classified as even 'more unfounded' than its realist opposite: the realist enjoys, at least, a self-perpetuating support of the common-sense practice, which it has succeeded in moulding in a way that constantly generates its own plausibility. Of this practice Husserl takes a disdainful view, which clearly shows through his description:[16]

Theirs and my worlds I see as the same world, which only comes to consciousness of different people in different ways. Each of us has his own place, and accordingly each has different phenomena of things. . . . Nevertheless we communicate with others. . . .

It is not this unreliable kind of communication Husserl is after. But in cutting it off in order to put a better one in its place, he cuts off the one foundation offered to seekers of secure knowledge which is ready-made, prefabricated by common sense.

Husserl does not bewail what has been lost; he has nothing but scorching criticism for the scientists who relish the deceitful security of the 'natural attitude':[17]

But how is it now, when any and every norm is controverted or empirically falsified and robbed of its ideal validity? Naturalists and historicists fight about *Weltanschauung*, and yet both are at work on different sides to misinterpret ideas as facts and to transform all reality, all life, into an incomprehensible, idealess confusion of 'facts'. The superstition of the fact is common to them all. . . . If the sceptical criticism of naturalists and historicists dissolves genuine objective validity in all fields of obligation into nonsense, if unclear and disagreeing, even though naturally developed, reflective concepts and consequently equivocal and erroneous problems impede the understanding of actuality and the possibility of a rational attitude toward it, if a special but (for a large class of sciences) required methodical attitude becomes a matter of routine so that it is incapable of being transformed into other attitudes, and if depressing absurdities in the interpretation of the world are connected with such prejudices, then there is only one remedy for these and similar evils: a scientific critique and in addition a radical science, rising from below, based on sure foundations, and progressing according to the most rigorous methods – the philosophical science for which we speak here. *Weltanschauungen* can engage in controversy; only science can decide, and its decision bears the stamp of eternity.

A controversy to end all controversy; an understanding to eliminate all misunderstanding; truth which is truly eternal; science which is not another *Weltanschauung*; these are not uncommon dreams and new ambitions. On the contrary, they are well founded in the tradition of western thought. But never before – certainly not since Plato himself – has the task been considered in such elitist terms. Ordinary people, immersed in their daily bustle, cannot be trusted with a mission which befits only the selected few. 'These men who set the goal in the finite, who want to have their system and want it soon enough to be able to live by it, are in no way called to this task.'[18] The dream of the universal and absolute truth results here in a lack of interest and attention to 'mundane' life and contempt to the people who live it. To face the absolute, to 'be sure', one has first to turn one's back to both.

The reasons for the phenomenologist's loneliness are clear enough; all bespeak the unavoidably aristocratic status of the 'absolute truth' and 'true understanding'. In the words of Robert Sokolowski, phenomenology[19]

does not deal with things that are perceptually given to the public; the 'givens' of phenomenology are disclosed only through the inquiry and speech that manifest them. We do not bump into, feel, see, hear, taste, or circumscribe phenomenological data, so we cannot enlist the help of such public, perceptual means to show what we are trying to say. Second, there is no inherited deposit of phenomenological evidences that we can take over and build upon. Everything has to begin afresh, even the naming of

objects and parts. Nor can we assume familiar habit of doing phenomenology; the style and method have to be established in a radical
beginning. Third, the 'unnatural' direction of focus used by phenomenology is a difficulty that no habituation will ever remove. Its objects, the
things it must learn to name, are not members of the world which is
normal business of consciousness. In phenomenology the mind must
inhibit its spontaneous concern with the world and things in it and focus
on this concern itself. . . .

The history of mankind so far has failed to bring us any closer to
certainty. Phenomenology must, therefore, start afresh, begin from
a zero point, having left behind the cultural lore of the past together
with its contemporary bearers. To make things even worse, nothing
in this lore warrants the fresh start; nothing at all can be relied upon
to force men and women to abandon the cosy blindness of natural
attitude. Phenomenology is possible only as the heroic decision of
the few solitary noble spirits who would settle for nothing less than
certitude. 'There is need of special motives if the one who is caught
up in such a life in the world is to transform himself and is to come
to the point where he somehow makes this world itself his theme.'[20]
It is not enough just to choose the special motive once and for all.
What is needed is constant vigilance, a truly monastic abstinence, a
never-relenting resistance to the allurements of the natural attitude,
of worldly interests, of life. And nothing sustains this perpetual
self-abnegation except the act of faith. For this reason alone one
would not expect phenomenological search of true understanding to
become a pastime of the masses.

For the same reason entering the enchanted world of phenomenology is almost as difficult as entering a promised land (be it the
Garden of Eden or a communist society): one cannot achieve the
required state of purity anywhere but inside its boundaries; but one
cannot be truly inside unless one purifies himself first. Given the
unsolvable paradox, one wonders how there can be any insiders. But
if there are any, they can afford to look down their noses on those
who remain outside; they are under no obligation to take the out-
siders' criticisms seriously. Prominent phenomenologists made this
curse-through-luxury explicit. In the words of Eugen Fink, to understand what phenomenology is to impossible without being a phenomenologist; according to Max Scheler, the phenomenologist could
quite calmly accept the fact that the rest of the world disagree with him;
he could be *sure*.[21] Indeed, if the certitude which phenomenologists
seek resides in the act of insight, not in discourse, and certainly

not in our engagement with the world we live in, then in order to be sure of my own certainty, I have to believe that the insight I have been offered is right. But then, 'I *may* deny that the statement is apodictically obvious. A phenomenologist, in such a case, can only answer that I am stupid and that is the end of the dispute.'[22] No arguments forthcoming from the world, which has not yet been phenomenologically reduced, bear credence or carry enough significance to be taken seriously. As it were, it was Husserl who declared that the phenomenological insights begin with annihilation (*Vernichtung*) of the world:[23]

> If one carries through the reduction, as the precondition for a thoroughly critical or radical philosophy, he must make it clear to himself that he has defined an artificial domain for inquiry. To disengage the thinker and his experiences from his natural and cultural setting is to introduce artificial conditions. 'Pure subjectivity' is not to be found in nature. It is a device of method, an abstraction, a falsification in fact.

But is this tremendous effort worth while? We have seen what has been lost in the process. Is there something we can gain instead? Are we closer to solving the problem of understanding?

If understanding ever becomes a matter for our practical concern, it is in the course of communication with other people. Understanding as a problem makes itself manifest through a worried question, 'What do you mean?', or a plaintive complaint, 'You do not understand me.' When our communication with other people suddenly grinds to a halt, when the flow of apparently 'transparent' words is interrupted by a challenge which has abruptly turned a word or a statement from an invisible window-pane into an opaque screen which conceals rather than reveals – then understanding reveals itself to us as a problem. Understanding is a problem of theoretical and practical import in so far as we need to see through the opacity begotten by contest; in other words, understanding derives whatever importance it may have from the need to do away with misunderstanding. But misunderstanding can arise only in a discourse; outside it it is inconceivable. Misunderstanding resides in the world. And, consequently, so does the problem of understanding.

It is, however, this self-same world which Husserl has asked us to abandon for the sake of true and secure understanding. The artificial world he invited us to enter instead, with its thin air rarefied by phenomenological reduction, is clinically clean and – so we are assured – dazzlingly transparent. The trouble is, however, that having miraculously negotiated the steep slope which leads to its entrance, we realize, to our dismay, that the very reason which sent us there has been lost on the way. What is our dearly gained understanding worth if it cannot be applied in our struggle to repair broken communication? What is the value of understanding which can remain itself only in the thinned, antiseptic atmosphere of phenomenological insight, only at the cost of its separation from daily discourse, only in so far as no attempt is made to return it to the discourse from which it has been separated? One is reminded of an attempt to draw deep-water fish up to the surface in order better to admire their bizarre shapes: they burst from their internal pressure before we can set our eyes on them. The truths brought back into the world from the rarefied stratospheric heights will be crushed by the multiple forces of interests, traditions, and other earthly powers. The truths were conceived when all these forces which make the ordinary discourse so difficult had been 'bracketed away'. They will die at the first attempt to remove the brackets. However glittering are the prizes promised for our renunciation of the worldly bustle, we will be allowed to enjoy them only as long as we agree to remain in exile.

And so the old problem, first brought to our attention by the allegory of the cave, is still with us: if I grasp the truth which resides outside the cave, how can I pass it over to the rest of the cave dwellers? Or, for this matter, how can I myself use it in my later life in the cave? Plato light-heartedly bypassed the question. Husserl asked it explicitly, but offered no answer. Instead, he proposed that we remain forever outside. Only the chosen few can afford to take up his offer. The rest will remain largely unaffected. They will have to continue to struggle with their misunderstandings using the self-same old and crude methods Husserl so disdainfully rejected.

It is true that Husserl spent the last part of his life haunted by the realization that his solution to the problem of understanding was evidently ethereal. He tried hard to build a bridge from the phenomenologically reduced, back to the 'life' world, over the gap between the two which he himself had dug. As Schutz remembers: 'When I asked him once why he had refrained from publishing the second volume [of *Ideen*], he answered that at that time he had not found a solution to the problem of the constitution of intersubjectivity.'[24] Drafts published posthumously revealed how painfully was Husserl aware of this fatal flaw in his system, and how feverishly he tried to rectify it. But having once settled down in the phenomenologically reduced world, he could only articulate his task as finding the way of 're-building' the full-blooded social and cultural world while using only the bricks and mortar permitted in his purified world. It is evident that this task is as artificial as the world in which it has been articulated; that it may fascinate only phenomenologists committed to their reduction; and that in no way can it, even if accomplished, claim a foundation more solid and universally acceptable than the act of faith on which the phenomenological project is founded. The task, no wonder, has not been accomplished. Husserl's efforts brought no cogent, or at least credible, results.[25]

Schutz asserts that the question, 'How is a common world in terms of common intentionalities possible?', has been never answered to anybody's, including Husserl's own, satisfaction. But let us note that the question makes sense only in a world already phenomenologically reduced. If it were not for Husserl's 'bracketing away' society, culture and history and reducing knowledge to whatever the 'pure consciousness' can intentionally produce, the question would hardly seem insoluble. It is a question only Husserl may be seriously worried by, and only in so far as he is concerned with finding a way back from his voluntary exile. Indeed, towards the end of his life Husserl intensely, though unsuccessfully, attended to the *Lebenswelt* he earlier wished to annihilate. In *Erfahrung und Urteil* (para. 10) a new slogan, *Rückgang auf die Lebenswelt* (return to the life-world), seems to replace an earlier exhortation, *zurück zu den Sachen selbst* (back to the *things themselves*).[26] The new slogan, however, could not count on sympathetic reception by those who had not followed Husserl on his earlier, distant voyages. For such a person Husserl's new worry would be, in all likelihood, an un-problem. And so it is for Schutz himself, though he would never admit that the one alternative remaining to him, as the loyal disciple of Husserl, was to join the master at the point *obviating* the journey which the master himself saw as his only life achievement.

And so Schutz has to start from the *Lebenswelt* not as it could be reached via phenomenological reduction, but as it was *before* Husserl set on annihilating it. Social sciences, he would admit,[27]

do not have to deal with the philosophical aspects of intersubjectivity, but with the structure of the *Lebenswelt* as experienced by men in their natural attitude, by men, that is, who are born into this socio-cultural world, have to find their bearing within it, and have to come to terms with it. . . . In the natural attitude I take for granted that fellow men exist, that they act upon me as I upon them, that – at least to a certain extent – communication and mutual understanding among us can be established, and that this is done with the help of some systems of signs and symbols within the frame of some social organization and some social institutions – none of them of my own making.

When another loyal Husserlian, Maurice Natanson, rephrases the domain of phenomenology as the study of 'the meaning social acts have for the actors who perform them and who live in a reality built out of their subjective interpretation', or, more concisely, as the study of 'the intentional life of actors in social reality'[28] – his retreat from Husserl's venture into apodictic understanding is complete. The name of phenomenology has now been appropriated for the study of precisely these real, empirical individuals whom Husserl wished to pare to the dry bones of 'transcendental subjectivity'. Good news perhaps for the social sciences threatened by Husserl's surgical knife; but bad news for the hope that absolute truth may be squarely faced and grasped in its uncontaminated essence. The empirical individual in his 'social reality' cannot but bring back all these noxious interests, prejudices, traditions, cultural constraints and social pressures, which in Husserl's view stood in the way to truth and understanding.

Husserl's was perhaps the most consistent and ambitious attempt to articulate the problem of understanding as the problem of context-free, uncommitted and *therefore* absolute knowledge. If he failed, the articulation is wrong. Geniuses never fail to no avail. Even in their defeat they illuminate. The giant's error is our discovery. We can now be sure that there is nothing at the end of the road which – as Husserl hoped and we, tentatively, hoped with him – led to the station called certainty. We now know that we must seek the solution to the problem of understanding along other roads.

In the later period of his life Husserl did realize that the method of transcendental reduction failed to achieve the objective called to justify its inhuman rigour and uncompromising anti-empiricism (as the posthumously published 'Crisis of European sciences' testifies). It did not facilitate the solution of hermeneutical problems. It did not bring us closer to the task of true interpretation. What Husserl in fact did was to reduce the question of being to the question of meaning, and the latter to the status of subjective intention; to advance, as it were, a new version of methodological idealism, with little, if any, practical consequences for the tasks relentlessly posited by the activity of understanding.

H.A.S.S.—E

The verdict passed by Paul Ricoeur, a prominent contemporary hermeneutician, is unsparing but just:[29]

> It is thus finally against the early Husserl, against the alternately Platonizing and idealizing tendencies of his theory of meaning and intentionality, that the theory of understanding has been erected. And if the later Husserl points to this ontology [of *Lebenswelt*], it is because his effort to reduce being failed and because, consequently, the ultimate result of phenomenology escaped the initial project. It is in spite of itself that phenomenology discovers, in place of an idealist subject locked within its system of meanings, a living being which from all time has, as the horizon of all its intentions, a world, the world.

It was not by Husserl, however, that the consequences of this discovery were fully developed.

6 Understanding as the work of reason: Talcott Parsons

There are two aspects to Parsons's sociological theory which permit it to be regarded as an application and extension of Husserl's programme. First, Parsons assumes that essentially subjective human action can be understood objectively, i.e. with no reference to the truly individual 'psychological events' taking place in the author's psyche, if only the effort of understanding concentrates on the necessary structures which must underlie any contingent, phenomenal form this action can historically take; these necessary structures, as they are timeless and transcendental, can be grasped by equally timeless and apodictic reason. The result is, by the same token, exempt from the work of history and can be viewed as truly absolute and immune to the plague of historical relativism; indeed, the validity of knowledge so produced is solely a function of method, i.e. the self-discipline and coherence of analytical reason. Second, the method Parsons applies in pursuit of such knowledge (in practice, in spite of many misleading comments as to the 'empirical' character of his work – made perhaps to appease the American sociological audience oblivious to the long history of German idealism) is one of phenomenological insight. Phenomenological inquiry into the transcendental structures of the human action supplies the only, but solid, foundation to the whole of Parsons's model of social system. The totality of Parson's description of the social system makes sense in as far as one remembers that the true object of Parson's investigation was never this or that specific form social action could historically assume, but the possibility of social action taking place at all, and the transcendental conditions of that possibility. One could say that Parsons's 'objective theory of social action' is the theory of its objective possibility.

In one crucial sense, however, Parsons's sociology is an extension, if not a transcendence, of Husserl's project. The subject around which Parsons's descriptions are organized is not the pure consciousness, the 'transcendental subjectivity' of early Husserl, but a sort of 'pure action', or 'transcendental actor'. Elements of social life entailed by this description are not, therefore, reduced, as they are by Husserl, to meanings, and through them to intentional consciousness. They are accorded a degree of autonomy and, indeed, 'materiality', which early Husserl's aseptic world of pure consciousness would not allow. Unlike transcendental subjectivity, social action entails from the outset that its objects be not just in the state of *Bewusstsein*, but in a truly existential modality; and these objects include, equally from the outset, 'human objects', i.e. other subjects, other meaning-generating and meaning-oriented actors. If the founding of a society or culture while starting from pure consciousness proved an unsurpassable obstacle to Husserl, society and culture have been shown by Parsons to be apodictically present, as its transcendental conditions, in the very idea of social action.

As a motto for *The Structure of Social Action*, his first and most seminal of books, which launched his 'voluntaristic theory of action' as a foundation for new sociology, Parsons selected a sentence from Weber stating that any thoughtful reflection on the ultimate elements of meaningful human action is above all related to the categories of 'means' and 'ends'. The selection is indeed a frank statement of the major message of the book and, for this matter, of the guiding idea of the entire majestic system of sociology which Parsons later developed.

The voluntaristic theory of action has been advanced as an alternative to the two closely related approaches which, in Parsons's view, stood in the way of scientific sociology: the utilitarian and the positivistic.

The major flaw of the utilitarian concept of action consisted, in Parsons's view, in its excessive voluntarism. It accepted that action is organized by the actor's orientation toward the end, and therefore can be understood in terms of this orientation. But having limited its vision to the individual and neglected all supra-individual entities, it had to leave the end entirely to the discretion of actors considered as free agents. It failed, in consequence, to consider 'the relations of the ends to each other'. 'The failure to state anything positive about the relations of ends to each other can . . . have only one meaning – that there are no significant relations, that is, that ends are random in the statistical sense.'[1] If, however, ends are indeed random, then, Parsons indicates, 'there can be no choice' between them.[2] What he probably means by this not immediately obvious verdict is that there is no choice which could be understood in the way human action can be, i.e. as a means leading to an end; unless the end of an action X can be portrayed as a means for a wider end Y, the criteria applied to its selection cannot be made intelligible. The voluntarism contained in the utilitarian concept of action leads, therefore, to positing action as essentially irrational and unpredictable, and consequently defies its scientific treatment. (One could hardly agree with Parsons on this point; he obviously cuts off the concept of action from the utilitarian total world-view, within which action's ends could be considered anything but random. For the utilitarians, ends were given once and for all by the human drive to gain and gratification, and therefore could justly be left out of focus as unproblematic. In fact, there is much less difference between the utilitarian and the Parsonian versions of voluntarism than Parsons would like us to believe.)

The positivistic alternative (or, rather, correction) to the utilitarian concept of action was to reduce the selection of ends to deterministic causes embedded either in hereditary features of the actor or in the immediate environment of action. The 'randomness' has been removed, but only at the cost of obviating the autonomy of ends: the ends, now genetically determined, became mere epiphenomenal appendices to the objectively given traits of the actor or traits of the actor's situation – both well beyond actor's control and conscious choice. Thus action was now amenable to scientific treatment, but it lost irretrievably its voluntaristic character. In the positivistic scheme of action the actor's subjectivity appeared only as a factor mediating between determining causes and determined effects; when the actor, behaving like a miniature scientist, collected the 'hard facts' about his situation and drew inevitable conclusions from the 'rational scientific appreciation' of 'non-subjective conditions'.[3]

The two dominant concepts of action have been, therefore, equally unsatisfactory, though for different reasons. The utilitarian concept paid its due to the subjective, voluntaristic nature of human action, but made its scientific treatment impossible. The positivistic concept, on the contrary, posited action in a form eminently suitable for scientific treatment, but deficient: a form in which the voluntary character of action has been reduced to non-significance.

It is clear from this criticism what Parsons's intentions are: he would like to construct a model of social action which could be, simultaneously, an object of understanding as a subjective, meaningful phenomenon, and an object of scientific theory, as a model amenable to objective analysis. To achieve this, one has to dissociate oneself from the error of utilitarianism, treating the selection of ends as entirely random, and from that of positivism, treating it as entirely determined by non-subjective factors. The obvious way of doing this is to postulate the actor's motives as the decisive causal factor in selecting both ends and means; but to find a way in which these essentially subjective motives could be dealt with in an objective way. This was to become the major preoccupation of Parsons:[4]

> Within the area of control of the actor, the means employed cannot, in general, be conceived either as chosen at random or as dependent exclusively on the conditions of action, but must in some sense be subject to the influence of an independent, determinate selective factor, a knowledge of which is necessary to the understanding of the concrete course of action.

The task consists, therefore, of elevating the analysis of subjective meanings to the level of objectivity and systemness attainable in the case of 'external' aspects of action. One could almost epitomize Parsons's project as the 'disenchantment' of hermeneutics.

Significantly, Parsons consistently uses the term *Verstehen* in its alien German form, meaning evidently that the term is not a part of the 'great tradition' which ought to be assimilated by the emerging theory of action. He deals with the term above all in the section headed 'Intuitionism'; *Verstehen* is, in his view, an idea forced upon people concerned with science by an essentially unscientific pressure group which insists on confusing the way in which the cognizing mind operates with the way in which its cogitation may be validated. In short, *Verstehen* is essentially an ill-conceived idea best kept in its strange German shell lest it spills over the problematics of understanding. Parsons seems to identify *Verstehen* with 'immediate intuitions' (compare Dilthey's empathy or *Sichhineinversetzen*) which, whatever their value in a particular case, cannot be admitted to the realm of scientific knowledge unless they pass a test of analytical propriety:[5]

> Our immediate intuitions of meaning may be real and, as such, correct. But their interpretation cannot dispense with a rationally consistent system of theoretical concepts. Only in so far as they measure up to such criticism can intuitions constitute knowledge.

In other words, intuitions which make for the difference between pre-scientific *Verstehen* and scientific understanding may be allowed into science only if they shed everything specifically intuitive.

Thus intuitions, empathy, 'putting oneself in the skin of the other', etc., are, admittedly, not the way in which the 'subjective' nature of human action is allowed to enter Parsons's voluntaristic theory. Indeed, Parsons freely admits that his schema of action is subjective 'in a particular sense'.[6] This particularity, one would conclude from the reasoning which follows, consists of admitting the 'subjectivity' of action only in the sense of the analyst's articulating it as such. It is the analyst's decision (though a methodical and not an arbitrary one) to so select his vocabulary and so describe mutual relations between concepts as to emphasize their reference to the 'point of view' of the actor under analysis, and not to those other elements which surround the action, which do not or cannot enter the actor's field of vision. Subjectivity is, in brief, a methodological principle. It stands for the 'subjective point of view' adopted by the 'scientific observer of action'.

Indeed, the crucial terms of the voluntaristic scheme of action, like ends, means, or conditions, would make little sense were it not for the 'actor's point of view'. It is trivially true that end, by definition, is somebody's end; there would be no ends without subjects (gods, human) positing them. It is trivially true again that once the end has been posited, the rest of the situation immediately splits into 'means' and 'conditions'. Having selected this vocabulary rather than an alternative one, the analyst simply sets limits to his interests – something which any theorist must do anyway: 'He is interested in phenomena with an aspect not reducible to action terms only in so far as they impinge on the schema of action in a relevant way – in the role of conditions or means.'[7]

The 'subjective point of view' becomes, therefore, an analytical device. Accordingly, understanding becomes a matter of scientific analysis. The 'subjective point of view' in Parsons's version, as in Husserl's, means eviction of the empirical subject.

True, the conceptual scheme Parsons designs may be used on two different levels; one of them is, in Parsons's terminology, 'concrete'; here we deal with a concrete action of a concrete individual. But what we can achieve on this level is, at most, the description of what has happened. The voluntaristic conceptual scheme helps us in the job of describing. We know which question to ask and how to classify what we see. In particular, we will try to find out what the end of action was and then to take a stock of means and conditions according to what we have found. But – Parsons reminds us – in this his conceptual scheme 'serves only to arrange the data in a certain order, not to subject them to the analysis necessary for their explanation'.[8] Human action, emphatically, cannot be explained (understood; Parsons uses the two words synonymously, stressing time and again that the intention to understand is the feature shared by natural and social scientists) on the level of a 'concrete' subject and his 'concrete' subjectivity.

The true understanding of subjective action is achievable only on a more abstract, 'analytical' level, where the action is still presented in the structure 'from the actor's point of view', but thoroughly cleansed of all idiosyncratic features ascribable to the 'concreteness' of concrete actors. On the analytical level, ends and means cease to be real entities inhabiting the actor's mind, and turn into conceptual units of a theoretical scheme. This allows us to 'bring out the functional relations involved in the facts already descriptively arranged'.[9] The fact that we can grasp such functional relations while abstracting from all and any concrete subject shows that these relations have their foundation in the conceptual scheme itself rather than in the minds of acting subjects. The task of understanding has been by the same token finally freed from 'intuitionist misconceptions' which insisted that understanding can be reached only in the mystical unity with the subject, and therefore cast the 'understanding' humanities beyond the bounds of science.

The tendency already conspicuous at the stage of *The Structure of Social Action* became still more pronounced in his later writings. In *Toward a General Theory of Action*, the 'actor', whose orientation is admittedly the feature distinguishing social action from all other conduct, has been already subtly re-processed by the theory; we read that 'action has an orientation when it is guided by the meaning which the actor attaches to it in its relationship to his goals and interests'.[10] The actor is still credited with an active role, with actually attaching something to something; but he is no longer free to choose what the meaning of action is attached to. The decision has been taken for him by the theory. Goal-attainment or interest-gratification is now what gives the action its meaning. In *The Social System* the small remaining step is taken: the distinctive feature of social action, we are told now, is that it 'has motivational significance to the individual actor' (and not that the actor attaches a meaning to it) – a subtle shift, but seminal. It is becoming increasingly clear that it is not the actor's initiative, but the type of objects to which this initiative has been turned, which qualifies his action as a social one. The next sentence makes this crystal-clear, asserting that 'motivational significance' 'means that the orientation of the corresponding action processes has a bearing on the attainment of gratifications or the avoidance of deprivations of the relevant actor'.[11] Clearly and unambiguously, conduct which the theory of action wants to analyse becomes identified with the rational type of behaviour of the individual whose demeanour approximates the hedonistically motivated *homo oeconomicus*. The same Parsons fourteen years earlier criticized the positivistic position for making the status of the normative elements of action exceedingly precarious: 'To speak of ends as determined by the mechanisms of pleasure is to . . . eliminate ends from the generalized theoretical system.'[12]

But the apparent shift consists more in the unfolding of elements present in Parsons concept of social action from the start, rather than in genuine change of mind. It has been said, after all, in *The Structure of Social Action*, that 'it is impossible even to talk about action in terms that do not involve a means–end relationship'.[13] This may pass, with some allowances made, for a Weberian statement; Weber probably would refuse to sign it for its uncompromising zest, but he too believed that we can best understand an action if we posit it as of rational type, that is to say as organized into means and ends. The resemblance is, however, superficial. In Weber, the selection of rational model as the objective method of approaching social action was related to his global view of history increasingly attuning us to understanding through rational models. In Parsons, the absolute superiority of the rational model has no relation whatsoever to the historicity of human understanding. It is an a-temporal attribute of human reason, and the only way in which history may be relevant to it is the moment when this truth has been discovered. And so we read:[14]

The action frame of reference may be said to have what many, following Husserl, have called a 'phenomenological' status. It involves no concrete data that can be 'thought away', that are subject to change. It is not a phenomenon in the empirical sense. It is the indispensable logical framework in which we describe and think about the phenomena of action.

The difference between this and Weber is obvious. Though he was not particularly consistent in its application, Weber repeatedly expressed his belief that the rational model of action is a historical product and by no means the only form of human behaviour in the society. He would not accept that something so clearly historical could be accorded a truly phenomenological universality.

Of more immediate interest to us, however, is the fact that Parsons invokes Husserl, though he invokes him mostly for his development of the Kantian idea of 'transcendental analytic'. Parsons, in fact, was deeply impressed by Kant's way of putting theoretical questions. With unqualified enthusiasm he remembered how Kant reversed the traditional articulation of the epistemological question 'by stating first: It is a fact that we have such valid knowledge. And only then he asked, How is this possible? While Kant's answer may not be wholly acceptable, his way of putting the question was of revolutionary importance.'[15] Obviously inspired by Kant's example, Parsons conceived of his theory of action as a similar analysis of absolute and universal, unavoidable conditions of its possibility. The language of his positive exposition of action leaves no doubt as to this intention. It is not a language of empirical description, nor of an empirical generalization of even the highest conceivable level; it is, unambiguously, the language of deductive analysis of 'necessities'. To select just two pages[16] as an example, Parsons writes of various elements of action that they 'cannot be random', 'must be integrated', are 'possible only because of', 'must be coherently organized', are 'necessary to reform', 'impossible without', etc.

The snag is that 'social action' (or society, to which the same transcendental approach has been applied, as we will see in a moment) is not a reality given as directly and unquestionably, as 'valid knowledge' in the case of Kant, or even 'life-world' in the case of Schutz (see pages 181–2). This is not a 'pre-theoretical' phenomenon, itself a precondition of all other phenomena, of existence itself. Social action as it comes under Parsons's transcendental analysis is already a 'conceptual scheme', an end-product of theoretical selection. In no conceivable way may it be seen as 'immediately obvious'. Thus the relevance of Parsons's 'transcendental conditions' to actual, empirically given human acts is, unlike the relevance of Kant's or even Schutz's, by no means automatic. As it were, only the rational or quasi-rational action comes under his analysis, and we do not know whether one can build a comprehensive theory of understanding while starting from this kind of action alone.

In all likelihood, Parsons was well aware of the weakness of his emulation of Kant. At any rate, he tried to compensate for it by insisting that his model is linked to concrete, empirical action, after all – since it has more dimensions than the purely phenomenological in the orthodox sense. Parsons reminds us that the means–ends schema, the backbone of his model of action, 'involves a real process in the mind of the actor, as well as external to it'. The word 'involves' helps by its equivocality; Parsons does not specify whether it involves 'real process in the mind' analytically, or empirically. If the first is the case, we have learned nothing new. If the second, however, Parsons wants us to take on his word the solution of the most haunting and vexing of problems posited by hermeneutical enquiry.

Obviously the ambiguity is convenient. The next sentence tells us that

on this level [again, which level? Analytical? Empirical? The dilemma repeats itself] then the action schema, including its central means–end component becomes more than phenomenological, it takes on not merely descriptive but also causal significance, and in so doing involves references to 'real subjective processes' of motivation.

This is clearly based on wrong understanding of phenomenology. The name 'phenomenology' stands not for what is being stated, but on what ground it has been accepted (or, rather, on what ground its claim for validity rests). One can postulate phenomenologically a 'real process in the mind' as an essence of the idea 'means and ends schema' without the schema becoming the slightest bit empirical. The reasoning throughout remains ambiguous as to the ground on which Parsons wants to base his claim that the means–end schema is, indeed, a suitable model for analysing social action. Weber, as it were, based similar claim on an unambiguously empirical (i.e. test-able, whether true or wrong) statement about history in general and modern capitalist society in particular. Parsons explicitly and con-sistently selects non-historical, transcendental grounds for his version of the means–end schema. By the same token he renders his model immune to empirical criticism, but puts in doubt the question of its empirical utility in the first place.

The following tautological statement comes, therefore, as no surprise:[17]

In order not to leave the reader feeling that the formulation of analytical laws on the basis of the system here worked out is in the structural context impossible, it may be useful to suggest tentatively that there already exists [where? In Parsons's vision of the later development of his theory?] the basis for the formulation of such a law of wide scope and high significance. The law may be tentatively formulated as follows: 'In any concrete system of action a process of change so far as it is at all explicable in terms of those elements of action formulated in terms of the intrinsic means–end relationship can proceed only in the direction of approach toward the realization of the rational norms conceived as binding on the actors in the system.'

The 'law' says that if we express an action in terms of the rational schema it will tend to be expressed in terms of the rational schema. True enough, though this is not what we used to expect from laws. Parsons's theory throughout consists of phenomenological insights, or of analytical statements in the Kantian sense, which play an 'explicative', but not an 'augmentative' role toward our knowledge of society. Parsons was for many years engaged in a determinate and assiduous effort to 'unravel' the deductive conclusions potentially contained in his few initial basic terms and axioms, and above all in the means–end model of action. One could describe his work as a painstaking investigation of a world which would exist if it was made of a multitude of men and women whose action consisted in selecting, rightly or wrongly, proper means to the given ends. This is the radical difference between Parsons's use of the means–ends schema and the use of the schema by Weber, who was interested in the model of rational action not as a set of axioms from which to build an abstract theory of society, but as a tool to understand objectively historically diverse modes of action.

The actual voluntary, indeterminate historical activity of men and women is of little interest to Parsons and of little import for his theory – beyond the initial supply of basic terms and axioms. The voluntarism of actor's selection of meanings remains the founding stone of the theory throughout, but all the attention is paid to the upper reaches of the edifice, where transcendental necessities are the reigning architectural doctrine. Parsons does not explore the impact exerted upon historical forms of society by choices made by people in their search for meanings; instead, he wishes to spell out the necessities which are contained *in nuce* in the very model of action seen as a means–end structure. The paradoxical effect of this approach is to make the role of the actor's motivation, crucial as it is to the structure of the theory, increasingly irrelevant. The object of understanding shifts from the actor's motives to the necessary relations between various elements of action's setting. To understand human action, in Parsons's theory, is to 'bring out the necessary relations'; to explore the transcendental logic of interaction between actors behaving according to the means–end model.

Thus in as far as the world is to the actor a pool of objects poten-

tially relevant to his interests, differentiation of these objects necessarily follows. The paramount distinction is the one between interacting and not interacting objects. (Parsons hastens to remind us
that 'this is a technical usage of the term interaction. It implies a
relationship both parties to which are actors in the technical sense.
It is thus distinguished from the sense in which interaction is synonymous with interdependence.'[18] It is crucial that we keep in mind this
comment relevant to all the terms appearing in Parsons's theory, lest
we should follow the common error of criticizing Parsons's system
for what it is not, a conservatively biassed description of society.)
Interacting objects are, of course, themselves actors. As such they
have complete action systems of their own, including their expectations as to the behaviour of the original actor and their own pursuit
of gratification. In the presence of other actors, the ego's action must
be oriented not just to their expectations, but to their possible
reaction to ego's expectations as well. From the point of view of the
general theory of action, ego and alter are, of course, mutually
exchangeable. What emerges, therefore, as an assumption of decisive
importance is that interaction is a relation in which expectations
'operate on both sides'.

Hence the 'complementarity of expectations', again a technical
concept referring not to the empirical identity of ego's and alter's
expectations, but to their mutual relevance, and hence to the importance of their mutual adjustment. One person's action is other
persons' sanction. Complementarity of expectations necessarily
entails a 'double contingency':[19]

On the one hand, ego's gratifications are contingent on his selection
among available alternatives. But in turn, alter's reaction will be contingent
on ego's selection and will result from a complementary selection on
alter's part.

This is nothing less than a statement of the logical necessity of
society. Indeed, if interaction is a relation involving actors' responses
to each other's expectations, a certain 'stability of meaning which can
be only assured by "conventions" observed by both parties', as well
as 'generalization from the particularity of specific situations'
become the indispensable preconditions of action, in as far as the
action is oriented towards the gratification of actors' interests.
Therefore, the necessity of society (generalization of typical patterns
of inter-situations) and cultural system (stability of meanings) are
logically contained in the means–end scheme of action.

This is a point of crucial importance. Both the strength and the weaknesses of Parsons's description of the social system are ascertainable solely when seen as an exercise in the phenomenological exploration of the transcendental conditions of the social action. If this point has been more often than not overlooked, and Parsons's description has been unjustly criticized for what it was not and could not be, Parsons himself ought to be held responsible: his frequent assertions of the 'empirical' status of his study obscured rather than clarified its true import. It is vital to see that social and cultural systems are introduced by Parsons as findings of the phenomenological analysis of the intentional meaning of means–ends concept; they are derived from the concept as the necessary constituents without which the concept is unthinkable. They are discussed as 'existing' in the Husserlian mode of *Bewusstsein*. Husserl starts with postulating the subjectivity of the transcendental ego in order to dissolve and overcome it in the objective necessity of meaning attributes and relations; Parsons starts with postulating the actor's subjective motives in order to dissolve and overcome them in the objective necessity of societally and culturally arranged networks.

Only the phenomenological project can give sense to the following statement: 'When, in the above discussion of action, we reached the point at which interaction of an actor with other persons or social objects became crucial, we disclosed the nucleus of the development of social system.'[20] (The only other possible interpretation is in terms of etiological myth, which would be totally alien to the letter and the spirit of Parsons's system.) There is a 'phenomenological necessity' link between the theoretical decision, that the 'organization of action elements is . . . above all a function of the relation of the actor to his situation', and the deductive necessity of a social system which[21]

consists in a plurality of individual actors interacting with each other in a situation which has at least a physical or environmental aspect, actors who are motivated in terms of a tendency to the 'optimization of gratification' and whose relation to their situations, including each other, is defined and mediated in terms of a system of culturally structured and shared symbols.

And there is a phenomenological foundation to ascribing, on the one hand, the 'law of increasing rationality' to Weber (depicting it as 'the most fundamental generalization that emerges from Weber's work'), while simultaneously castigating Weber for his tendency to 'reify his ideal type concepts'.[22] The law of increasing rationality is in Weber a historical generalization; in Parsons it is a phenomenologically discovered intentional meaning of the concept of purposeful action.

The utilitarian concept of social action is criticized by Parsons for its failure to 'see through' phenomenologically the logical consequences of the purposeful model. As we remember, Parsons's main objection to utilitarians was that they consider the ends of action to be chosen at random. The ends can be so considered only in so far as 'generalization of patterns' and 'stability of meanings', i.e. social and cultural systems, are not revealed as necessary derivatives and transcendental conditions of all purposeful action. The moment they are so revealed, the non-randomness of values, meanings, etc., become immediately obvious. It becomes analytically clear that[23]

Selections are of course always actions of individuals, but these selections cannot be inter-individually random in a social system. Indeed, one of the most important functional imperatives of the maintenance of social system is that the value-orientations of the different actors in the same social system must be integrated in some measure in a *common* system.

We learn, again by the way of the phenomenological analysis of the necessary meaning of concepts, that this common system includes the necessity of shared value orientations, ideas, and expressive symbols; that it includes as well the necessity of component personalities being motivated to 'act in the requisite ways' and receiving germane gratification for being so motivated; that functional imperatives must necessarily limit the tolerable incompatibility of motives and values; that, in other words, a 'voluntary selection of ends and means' includes, as its necessary condition, social and cultural systems bent on eliminating whatever may be the material effects of this voluntarity. The voluntarity itself boils down to the assumption that the actualizations of socially anchored norms are 'mediated' by conscious actors; a fairly trivial idea, of no visible consequence in the analysis of either of the three analytical systems (personality, society, culture) generalized from the model of purposeful social action. If anything, the invocation of the 'voluntary' nature of ends and means selection serves to bring into sharper relief the normative, limiting, anti-voluntaristic and anti-random requisites of all three systems. It renders possible, for instance, the following proposition: 'It is not possible for the choices of the actors to fall at random and still form a coherent and functioning social system.'[24] The main function of the stress on the voluntary character of action is to emphasize the paramount importance of de-randomizing factors among the conditions of purposeful action.

We have moved now a long distance indeed from the idea of understanding as penetrating, this way or another, the depths of subjective mind. The meaning of understanding has undergone a fateful change. It consists now of exploring the de-subjectivating factors; mechanisms and pressures which prevent actors' choices from being random in defiance of systemization and predictability. Husserl's methods have been applied to postulate such mechanisms and pressures as are necessarily contained in the very idea of the ends–means model. What Weber would portray as a resultant of the play of historical forces is for Parsons a stern and unquestionable requirement of reason. If rational action is a value, here are the unavoidable consequences, up to the requirement of 'apportioning sufficient power and prestige' to 'allocative and integrative roles' in society, i.e. to the people who are appointed (or self-appointed) to distribute differentially rewards and punishments and to spread the dominant ideas.

To understand human action is, therefore, to 'see through' the structure of social and cultural system. It is, solely and indivisibly, the work of reason trying to penetrate its own structural requirements. Once this has been done, one acquires the right standards to judge the meaning of actions invisible even to the actors themselves, as well as to portray the empirically discoverable gaps between the standards and the actual conduct as technical faults in meeting the prerequisites of rationality. The activity of understanding human action is dissolved in the phenomenological analysis of social structures and their transcendental conditions, called 'functional prerequisites', as well as empirical investigation of the failures in their practical applications. Understanding, therefore, becomes identical with structural analysis; it does not need the subject any more. On the contrary, it fulfils its task when it succeeds in dissolving the subject in the three interlocked systemic structures of personality, culture and social system.

In its ultimate effect, methodological and philosophical differences notwithstanding, Parsons's theory may be seen as a more sophisticated version of the central idea of Durkheim's sociology: to show the common-sense experience of 'social reality' as a reflection of transcendental necessity. There are, though, two significant differences between Durkheim's and Parsons's applications.

The first is between the moral and the rational. To Durkheim, society as a system of external sanctions is necessary for the individual to be a moral creature, as opposed to an organism set in motion by animal drives. Society is substituted in his version for God as the ultimate foundation of ethics. Parsons would in all probability dismiss this argument as one more metaphysical prop (though he does not seem averse to Durkheim's view of the society as a basically 'ennobling' force). Instead, Parsons argues for the necessity of external constraints in terms of the prerequisites of rationality. Society is the structure of the only setting in which rational action is plausible and, indeed, conceivable. It is, therefore, necessary for the individual to be able to act rationally, i.e. to select the right means to the selected ends. Societal regulation of individual's action is, to Durkheim, above all a moral commandment; to Parsons, it is a demand of technical reason.

The second difference lies in the treatment of the relation of individual and society. To the realist Durkheim, this is a relation between part and a whole, both part and whole being real entities in their own right. Hence the notorious difficulty inherent in Durkheim's system, with defining the exact meaning of the phrases 'the whole is more than the sum of parts', society 'is not reducible to the multitude of its members', etc., and of the terms like *conscience* or *mentalité collective* which stood for this supra-individual entity. The objections most often raised against Durkheim were in one way or another related to this, as many conceived it, essential incongruity of Durkheimian sociology. Parsons bypassed the difficulty by transplanting the whole problem from the empirical to the phenomenological. Personality (the individual) and society are *both* abstract concepts, once or several times removed from the only 'immediately given' entity, the unit act. Both are made of elements into which the unit act is split in the process of analysis. The building material being identical in each case, personality and social system differ as analytical concepts in the way the constituent elements are organized: whether around many acts performed by the same actor (personality), or around repetitive patterns of interaction between actors (social system). Neither is, therefore, primary. Personality, social system and, as we remember, the cultural system are three alternative directions of generalization into which the analytical reason can move, each time starting from the same initial point: a single social act. All three are 'modes of organization' of elements of action.[25] Neither can be seen, therefore, as a 'sum' of any of the others, and the metaphysical traps which plagued Durkheim's sociology are safely avoided.

The phenomenological sociology of Parsons has achieved, in purely methodological sense, what Husserl's tried to achieve in vain. Proceeding by purely phenomenological analysis of the intentional content of selected concepts (occasional, but abortive, forays into empirical world notwithstanding), it arrived at the concept of society and culture as 'objective necessities' without sacrificing the essentially subjective character of experience of which they are constructed. This remarkable feat has been accomplished by substituting 'social action' for transcendental subjectivity as the starting-point. We have seen how Husserl (inadvertently) proved that one cannot phenomenologically deduce the concept of supra-individual networks of any kind while leaving only the 'transcendental subjectivity' at the end of phenomenological reduction. Now we see how Parsons arrived where Husserl could not, by positing the means–ends scheme as his irreducible 'given'. And he never once let the suspended empirical reality interfere with his grounds of validation.

The important consequence for our problem is, however, that not the subjective aspect of the actor, but the action itself, is now the locus of meaning; and that the effort of understanding this meaning, instead of focussing on the actor's subjectivity alone, must now be a complex tri-partite analysis of action. None of the three screens on which the action may be projected to elucidate its structure is sufficient for understanding. The meaning we seek is suspended, so to speak, in the analytical space defined by the three dimensions of analysis. As everything else in Parsons's phenomenological sociology, the meaning is no longer an event of the world (in this case a psychic event in the mind of the actor); it is, instead, an analytical construct which refers to a certain relation of a given action to the three analytical systems.

From a sociologist's point of view, Parsons achieved more than Husserl. This does not mean that he escaped the notorious weaknesses of Husserl's phenomenology which seriously reduce its utility for the problems of understanding as they arise in social practice. Parsons, like Husserl, suggests understanding as the work of an expert analyst operating in the aseptic space of models only partially corresponding to social reality. Like Husserl, he fails to give a satisfactory answer to the question of how and when his analytical findings can be ploughed back into practical problems of understanding as raised by the practice of communication and disagreement. The validity of his findings, as we have seen, is confined to the realm designated by the initial basic concept of purposeful, rational-like action. His model is therefore equivalent to the empirical description of reality only in a rational world of rational actors. Parsons's theory neither gives us a clue as to the plausibility or probability of such a world, nor indicates how such a world could become the reality of social action.

7 Understanding as the work of life: Martin Heidegger

The driving force of Husserl's work was his urge to design a fool-proof and fully trustworthy method leading to an equally reliable, ultimate interpretation of meaning. In the course of his search Husserl turned away from the mundane, unmethodical and therefore precarious methods which ordinary men and women employ matter-of-factly to sustain and orient their life-in-the-world. Distrustful of such mundane understanding as notoriously ambivalent and volatile, Husserl postulated, as the only remedy, a radical disengagement of the interpreting subject from its wordly entanglements. We traced his efforts to achieve this, and we saw his ultimate failure; the truly radically disengaged subject turned out to be pure consciousness, incapable of returning to the world, much less of coming to grips with the task of understanding in the only form which counts: as it is posited by, and in, life-in-the-world.

Heidegger's is the earliest and most perceptive criticism of the irrealism of Husserl's project, voiced well before Husserl himself realized the self-defeating character of his efforts. The decisive departure entailed in Heidegger's approach to understanding expressed itself in the discovery that understanding is a mode of being, rather than a mode of knowledge; consequently, the mystery of understanding is an ontological, rather than epistemological problem. To Heidegger, the activity of understanding can be grasped solely as an aspect of being, as an essence of existence. As Ricoeur put it, instead of asking what is to be done in order to obtain correct understanding, Heidegger took another question as his major concern: what, in the human mode of being-in-the-world, determines both the possibility and the actuality of understanding?

Heidegger is not, therefore, concerned with a method which – once designed – could be learned and employed by professional hermeneuticians to resolve their conflicts of interpretation. Heidegger has little, if anything, to tell all those who want to know why they ought to prefer one particular interpretation to another. Instead, he painstakingly explores the ontological foundations of the understanding which men and women reach by the very fact of being-in-the-world. This understanding is a necessity, rather than an exceptional achievement; a necessity constantly arising from their very existence, as this existence stubbornly and incessantly reveals to them the variety of possibilities in which they might be-in-the-world. *Das Dasein ist seine Erschlossenheit*[1] (existence is its own disclosure).

This is the central message of Heidegger.

Though Heidegger and his doctrine are rarely quoted as paragons of lucidity, his main idea is clear and unambiguous. Understanding is a problem *in* the world, and if it can be solved at all, it is to be solved in the world. People do solve it day by day. If their solutions fall somewhat short of the philosophers' ideal of purity and precision, so much the worse for philosophers – because understanding can be found only where it is. If absolute truth and true understanding can be found only in an imaginary, prejudice-free, antiseptic world emancipated from its earthly commitments, there are no such things as absolute truth and full understanding. But then it does not matter much for human understanding to go its course.

In his exploration of the mystery of understanding Heidegger invites us to embark on a journey no less protracted and adventurous than Husserl's voyage to 'transcendental subjectivity'. But his expedition is in a totally different, if not the opposite, direction. It shies away from philosophers' concern with timeless extremes and instead returns to the foundation of human existence. Heidegger's hopes are lodged with a worldly existence uncontaminated by false philosophy, rather than with a consciousness unpolluted by existence. The true answer – the only answer accessible – lies there, in our pristine, straightforward, 'pre-reflexive' being-in-the-world, which philosophical abstractions beclouded rather than disclosed.

Heidegger seems to identify the foundations of existence with the beginnings of western history, much like those early anthropologists who hoped to find in 'savage', uncivilized life the sought-after truth of the 'natural man'. Free from the effete sophistication of later philosophy, early Greeks could articulate the truth of human existence with a lucidity never surpassed. It has been the misfortune of western civilization that it took over Greek philosophical lore with this simple articulation already hidden beneath a thick layer of pseudo-refinements.

The original Greek word for that what exists, for the being (*das Seiende*; translated by Ralph Manheim as 'essent'), was *physis*. It

was translated into Latin, through which it entered our own thinking, as *natura*. This unfortunate translation triggered off a long
series of imperceptible modifications of the original meaning, particularly within the Christian philosophical tradition, which eventually
brought us into the blind alley in which the battles of contemporary
philosophers are being fought. One can hardly remember now what
physis originally meant. One still has to recover and re-appropriate
the richness of its original meaning, since it succeeded where later
philosophers failed: in encapsulating the very essence of existing:[2]

What does the word *physis* denote? It denotes self-blossoming emergence
(e.g. the blossoming of a rose), opening up, unfolding, that which manifests
itself in such unfolding and perseveres and endures in it; in short, the realm
of things that emerge and linger on. . . . *Physis* means the power that
emerges and the enduring real under its sway. . . . *Physis* is the process of
a-rising, of emerging from the hidden, whereby the hidden is first made
to stand.

The Greeks coined their concept of *physis* through a fundamental
poetic, existential experience of being, rather than through generalizing from natural studies. From the distorted perspective of our
scientific age, in which *physis* has become above all the spatial
movement of atoms investigated by physics, the poetic, existential
richness of *physis* is no longer visible. The Greek idea of *physis* is
mistranslated as their incipient science of nature, just one 'ethno-
science' among the many recorded by ethnographers; 'the Greeks
become essentially a higher type of Hottentot, whom modern science
has left far behind'. In actual fact, the alleged 'natural philosophers'
were ahead of us, lost as we are among concepts misconceived in
later philosophical history; the truth of existence, which we vainly
try to paste together out of the scraps of empirical evidence, appeared
to them in its pristine, unmediated fullness. They knew what we
forgot – that truth is not this or that relation to being, an attitude
taken toward it, but the being itself:[3]

The essence of being is *physis*. Appearing is the power that emerges.
Appearing makes manifest. Already we know then that being, appearings
causes to emerge from concealment. Since the essent as such *is*, it places
itself in and stands in *unconcealment, alētheia*. We translate, and at the
same time thoughtlessly misinterpret, this word as 'truth'. . . . The essent
is true insofar as it is. The true as such is essent. This means: The power
that manifests itself stands in unconcealment. In showing itself, the
unconcealed as such comes to stand. Truth as un-concealment is not an
appendage to being.

Later, however, truth has been recklessly evicted from its natural dwelling – existence. It has become a property of the Spirit, carefully separated from earthly engagements, from the toil and sweat of earthly labour; the Spirit nobly suspended well above the world of things, of implements, of work, high enough to make its contemplation of the world pure and undisturbed by earthly concerns. One would wonder to what extent epistemology as we know it, the pursuit of truth interpreted as the assessment of being by an independent Spirit, reflected the philosophers' own existential experience: thinking as the leisurely pastime of free men who detested labour as the activity of slaves; thinking as the attribute of those who dominate, handling of things as the attribute of those who are dominated. Whatever the reasons, truth came to signify the power of Spirit who rules, rather than the quality of being; being itself has been deprived of its original self-propelling capacity and transformed into passive matter, blind and invisible to itself, dependent for its completeness on something external and alien to itself. Thereby the problem of truth has been wrongly posited as the problem of the relation between idea (Spirit's product) and facts (the product of nature). Wrongly posited, it has been insoluble from the outset and is doomed to remain so until abandoned.

Again, the early Greeks show what to replace it with:[4]

We know from Heraclitus and Parmenides that the unconcealment of being is not simply given. Unconcealment occurs only when it is achieved by work: the work of the word in poetry, the work of stone in temple and statue, the work of the word in thought, the work of the *polis* as the historical place in which all this is grounded and preserved.

Alētheia, the truth, the not-being-hidden, is constantly turned out by the work in the world and only there can be found. The idea of truth which can and ought to be conceived outside this world, as a product of a non-worldly agent disentangled from the worldly bonds, is an absurdity.

This is nothing less than a complete and irrevocable reversal of the position taken and vainly pursued by Husserl. It was Husserl who demanded that 'one must "step back" from one's situation through an inhibition or destruction of interest or involvement in order that the appearance of brute facticity pervade uncontrolled experience'.[5] It was Husserl as well who at the end of the road discovered, to his dismay, that 'the original problem remains: how can there be an identity between the solitary, unworldly Ego, and the intersubjective society of natural human beings in their cultural world?'[6] To Heidegger, this was the result one ought to expect, once the interest and involvement have been destroyed. No 'facticity' is to be revealed to a person who 'steps back' from his world. The unworldly Ego is condemned to a solitude which no amount of philosophical antics will ever remove. Being-in-the-world, so Heidegger would emphasize over and over again, is proper to human existence: 'Yet, ultimately this is most trivial and empty thing we can say; it simply means that [human existence] is found amidst other beings and so can be met with there.'[7] Trivial to the point of emptiness. Yet it took two millennia to recover this pristine, clear truth. More difficult still, the restitution of the lost or forgotten truth flew in the face of the *sanctum sanctorum* of our scientific age: the belief that the pursuit of truth is a struggle between pure, interest-free theory and a prejudice arising from partisanship. It is, after all, a conviction only seldom questioned, that true knowledge is without presupposition, that earthly passions blind the inquisitive mind, that concerns with other things than pure knowledge may result only in distortion of truth. To Heidegger, this very belief is our original undoing; since its acceptance our pursuit of true understanding is led astray.

Never denying the historical importance of scientific achievement, Heidegger was keen to emphasize that the nature of this achievement is bound to constitute its limitation: science is just 'practical intelligence', which can operate only by dismembering human existence both theoretically and practically. Less harm is done when the scientific achievement is set soberly in its true context – as an aspect of utilitarian specialization, which makes practical tasks more practical and easier done. The harm is, however, boundless, when such an activity is presented as a cultural value; as *the* cultural value of our age, as it were. In Heidegger's view, it is a lie that something so heterogeneous and dismembered, so unlike human existence itself, can be a cultural value. In his early work, *Was ist Metaphysik?* (1929), he announced the verdict never later changed:[8]

Today this hodgepodge of disciplines is held together only by the technical organization of the universities and faculties and preserves what meaning it has only through the practical aims of the different branches. The sciences have lost their roots in their essential ground.

Detached from this essential ground and engrossed in their partial, highly specialized practical concerns, sciences cannot offer any significant answer to the fundamental questions of human existence. There is no way which leads back from sciences to the totality of human existence.

Elaborating upon essential ideas of Plato, the scientific tradition tended to see the mind as a mirror which merely reflects external objects; the better this mirror is polished and cleaned up, the more it 'effaces itself', the less it interferes with the look of the reflection. To Romantics, on the contrary, the mind became 'a lamp, a radiant projector'.[9] Whatever has become part of human reality, parcel of human existence, has done so only by the light of this lamp which 'snatched' it from the eternal darkness. Men are not recorders of the world, they are its existential conditions. The fundamental attitude of the Romantic is his sense of a fuller, more real because more total, world, which[10]

ends paradoxically by making him attach more value to the sensations and appearances which constitute his daily life. They sharpen his insight and make him find charm and significance in much that others dismiss as trivial or fail altogether to notice.

This has been to a great extent Heidegger's attitude and his style of philosophizing. If one accepts Novalis's definition of Romantic activity, 'By giving the common a noble meaning, the ordinary a mysterious aspect, the known the dignity of the unknown, the finite the appearance of the infinite – I romanticize'[11] – then, and to that extent, Heidegger was a Romantic.

In the fullness of the Heideggerian notion of existence all the traditional distinctions which provided philosophers with their problems and the subject-matter of their debates are merged and restored to what Heidegger considers their primeval unity. Thereby most haunting philosophical difficulties are exposed as artefacts of wrong distinctions, which unnecessarily impoverish human existence. It is because 'Nature' has been substituted for the genuine phenomenon of the world that 'the perennial problems of cognition and knowledge' have been generated, 'for whose solution countless "theories of knowledge" have been constructed'.[12] The false dilemma hopelessly split philosophers into realists and idealists. Both camps spent most of their time and energy trying to prove the existence of an external world. But[13]

to 'prove' the existence of an external world is to overlook the *a priori* nature of Being-in-the-world. . . . Rocks and trees do not depend on man for their occurrence in the universe, but reality, which is merely a mode of man's interpretation of the world, does depend on man's existence.

If we only remember that the human existence is not laboriously patched together from bits and pieces of empirical evidence, but the fundamental *a priori* of the world as we know and can know it, including all the philosophical inquiries which can be made about this world – then it becomes clear that consciousness and 'external nature', so sharply opposed in our philosophical tradition, far from being autonomous partners in contractual relations with each other, are inextricably welded into one, inside the all-embracing phenomenon of our being-in-the-world.

Similar reasoning will expose the artificiality and groundlessness of other hallowed problem-generating distinctions: between actuality and potentiality (neither can exist without the other), and – most important for our concern with understanding – between me and the others. Communication with others is in no way a mystery, but an *a priori* condition of existence. Being-in-the-world is from the outset organically and irretrievably being-with; it is an illusion, trained by misleading abstractions, to suppose that it has to be first 'proved' that this may be so, or brought about by the application of special, technologically sophisticated, exertions. *Das In-der-Welt-sein is gleich ursprünglich das Mitsein und Mitdasein.*[14] (Being-in-the-world is, from the outset, being-with and existing-with.)

We have now, I hope, enough preliminary information about the nature of Heidegger's project to consider the solution it offers to the problem of understanding.

Consider the following case:

I have a pet dog. I am fond of him, I enjoy his wagging his tail when I return home, his peaceful sleep at my feet when I rest in my chair. I feed him, I take him for a walk. I protect him from the hazards of the outside world. If I gave enough thought to it, I would perhaps say that my life is full of my pet, that it is brightened by his presence, that I like my pet because of all the little pleasant acts I perform thanks to this presence. But I would hardly say so unless forced by a sudden interruption of our happy routine co-existence; I would hardly say so because I have no reason to think about the nature of our co-existence. Not that I do not understand this nature: we happily and unproblematically co-exist, experiencing no obstacle in what has become already our habitual way of being, our existence itself. And so I am never given any reason to subject this co-existence to scrutiny, to ask about its nature, to analyse the similarity or dissimilarity between what it actually is and what it could or ought to be. Normally, I would never have occasion to define – even to myself – this co-existence as a specimen of a wider category, a case relation of a pet and his master. As long as our life together runs its normal course, there is no reason for questioning. This existence without questions is not, however, a case of ignorance, of the lack of understanding. It is only that the understanding, implied to an external observer by the smoothness of my routine, remains to me inarticulate. And it may as well remain silent until the abruptly disturbed routine reveals the brittleness of daily habit and cries for analysis.

There are several ways in which my routine can be disturbed, and, therefore, a need to question it arises. My dog may disappear: he may be run down by a passing car, stolen, lost on one of his lonely escapades. His disappearance makes a hole in my existence. Some-thing is missing, there is emptiness where there was wholeness before, nothingness instead of something. This nothingness reveals to me my missing dog as indeed something, as an object, as a pet: member of the category of pets, a definite object, a definable object. This thought may occur to me for the first time. Only when I suddenly lack it, I begin to ask just what it was in the first place: what it is appears to me in the form of 'what have I lost', and only when it can take that form.

Or my pet, so lovely and gentle a creature, can all of a sudden bite me. To the best of my memory, he has never behaved like that. To be sure, it is only now, sucking my bitten finger, that I begin to scan my memory in search of the record I normally do not delve into, to set one fact against the other, compare, draw conclusions. At the end of my investigation a picture will emerge – of a pet as it ought to be *and* as it 'normally' is. 'Pets ought not behave like this.' 'But then my pet never behaved like this.' What is being formed in my mind is the essence of 'petness', the awareness of what being a pet can mean. I can now spell out the meaning of being a pet, something which was hardly my habit before. Let us be clear what has happened: I can now articulate the meaning of 'petness' only because a possibi-lity of my dog being something else (an obstreperous, dangerous beast) has been revealed to me. I now understand what a pet is, only because I know that not all dogs are like that all the time and that a dog being a pet as I would understand it is merely a possibility.

Finally, I may be asked, with amazement or reprobation: 'Why do you make so much fuss about such an ugly brute? If I were you,

I would not let him near my house.' I hear the question, and it suddenly dawns upon me that my pet dog is an object which can be looked upon, assessed, praised or censured, liked or detested, admired for his beauty or condemned for his ugliness, played with or rejected. Inevitably, a question occurs to me: what is my dog truly, whatever people may say of him? And what is this dog to me? What meaning has he? Indeed, why do I make all this fuss? These questions, and perhaps many similar ones, come to my mind only because I have been faced with a clash of opinions. The question I heard bumped against an obstacle which prevents it from being quietly absorbed by me. I suspect that this obstacle is my own view of my dog, at odds with the intention I sensed in the question. I suspect it only, since I never felt any need to clearly articulate this view of mine. Now, for the first time, am I forced to. Between the two clashing opinions, the presence of my dog, this creature familiar to the point of triviality, lost its previous transparency and became a subject in its own right, something I can and ought to ask questions about. It is only at this moment that I consider him a carrier of a meaning which I am keen to understand.

Let us sum up in the words of Arland Ussher: 'The world as world is only revealed to me when things go wrong.'[15]

According to St John, 'when all things began, the Word already was'. According to Heidegger's gospel, for all things to begin, there must be already Existence. I start looking for words when existence reveals to me its rough edges; I need words to patch up the cracks in my world. I do not start from looking at my world, contemplating it, analysing: I start from living it. Whatever my world may consist of, it is all there 'naturally', as unnoticeable parts of the totality of my existence. It becomes an object of my contemplation only when it is brought into salience because it is missing, or when it strikes me because of its unsuitability. Or, alternatively, when it resists its assimilation into my world because of its unreadiness, its obstinate resistance to usability.[16]

In his second meditation Descartes set about explaining what the knowing 'that things exist' may mean. He chose a piece of wax as his example. This piece has something of the sweetness of honey and the odour of flowers: it has an apparent colour, size, figure; it is hard and cold. 'But notice that while I speak and approach the fire what remained of the taste is exhaled, the smell evaporates, the colour alters, the figure is destroyed, the size increases, it becomes liquid, it heats. . . . ' So what is there that exists? In what sense can

one say that this piece of wax exists? Is not existing equivalent to
having attributes? To being thereby itself? In what sense can one say
that wax has attributes? Which attributes would these be?

Heidegger's rejoinder to this reasoning goes, roughly, as follows.

Descartes took off on a wrong track in his preliminary decision to
locate the question of existence 'out there', in this piece of wax, in
that fire, and to articulate his problem as the question of attributes
which things possess in themselves, outside, or potentially outside
our life-world: this determined both the impossibility and the
irrelevance of his project. The next thing he will have to grudgingly
admit is that *nos non docent, qualia [corpora] in seipsis existant*. The
endless chain of epistemological theories will be soon produced,
vying with each other for a less absurd and outlandish solution to a
problem which daily existence solves effortlessly and without interruption. Descartes' original sin was to posit objects as having from
the start the mode of *Vorhandenheit* alone, i.e. of being out there,
occupying a spot in space, self-enclosed, safely entrenched outside
human practical existence, from inside which they can be only looked
at, contemplated. Having first reduced his Ego to the pure thinking
capacity, having allowed this impoverished Ego to communicate
with the world only via contemplation, Descartes severely limited
his own chance of coping with the problem he set out to solve: he
left, as it were, contemplation as the only meeting-point between
objects 'out there' and human existence. Of course, the end has been
already determined by the choice of the starting-point. Of course,
what things are cannot be established by contemplation alone. Of
course, we will be never sure whether our thinking about objects
truly reflects what they 'truly are'. Of course, if measured by the
standards of constancy and solidity we tend to ascribe to things in
themselves, our knowledge will always look pitifully fragile and
contingent. The point is, however, so what? Why should it worry
us?

It does worry us only because we have already transgressed the
obvious, homely life-world in which there are rarely grounds to doubt
what wax is. It is a philosopher's illusion that we first meet wax
when we try to attribute to it abstract qualities which it allegedly has
entirely by itself. This attempt is not our first encounter, but a fairly
radical departure from the life-world where we used to meet wax
matter-of-factly, never fixing our gaze on it like an alien object,
separate from our own being-in-the-world and, consequently, a locus
of separate attributes. Above all, we *used* wax; we poured it molten

into candle moulds, we sealed letters with it, we carved sculptures in it. Wax was there, together with us, in the world, hardly ever noticed as a problem in its own right. One would say, we knew it rightly in so far as we handled it the right way. And we had no reason to ask or to think whether we indeed knew it, as long as we continued to do the right things and the right things were done without obstacle. All this we did without ever needing an answer to the question, 'What are the attributes of wax?' – the question which we continually answered in our handling of wax and therefore had no need to ask as a question. This is exactly what Descartes failed to consider. He wanted us, therefore, to grasp the essence of wax away from the very context of the life-world in which this essence is given to us in all the clear obviousness of wax's existence. By locating his problem in this artificial realm, he deprived himself of the only possibility of answering his own question. And so did all the epistemology, founded on the separation of subject and object, and set on finding out what the objects are independently of their natural context, the life-world.

According to Heidegger, the *Dasein* – the existence typical of humans – entails the 'objects' as *Zuhandenheiten*, implements (Vycinas), handy reality (King), given to hand. Like wax, entailed matter-of-factly in the moulding of candles or sealing of letters, like the pet dog contained naturally by my evening rest, they are dissolved in our daily existence so completely that in ordinary circumstances they do not appear as opaque objects which invite questioning as to their meaning. We take them for granted. They are just there, naturally and unproblematically. All knowledge starts from there. Being given-to-hand is, to be sure, the condition without which 'knowing things' is unimaginable:[17]

In its familiarity with significance, existence is the ontic condition of the possibility that the beings be disclosed, which he meets in the world in their mode of being circumstanced (*Bewandtnis*), given-to-hand (*Zuhandenheit*).

'Being circumstanced' is the existential quality of all given-to-hand. They are fully determined within my life-world, though I rarely attend to their determination and attempt to articulate it. I am, indeed, familiar with their significance; I know somehow that the wax is there to seal with, that the hammer is there to hammer with and the pet to play with. I know all this of which my existence consists, though I do not know it *theoretically*; to wit, I do not distance myself from the object of my knowledge. The distinction between subject and object is a theoretical distinction, as perceived *after* the 'distantiation' took place. It does not overlap with the distinction between my existence (*Dasein*) and the world of my existence, which is given to me all the time, always as unity, and before any other distinction (including this between subject and object) could be made, before I could even commit this act of self-distantiation with which all the distinction-making starts.

'Normally' we have, therefore, no occasion to posit theoretical knowledge, understanding, as a task; and we can easily do without it. Or, rather, we could, if the world functioned smoothly and without interruption, if there was a perfect harmony between my hand stretched towards the world and the shape of the world the hand is stretched to handle, if the two were perfectly geared to each other. But there is no such harmony. The hand stretched towards the world is likely to hang in the void, or touch a rugged surface, or catch an object too large or too unwieldy to be grasped. The world is fraught with such incongruities, and in this quality the constant possibility of theoretical knowledge is ineradicably present.

The process leading to theoretical knowledge is triggered off when things reveal that their givenness-to-hand, their readiness to be handled, their obedient fitness, are not qualities which can be taken for granted. Suppose I need to nail a lid on a box, but I have nothing to hit the nail with; it is then that I start thinking about the qualities of an object which I could use to do the job. It is then brought to my attention (I am becoming aware of) that the object ought to be heavy, unbreakable, tough and have a flat surface with which to hit the nail. In the process I have distanced myself, without noticing it, from the object I sought: I have created a theoretical image of it, I have posited it as an object which can be analysed, as a *Vorhanden*, disposable (Vycinas), substantial reality (King), a thing in front of me, a thing 'out there'. Or suppose I have a hammer which could serve the purpose, but I cannot lift it; it is too heavy. Again, although 'being too heavy' is ultimately a feature of my relation with the hammer rather than of the hammer itself, I would rather posit the frustrating 'heaviness' as a property of the hammer. Heaviness is revealed to me as an attribute of the hammer, a feature which protrudes from our matter-of-fact relations and stops them from being such. Again, the hammer becomes a *Vorhanden*, posited as an object of theoretical knowledge by the distance which arose between us. Or suppose that while I hit the nail the hammer broke, and I could not finish my job. The broken hammer shows me what the hammer was when it was not broken: a heavy, tough, etc., object which I wielded in order to hit the nail. All this is revealed to me when the smooth, routine use of the hammer grinds to a halt. It is then that I start asking what the hammer in fact is. I start asking this question when it ceases to be a part of my familiar life-world, and therefore sets itself in front of me as a thing-in-itself, an opaque object, which ought to be pierced through by theoretical analysis.

All these instances of the passage from the mode of *Zuhandenheit* to *Vorhandenheit* have one feature in common. They all take place when acting-from-familiarity fails, when the 'natural' course of 'in-order-to' action has been broken, clashed with the absence of its natural component or with a frustrating situation in which the components are not what they 'used to be'. In other words, a 'given-to-hand' becomes a 'thing-out-there', an object waiting for our theoretical knowledge to attribute to it qualities, when it reveals that it may not be there or that it can be different. Theoretical knowledge starts from the disclosure of possibilities; from the discovery that familiar actuality does not exhaust the realm of possibilities; from a 'bumping' against the lack of fit between actuality and possibility. We start thinking of the 'essence' of things as their own property when we disclose the possibility of things not being there or being different.

And so it is not the actuality which requires (and, indeed, makes possible) theoretical knowledge; it is the possibility which does. The question, 'What is X?' makes sense only when the possibility that X can be something else has been discovered. In a world in which that discovery could not be made, theoretical knowledge would not arise; it would be unthinkable in a world in which all possibilities were identical with actuality. But our world is not such a world. To be exact, our existence is specifically human existence, *Dasein*, only in so far as our world is not such a world. Our world not being such a world, and our existence being human, are in fact two wordings of the same truth. In as far as our existence is human, the lack of identity between possibility and actuality, and therefore theoretical knowledge, is not just conceivable, but inevitable. The theoretical question about the essence of things, whether articulated within realistic discourse (what are they in themselves?), or in the empiricistic discourse (how do they appear to us?), or in a phenomenological one (how do they exist in the mode of being?), is not a feat accomplished by the philosopher; in its rough form it continually emerges, and cannot but emerge, in the very midst of our ordinary existence. Theory is our fate.

But how is it so? Why is existence doomed to discover possibilities and therefore to theorize? The answer is not immediately obvious. It requires a closer look at the structure of existence; so far we have concentrated on the world of existence rather than on existence itself. We have distinguished, following Heidegger, two modes in which the world may confront *Dasein*. We do not know yet in what mode *Dasein* confronts itself. According to Heidegger, in this mode – or modes – the answer to our question can be found.

One searches Heidegger's writings in vain for the notion of the human being as an empty vessel, yet to be filled with content (by perceptions, socialization, or what have you). Not that Heidegger is just not interested in the biographical – true or imaginary – beginnings of consciousness, but that he would not attach to such beginnings, when imagined, the label of 'existence'. Perhaps individual humans do start their individual life as clinically clean empty vessels, but whether they do or do not has no relevance to our problem. Existence is from the outset irretrievably being-in-the-world, and only as such can it be analysed. And being-in-the-world, in its turn, means from the outset *being with*, with things and with other people. As we have seen, theoretical knowledge is a secondary, derivative feature of being-in-the-world. Existence is above all surrounded by givens-to-hand; its cognitive concerns may arise only at a higher stage, as a result of something which has happened already before in the 'handy', familiar realm. This realm, we remember, consists primarily of things which are handled and known only through being handled. The emergence of theoretical knowledge is, therefore, not a question of cognitive curiosity, but of much wider practical concerns and occurrences. And to reconstruct it is not to see how an empty consciousness comes to be filled, but how the existence which can do without theorizing reaches a point at which theorizing becomes necessity. We can put it this way: the problem of knowledge, articulated by most epistemologists as the passage from emptiness to fullness, Heidegger re-phrases as the question of passage from pre-reflective (but full all the same!) existence to an existence which includes self-reflection.

And thus we meet existence when it is already itself – being in, and together with, its densely populated world. In this first encounter we find in it nothing even remotely reminiscent of an 'empty cabinet', '*tabula rasa*', or other favourite images of epistemologists. We meet existence in the state of *Befindlichkeit* ('being situated'), or *Stimmung* ('tuned'). The two terms mean in fact the same; as it is often the case with Heidegger, the first term gives the concept its own, distinctive name within Heidegger's ontology (pointing out, in a sense, where the concept belongs and within which universe of discourse it ought to be interpreted); the second sends us to the nearest analogy, enlisting thereby the powers of imagination to assist the assimilation of the novel idea.

Befindlichkeit is, in Heidegger's words, an ontological name for 'being tuned'. This is a fine image, which does help to understand what Heidegger has in mind. Our existence has been from the start 'tuned' to become a specific existence, this existence here, located in (or, again, in Heidegger's imaginative expression, 'thrown in') the world which contains what it contains. Existence enters this primary mode already prefabricated; it is ready-made, 'tuned up' the first moment we meet it. It did not exist before this 'tuning up' was accomplished, and we can say nothing about the way in which it could exist then. Emphatically, Heidegger harps on this point, selecting powerful expressions like *'ursprünglich'* (from the beginning), *'hartnäckig'* (obstinately), *'immer'* (ever) to denote the way in which the 'tuning up' is predicated on existence.

We can depart a bit from specifically Heideggerian vocabulary, and come closer to the form in which problems usually appear in sociological discourse, by saying that we can only comprehend what 'understanding' involves and what role it plays in human life if we begin our analysis with the man already 'immersed' in his world, 'infested' with prejudices, with his consciousness 'committed' in the sense of being sharpened in some directions and blunted in some others. We are asked, therefore, to forget 'unprejudiced' understanding; pure consciousness, cleansed of the life context, is an incongruity; one would be hard put to show what it would mean. To imagine such consciousness would be equivalent to demanding that we know a world which is empty of would-be objects of our knowledge. The objects of all future knowledge must be already constituted 'at hand' before knowledge becomes possible. But together with these objects, the 'tuning up' takes place, and with it the prejudices which many an epistemologist wishes away.

The German word for 'prejudice' (or, rather, pre-judgement), *Vorurteil*, stands in one line with other Heideggerian terms, *Vorhabe* (purpose), *Vorsicht* (circumspection), and *Vorgriff* (anticipation), all considered as denoting the necessary conditions of knowledge. They all combine to produce a situation in which the given-to-hand is finally transformed into an object-out-there and subject to theoretical scrutiny. All must somehow precede this transformation, therefore be present already in the state of 'being situated'. Hence the dialectical nature of *Befindlichkeit*: on the one hand, it closes up the human being by the very act of 'tuning'. Having done so, it jealously guards its prisoner, the fact which is distinctly felt the moment an attempt is made to go beyond the enclosure (to see something with eyes untinted by what they have seen so far, with an 'unprejudiced' eye). On the other hand, however, it is exactly 'tuning up' which makes the human being a being-in-the-world, therefore a being opened up to things of this world, and (as we have already seen) bound to come across disobedience of things and to be pushed into the effort called theoretical knowledge. The 'tuning up' is freedom disguised as fetters. The prejudice it entails is the condition of our knowledge. Not that 'prejudiced' knowledge is better than an unprejudiced one; it is rather that if it were not for 'prejudice' there would be no knowledge.

While remaining just 'situated', 'tuned up', men may reach the stage of theoretical knowledge, to distance themselves from the 'things out there'; and still fail to distance themselves from themselves, to look at themselves as objects. I say this in order to emphasize that the two acts are different and require different sorts of efforts, not in order to suggest that one does happen without the other (which, as we shall see later, cannot be the case). Distancing myself from oneself is, in a way, much more radical and fateful than distancing oneself from others. As we have seen, knowing things theoretically means revealing the possibility of their not being there or being different. The same discovery in relation to ourselves means more than just the passage from familiarity to theoretical knowledge. It means lifting ourselves from the mode of 'being situated' into the mode of 'understanding'. It is the disclosure of the possibility to be free, which the state of 'being situated' contains and conceals at the same time.

How does it conceal this possibility of freedom? In a way similar to that in which 'givens-to-hand' escaped losing their matter-of-fact familiarity and 'homeliness'. In both cases, 'things must go wrong' before they can reveal themselves as problems, as not-necessarily-what-we-take-them-for, as capable of not being there, or being there in a different way. What prevents my own existence from losing its matter-of-fact familiarity is (we can put it this way, which is not necessarily Heideggerian) its practical transparency, which prevents it from revealing to us its intellectual opacity; a certain smoothness, unchallenged obviousness to its daily course; in sociological terms again, its habitualized, routinized character well geared to the conditions in which it takes place. What gives our existence an additional but powerful support in guarding its matter-of-factness is the presence of a resourceful authority, which adds a touch of righteousness to the obviousness of the way in which we are situated in the world. This authority Heidegger calls *das Man*; a term resisting an English translation, as it owes all its formidable poignancy to the way in which it violates linguistical rules obligatory in German or French but absent in English. One says in German, '*man sagt*', which in English will mean, roughly, 'It is being said'. A lot of *man*'s character is lost in the translation. The most important thing which has been lost is the fact that *man* plays the grammatical role of a personal pronoun, therefore suggesting that it stands for a person (a German–English dictionary translates '*man*' as 'one; a man; we, you, they; men, people'). But in fact it stands for nobody in particular, only for a widespread habit which is prominent above all for its anonymity, for its lack of attachment to any authorship in particular. Having added '*das*' to '*man*', and written '*Man*' with a capital letter, Heidegger puts this nothingness, this anonymity, in the grammatical form of a substantive, suggestive not of an emptiness but of a solid, space-filling thing. *Das Man* is all-powerful precisely for its elusiveness, for the fact that it has been made of a condensed void and therefore is immune to assaults, which go through empty space as a knife through butter, destroying nothing and leaving everything as it was. This *das Man* is, in Heidegger's words, as *ursprünglich*, primeval, as the state of 'being situated' itself. '*Das Man* is a *nobody*, to whom all our existence, in its being-together, has already surrendered.' This surrender is an original act which normally has lasting consequences: 'At the beginning, I am not "me" in the sense of my own self; to start with, *Dasein* is *Man* and tends to remain so.' What is being *das Man*, instead of being myself, like? *Das Man* is, above all, the Average; it is the 'levelling up' of diverse possibilities of being.[18] When reflected in myriads of mirrors, our existence has no chance of striking us as bizarre and therefore demanding analysis, invite us to turn our spotlights upon it and posit it as a problem. It is not that we are reassured when we look around and notice the universality of the 'matter-of-factness' with which our fellow men live their lives, so similar to each other in their appearance of being determined, shaped in advance; the real problem is, that as long as the discreet authority of *das Man* holds us in its grip, the very occasion which would require reassurance is unlikely to arise. 'Being situated', remaining under the rule of *das Man*, has tremendous advantages which become visible when they are lost: homeliness, familiarity, security, sheltered existence, none of which could be sustained without the powerful prop of *das Man*.

These advantages I have to forfeit when seeing through my existence as a mere 'being situated', and through *das Man* as a mere nothingness. This is why my emancipation is not easy; and this is why, even if given a chance, I could still be tempted to run back under the cosy shelter of *das Man*. It is precisely the *Unheimlichkeit* (unhomeliness) of the existence 'outside' which brings into sharp relief the unique attractions of *das Man*.

And yet, the transcendence of the state of 'being situated', the escape from the iron grip of *das Man*, is inevitable, for the same reason that 'givens-at-hand' must turn time and again into 'things out there'. Our existence is bound to reveal itself to us as a mere possibility. Worse still, what is bound to reveal itself to us is the possibility of our non-existence: we know, after all, that we will die. Once we are aware there is no solid foundation for the very state of being alive, of existing, the possibility of existing differently appears as well. Since our existence may not be, it may be also different from the shape it has assumed by being 'situated', 'tuned up':[19]

The key phrase, *es geht um*, it is at stake, gives us the first hint of how the *not* is originally manifest to man. How could his own being be at stake for him, unless it were in advance disclosed as a being he stands to lose? Man exists, i.e. understands himself in his being from the constant possibility that he can also *not* be. . . . It enables man to understand the possibilities of his own being and those of other beings; it is the source of possibility as such.

Our life is always, and from the outset, life-towards-death. In Heidegger's formidable expression, man is dying already *as* born. Stubbornly present as a possibility, death 'relativizes' our existence and discloses it as another possibility. In this sense, indeed, the knowledge of my own death is the ultimate source of all the possibility, of the very notion of it; one could say that the very act of 'distancing' ourselves from the world and from our own 'situated' existence has its roots in the discovery of death, as if Heidegger's model of human existence were an obverse of Freud's; it is the 'death trauma', rather than 'birth trauma', which structures it.

The discovery of death is inevitable, but at the same time the most heroic and fateful of all acts man can commit. It means passing from the state of *Befindlichkeit* to *Verstehen*, from 'being situated' to understanding, the only state which can be called an authentic existence; the first is plankton-like, other-directed, just-so-existence. Only when I understand my existence as one possibility among many, does my existence become authentically human. Authenticity, understanding, and disclosing actuality as potentiality, are in fact different names referring to the same act or state. All of them refer as well to an opportunity which is always and organically available in all existence; to an opportunity, however, which has to be yet picked up, transformed from a historical offer (*Wahl*) into a choice (*Auswahl*).

And so understanding is an achievement, but an achievement within reach of all men and women. Understanding is, in fact, our fate, against which we can fight, but from which we cannot escape.

Understanding is not to be confused with the mere unreflective ability to act. All our 'moving around' in the world, including what does not require any transcendence of the 'situated' state, entails comprehension, choosing, using language, etc. Understanding, however, begins when a particular form of distancing takes place: the opening of a gap between my facticity, the way I am already, and the realm of my possibilities. Understanding, as we already know, means seeing possibility as possibility. In other words, understanding consists in projecting (*Entwurf*). This is a two-pronged act: on the one hand, possibilities are 'thrown' into future, into what-is-not-yet; on the other, possibilities so projected are re-projected, thrown back upon the actuality, thereby exposing it as an object of potential questioning, challenge, and change.

On the other hand, understanding ought not to be taken for a purely intellectual act in a drama of the thought facing the world, the Spirit gaining mastery over the matter. However often one repeats that the essence of human existence lies in its facticity – one would, indeed, never repeat it once too often – one has to accept this statement 'in all earnestness',[20] and patiently see through its manifold consequences. If understanding is the disclosure of possibilities, it can happen only in the world, in the context of the 'throwness' of our existence in a 'location' which includes things and other people. Possibilities must be there, in the world, if they are to be disclosed.

They are there because the past brought them up. But they would not be disclosed if our existence was not, in Heidegger's words, always 'ahead of itself', i.e. illuminating itself from the prospective projections of the present, from the standpoint of the future, which reveals the present as a cluster of possibilities. The moment I begin to see myself as a flexible, developing, unfinished, underdetermined possibility – I am 'opening myself up' not only to the future (that far Heidegger's view would not conflict with the image of 'knowledge as mastery' which underlies the model of science as bequeathed by the nineteenth century), but to the past as well. Only then can I truly assimilate the past, receive this history which has been handed over to me in the facticity of my existence. Because only then history reveals itself to me as an endless run of possibilities, as unfinished and underdetermined as my existence. Only then my existence will reach this fullness, this authenticity, in which *Sein* is *Zeit*, facticity *is* historicity:[21]

When I turn to the past as though it were a passive 'object' waiting to reveal its secrets to me, I am overlooking the fact that the past reveals itself to me in terms of human possibility, and that it is my projections, i.e., what I count possible, that determines what I shall objectively 'see' or overlook.

This summary is not entirely correct: it is not just what I *count* possible, but what *is* my, historically shaped, possibility, which determines what and how the past can be revealed to me. My understanding of history is not, therefore, a process between a timeless intellect aiming and the absolute and the contingent, protean facticity of events and facts. My understanding of history is itself history. I can understand history only when I have fully realized my potential of a historical being. History I try to understand and my existence – which incorporates this understanding, which is both the light thrown upon history, and its shadow – are made of the same stuff. And so historical cognition never truly ends. History is *die stille Kraft des Möglichen* (the silent force of the possible): history is a force powerful enough to turn out possibilities, but not to make them speak up. They remain silent until drawn into the limelight by authentic existence. Making them speak loudly, the authentic existence illuminates its own potential. What the possibilities of the past, when forced to speak, will tell, depends on this potential. But the potential itself depends on the message these possibilities are capable of conveying.

And so – a difficult piece of dialectics again – assimilation of history is always a historical event. We can learn our history only from inside it, never for a single moment mounting a 'supra-historical' peak from which to see history 'as it truly was'. History and its assimilation merge into one never-ending process in which being and time are one.

In practice this means that a timeless, absolute, full, irrevocable understanding of history is inconceivable. It cannot be achieved by and within *Dasein*, the human existence. Our understanding of history is continually being pursued and never finally reached in an endless process of *Wiederholung* or *Überlieferung* – recapitulation and delivery – which go in circles. The famous 'hermeneutical circle' in Heidegger's philosophy becomes a feature of existence itself, which endlessly incorporates its own recapitulations and thereby enriches its own delivery, setting the stage for a next recapitulation, and *da capo*.

Let us remember: understanding is always an understanding of history. And understanding is always historical. But this historicity of understanding is a-historical. Like understanding itself, it is an eternal quality of existence. Understanding is working in the world, but nothing is to be done to or in the world to make such understanding possible. It is already a possibility, always waiting to be discovered.

Heidegger's concept of historicity leaves many a problem unsolved. The sociologist would ascribe paramount importance to one, the role of human interaction, to which Heidegger pays only cursory attention. He satisfies himself with settling his differences with Husserl and declaring 'the other' as originally and unavoidably present in my existence. But here his interest in 'the other' lapses. The fact that there are many people co-existing and engaged in manifold relations (linguistic exchanges being an aspect of virtually all of them, but only an aspect) does not seem to strike him as a profound and fateful feature of existence – and, consequently, of the practice of understanding. His *Dasein* is engaged in the dialogue with history, with the past and the future, much more often, much more intensely and passionately, than with his contemporaries. Heidegger effectively did away with most timeless essences attributed to man. His *Dasein* is neither *homo oeconomicus*, nor *homo faber*, nor even *homo creator*. But he has an essence all right, timeless in its time-dependence: he is now *homo historicus*. Rather than a species being, the is now an age-being; or, rather, his existence as a member of the species takes the form of the age-being. It seems, furthermore, that the historical age is the same for everybody thrown into it. Tradition is the only factor which sets apart a chronologically given era, but the specificity of the tradition seems to exhaust its peculiarity. There is no further differentiation. Diversity of tradition may account for the differences of substance in which the era reveals itself to various contemporaries; and so the idea that people, in spite of being chronologically contemporary, may still differ from each other can be easily accommodated in the Heideggerian system, however little Heidegger himself is concerned with the problem. What protrudes as a problem whose accommodation would present insuperable difficulties is, however, that differentiation of contemporaries which gives them an unequal start in their emancipation from their respective 'tunings' and 'situations'. For Heidegger, the passage from 'being situated' to 'understanding' is an opportunity equally open to every denizen of an era, limited only by the richness and ripeness of related 'recapitulation' and 'delivery'. But this is patently not the case. There is no such equality.

Other people are present in my world not just as other existences – a constant invitation to, and potential objects of, communication. What happens between us is not just linguistic exchanges. But *Rede* and *Gerede* – speech and chatter – is the only typology of inter-human relations Heidegger is concerned with. We vainly search his writings for an account, or at least an acknowledgement, of the rich variety of ways in which one human existence can enter the existence of another: conflict ranging from quarrel to war, physical violence, political and economic subordination, barring access to information, etc. Are all these types of inter-human relations devoid of significance in shaping both actuality and potentiality of understanding? Can the most acute and stubborn problems of understanding be truly posited if no account is taken of them?

This neglect lies, or so it seems, at the foundation of the charge frequently levelled against Heidegger and against existentialist philosophy in general: the unremediable paucity of its ethics. All human existences having been '*ursprünglich*' equal in their only significant predicate, their universal historicity, no further difference is left which can generate moral problems. Morality is, therefore, dissolved in understanding, as much as understanding is dissolved in historicity. No wonder that *Schuldigkeit*, the existential Duty, elevated by Heidegger to the rank of the highest (indeed, the only) moral imperative, is spelled out as the obligation to return to itself from the state of being lost in *das Man*, and to accept that difficult mode of existence which is tuned by nothing.[22] To understand is to be moral. To be moral is to make use of the opportunity to understand. Perhaps one can blend back in this way theoretical and practical reason, so unjustly set apart for too long. But the price of bridging the gap is, for Heidegger, enormous. To believe that it is possible to reach one's authentic engagement with the world by talk and understanding alone means to turn a blind eye on those aspects of the world situation which truly decide when the meeting of understanding and engagement can occur, and what the consequences of this engagement will be.

Is it enough to understand to eradicate misunderstanding? And is not misunderstanding a relation between people before it can turn into the stultifying *das Man*?

There are neither these questions, nor answers to them, in Heidegger.

Dilthey, as we remember, never ceased to be fascinated by the ideal of objective understanding of history, i.e. understanding which itself would not be historical; he earnestly sought a vantage-point above or outside historical human existence, from which history could be seen as an object of objective study. We found his search unsuccessful; Dilthey could only offer the end of history as this point from which true understanding would become a possibility. Husserl can be seen as a philosopher who has drawn logical conclusions from the failure of historical hermeneutics to offer solid foundations for objective understanding: he assumed that objective understanding can be reached only outside and in spite of history, by reason, which by its own effort lifts itself above its existential historical limitations. Heidegger's is the opposite solution of Dilthey's dilemma. There is no understanding outside history; understanding is tradition engaged in an endless conversation with itself and its own recapitulation. Understanding is the modality of existence, always incomplete and open-ended as the existence itself. The end of history, instead of revealing the true meaning of the past, would mean the end of understanding: understanding is possible only as an unfinished, future-oriented activity. Far from being unfortunate constraints imposed upon true understanding, prejudgements shaped by tradition are the only tools with which understanding can be attained.

Existence is its own disclosure; the act of understanding, like existence itself, spans the past and the future. It cannot be otherwise. As existence itself, understanding derives its actuality from the historical totality in which it is immersed. The meaning is produced by countless relations inside this totality. It is not the ego, whether empirical or transcendental, who conjures up the meaning out of his intentions. Like his existence, his meanings are pre-formed for him by his world. His understanding, therefore, is mastering this supra-individual totality of meanings called language. In Gadamer's description,[23]

Thought is dependent upon the ground of language insofar as language is not merely a system of signs for the purpose of communication and transmission of information. Where there is real language, the thing to be designated is not known prior to the act of designation. Rather within our language relationship to world, that which is spoken of is itself first articulated through language's constitutive structuring of our being in the world. Speaking remains tied to the language as a whole, the hermeneutic virtuality of discourse which surpasses at any moment that which has been said. It is precisely in this respect that speaking always transcends the linguistically constituted realm within which we find ourselves.

The task of hermeneutical theory does not, therefore, consist of the constitution of understanding. Understanding is already given in the reality of language. The only task hermeneutics may reasonably hope to fulfil is to discover how, exactly, meanings are constituted and sustained in language and the endless linguistic sociation.

8 Understanding as the work of life: from Schutz to ethnomethodology

On one occasion Sir Karl Popper told his audience a story which had obviously shaken him.[1] It concerned an anthropologist invited to join some other first-class brains in discussing an important matter in the methodology of science. At the end of long and heated argument, to which the anthropologist listened in silence, he was asked to express his view. Much to the dismay of everybody present, the anthropologist replied that he paid little attention to the actual content of the dispute. The content was, he thought, the least interesting of what he saw and heard. Of incomparably greater interest were other things: how the debate was launched, how it developed, how one intervention triggered off another and how they fell into sequences, how the contributors determined whether they were in disagreement, etc. Our anthropologist, presumably, viewed the topic which aroused so much passion as just one of those 'native beliefs' whose truth or falsity is largely irrelevant for a scholarly study. This was why he was not particularly interested in the topic. Instead, he recorded with genuine interest the interaction in which the learned experts engaged and which the declared topic of the discussion 'occasioned'.

Sir Karl was, of course, indignant. For him statements are about something, and are to be judged, in this way or another, by being tested against this something. Whatever importance they may have arises from the degree of exactitude and veracity with which they grasp the subject of which they speak. When confronted with a statement, Sir Karl would presumably consider the 'immanent interpretation' the only worthy way of dealing with it. He would try to extract from the sentence the message it contained, and then attempt to put the truth of the message to the test.

Sir Karl perhaps was not aware that the odd behaviour of this unnamed anthropologist would soon become the paramount rule of a powerful school of sociological theory and research; that the father of this school, Harold Garfinkel, would codify the bizarre conduct of our anthropologist into an alternative methodology:[2]

An alternative conception of the task may do better. Although it may at first appear strange to do so, suppose we drop the assumption that in order to describe a usage as a feature of a community of understandings we must at the outset know what the substantive common understanding consists of. With it, drop the assumption's accompanying theory of signs, according to which a 'sign' and 'referent' are respectively properties of something said and something talked about, and which in this fashion proposes sign and referent to be related as corresponding contents. By dropping such a theory of signs we drop as well, thereby, the possibility that an invoked shared agreement on substantive matters explains a usage.
If these notions are dropped, then the parties talked about could not be distinguished from *how* the parties were speaking. . . .
In the place of and in contrast to a concern for a difference between *what* was said and *what* was talked about, the appropriate difference is between a language-community member's recognition that a person is saying something, i.e. that he was *speaking*, on the one hand, and *how* he was speaking on the other.

Thus a school emerges which calls on its members to stop asking *what* has been said, and concentrate instead on exploring *how* it was said.
The field which the school declared its territory has been given by Garfinkel the name 'ethnomethodology'. The new word is intended to be self-explanatory, by exposing its family resemblance to a whole group of terms already used by descriptive anthropology: ethnobotany, ethnomedicine, etc. All these terms stand for the activity of describing how the *ethnos* – the people under study – go about accomplishing the tasks normally classified as belonging to the field, say, of taxonomy of plants or of defining illness and treating the ill. In a similar way, ethnomethodology was meant to engage in the description of 'native ways' of performing the task of living. Except for this similarity, the analogy made conspicuous by the name of the new field of study has been, however, misleading. The extant anthropological terms all connoted anthropologists' intention to concentrate on differences between various *ethnos*; say, on the differences between medical practice of Hopi Indians and Zuni Indians. Ethnomethodology, on the contrary, employed the *ethno* in its name in an entirely different way, as denoting human beings as such, with no reference to tribal or cultural variations. The second part of its name, 'methodology', was equally general: instead of

referring to a specified, selected field of activity, it pointed to the method of 'being active' in general, to the method of doing whatever happens to be done, and manifested therefore what no other of the apparently analogous terms did: indifference and lack of interest in the 'substance' of analysed activity, in the 'whatness' of human practices. Ethnomethodology aimed from the outset to be a most general science of human action, to operate on a level so general as to neutralize the substantive differences between *ethnos* and between their diverse activities.

It is perhaps this generality, this suspension of the project high above the level on which variations of cultures, classes and other 'particularizing' groupings become obtrusive and seem relevant, that justified the description of ethnomethodology by Garfinkel (and more implacably still by his followers) as the 'phenomenological sociology'. I have not found much evidence that Garfinkel (at least at the time when *Studies in Ethnomethodology*, the most seminal work of the school, was published) read Husserl (he quoted Husserl after Marvin Faber). More important, apart from its generality, his project bears little resemblance to the gist of phenomenology as outlined by Husserl. First, the question of 'whatness', of essences of things, which Husserl's phenomenology was all about, has been completely discarded in favour of the 'how' question. Secondly and more importantly, Garfinkel selects as his field of study precisely this realm of reality which Husserl considered necessary to 'put in brackets' and never 'unbracket' again in order to make phenomenological project feasible.

Indeed, the original phenomenological project, as we know it from Husserl's writings, must have undergone considerable transformation before it could be invoked as the legitimate ancestor of ethnomethodological activity. This transformation had been accomplished by Alfred Schutz, and to his work we must now turn.

Alfred Schutz was concerned with understanding, with the possibility of grasping the meaning of human activity. Like Husserl, he assumed that understanding, if achievable at all, must be the work of reason; and that reason, to attain true understanding, must climb (or descend to) the most general level where the work of universal human subjectivity is given in its pure form, unpolluted by contingent and particularistic admixtures. Like Husserl again, Schutz did not believe in understanding as grasping the work of another subject in its uniqueness, given in a fully individual experience which nobody else can share. He was after features common to all humanity, which may serve as a basis for understanding precisely for their commonality. 'Other cultural humanity and other culture can become accessible only by a complicated process of understanding, namely, on the basic level of the common nature.'[3] He quotes with approval Husserl's characterization of the intellectual foundation of such understanding as the '"science of essences", which has to examine the invariant, peculiar, and essential structures of the mind'.[4] Like Husserl, Schutz wished to explore the possibility of an 'objective' study of 'subjective' meanings; the feasibility of attaining the necessary, essential knowledge of human reality in contradistinction to the knowledge of contingent, merely existential features of this reality; of 'objective essences' and not just of the arbitrary meanings which a given subject wants to give them. The strategic end which gave Schutz's project its structure was therefore very close to that of Husserl. But there the similarity ended.

Perhaps the crucial divergence between Schutz's and Husserl's strategies has been best expressed in one brief statement, concerning the peculiarity of understanding of social phenomena: this, according to Schutz, consists in 'reducing them to the human activity which has created them'.[5] If Husserl wished to refer social phenomena to their intentional meanings located in the 'transcendental ego', Schutz refers them, Heidegger-style, to human action. Having addressed the problem of understanding to the social process of the production of meaning, Schutz posited the 'objective study of the subjective' as sociology, something which Husserl either did not want, or could not do. But by the same token Schutz brought into focus in his study exactly those 'existential' aspects of human life which Husserl thought necessary to 'put in brackets' and 'suspend' for the duration of the effort at understanding.

Like Heidegger, and unlike Husserl, Schutz sees the 'naïvely, pre-reflexively given' life-world not as something to 'put in brackets', but on the contrary, as the field which the student of social phenomena should never abandon; as the 'natural habitat' for the problem of understanding. Like Heidegger's, Schutz's 'life-world' is complete from the start. It already includes, when our investigation starts, all the reasons for which understanding becomes necessary, and all the resources one may need in order to meet this necessity. The life-world, according to Schutz, includes everything which is taken for granted, and normally not reflected upon, in the attitude of common sense: it includes, therefore, also other men, 'and indeed not only in a bodily manner like and among other objects, but rather as endowed with consciousness which is essentially the same as mine'. The others are not merely present as a potential object of contemplation: 'It is self-evident to me in the natural attitude not only that I can act upon my fellow-men but also that they can act upon me.'[6] The others are given to me from the start as conscious, i.e. autonomous, springs of action; by the same token I confront the necessity of mutual adjustment, the threat of friction, acting on cross-purposes, misunderstanding; they are autonomous subjects, therefore whatever I do to them will evoke a response on their part; we need to agree, and in order to agree we must negotiate. Therefore, the necessity of understanding is organically contained in the very structure of the life-world. Indeed, it is the very condition of its existence. Understanding is not a philosophers' feat, as in Husserl. It is human fate, as in Heidegger. The fact that the life-world exists shows that men somehow cope, in their common-sense, routine way, with the need to understand each other. If we only penetrate the way in which they do it, we will be able to reveal the mystery of understanding. To know how understanding is achieved means to know how understanding is possible.

In a truly Heideggerian manner, Schutz considers other persons present in the life-world (and, indeed, all other objects present there), as given in the mode of *Zuhanden* – things 'at hand', parts and parcels of my routine life, hardly ever giving me reason to constitute them as objects of deliberate reflection. Normally, I deal with them matter-of-factly, in passing, without stopping for a moment of reflection. It takes a shock to shift objects from the mode of *Zuhanden* to that of *Vorhanden*, to cast them in the focus of my attention. The following statement sounds almost as a quotation from Heidegger:[7]

The world of everyday life is taken for granted by our common-sense thinking and thus receives the accent of reality as long as our practical experiences prove the unity and congruity of this world as valid. Even more, this reality seems to us to be the natural one, and we are not ready to abandon our attitude toward it without having experienced a specific shock which compels us to break through the limits of these 'finite' provinces of meaning and to shift the accent of reality to another one.

In the world of routine, everything is taken for granted and therefore unnoticed. To put this in a different way, most routine tasks of daily life are accomplished without engaging human analytical powers, 'on the way', 'unconsciously' (in the sense that no reasons for doing them this rather than that way are brought into awareness and no rules of doing them this way are consciously invoked). The world we act in seems to us 'naturally' organized into 'relevant' and 'background' parts, and the knowledge that our own 'shifting of relevances' hides behind this 'natural' organization escapes us. We do not notice, and unless things 'go bust' on us, we do not need to notice, that our motivations are largely responsible for organizing the world around us, and in particular for differentially distributing 'topical relevances' among its sections:[8]

Once taken for granted, the system of motivational relevances determines a system of topical relevances which, paradoxically expressed, are topical merely as a matter of course – that is, topical not as a theme, as a problem to be solved, as something to be questioned anew, but as 'topics at hand', as formerly thematic questions which have been 'definitely' and exhaustively answered, problems 'once and for all' solved and stored away. So to speak, those topics-at-hand have lost their interpretational relevances. . . . By becoming routine, by bringing it 'at hand', the open inner and outer horizons seemingly disappeared. Or, expressed more adequately: they were just cut off, and therewith were cut off all possibilities of reinterpreting the topic-at-hand.

The world of routine, which consists entirely of such *Zuhandenen*, is not, therefore, an object of active interpretation or re-interpretation. Unless challenged, we have no need to 'motivate' our routine actions to others and to ourselves. To us our routine actions appear parts of nature almost as much as their objects. Their 'horizons disappear': that is, we do not normally consider the course of action we take as just one of a whole set of alternatives; neither do we see the ends we wish to accomplish as objectives whose selection requires justification. In the world of routine, routine does not occasion analysis, neither does it require one in order to go on. Neither the motives nor the ends of routine action are 'topical as a theme'.

For somebody concerned with studying the subjective aspect of human action, with grasping the motives of action, with understanding action and not just putting on the record its external, observable forms, this discovery is crucial. It shows the futility of traditional 'understanding' strategies. More often than not it is assumed that in order to pay due attention to the subjective, motivational character of human action one has to employ the special power called 'empathy'; that is to say, put oneself in another person's skin and attempt to revive in one's own head thoughts and psychic states which allegedly had to accompany the other person's action. Empathy is considered a useful tool of study because it is assumed that it can yield rich results: there are thoughts and psychic states which, once reconstructed, will offer a particularly deep and exhaustive understanding of action. Schutz's description of the world of routine devalues empathy so understood. There is little to be gained by it simply because there are few or no motives to be discovered by reconstructing the conscious contents of another psyche. In ordinary circumstances, motives simply do not appear in the actor's head as articulated acts of consciousness. They are pushed into the unlit background, 'stored away'. If asked about his motives, the actor would hardly be able to give account of those reasons which actually give sense to his action, or of the many assumptions which 'had to be taken' (though by no means consciously) in order to make his action possible. As one of the most original of Schutz's followers, Aaron V. Cicourel, would say, 'Participants in social interaction apparently "understand" many things . . . even though such matters are not mentioned explicitly.'[9]

The above statement can be only interpreted in one way: actors' understanding does not take the form of thoughts actually thought, brought by the actors themselves in the light of consciousness. If the word 'understand' is put in inverted commas, it is because this understanding, which is clearly not an empirical 'event' in time and space, is not what we usually mean by understanding: a purposeful act of consciousness. It appears in our analysis of action rather than in the heads of actors, and it appears as a necessary condition of the actor's occurrence, rather than as a report of what has actually happened 'out there'. If we say that actors 'apparently' understand many things they do not give any account of, what we mean is that, unless those things were 'understood', we would not be able to give a logical account of the action we observed. The action simply would not make any sense.

So how can one go about understanding a meaningful act? How can one grasp the meaning of human action or its linguistic symbols if there is little hope that this can be achieved by empathy, by discovering what has actually happened 'in the head' of the actor? Heidegger, as we remember, was not particularly concerned with this problem. Understanding interested him as the mode of existence, not a methodological issue for a professional student of human affairs. It is rather in the later work of Ludwig Wittgenstein that one can find many an idea capable of elucidating Schutz's view of the task confronting a social scientist bent on grasping human action as a meaningful behaviour (though, of course, it would be difficult to prove that either of them influenced directly the thinking of the other one).

Wittgenstein defines the task of finding out 'what gives the words their meaning' as that of discovering 'without what they would have no meaning'. In other words, the task is not one of empirical observation and ensuing description of events (whether 'material' or psychical), but of analysis of necessary conditions of meaningfulness: what *has to happen* for a word to have a meaning. If we follow this rule, we soon discover – with Wittgenstein's help – that common-sense notions of meaning would not help much. For instance, if it is the 'referent', an object out there (like the bearer of a name), which gives the word its meaning, why is it so that words remain meaningful long after their physical referents disappeared? If it is some definition-like knowledge in the head of the speaker which gives words their meanings, what are we to do about the only-too-common cases of 'something that we know when no one asks us, but no longer know when we are supposed to give an account of it'? Surely it follows that 'to know' in the sense of the first part of the sentence is not the same thing as 'to know' in the sense of the second part: to understand the meaning is not the same thing as to be able to give account of it, for instance to define the word, or to tell the motive of my action. What is it, then?

Try not to think of understanding as a 'mental process' at all. – For *that* is the expression which confuses you. But ask yourself: in what sort of case, in what kind of circumstances, do we say, 'Now I know how to go on' . . . ?

Understanding the meaning is to know how to go on in the presence of a word, an act or other object whose meaning we understand. 'The change when the pupil began to read was a change in his behaviour.'[10]

We can now interpret Cicourel's words more fully. When he says that actors 'apparently understood' many things they did not give any account of, he may mean that they obviously knew how 'to go about' what they did. If we now wish to understand what they understood, let us not try to re-create their 'mental processes', but to watch their behaviour closely. For instance, let us faithfully record their dialogue. The fact that the dialogue took place shows that the conversationalists understood each other; otherwise they would not know 'how to go on', and dialogue would not be possible. This is one thing we know, and it is all we need to know in order to understand the conduct we saw. Reading is not 'an expression' of 'knowledge how to read'. To understand the act of reading is to spell out the conditions under which the act of reading is possible. Understanding is not an act of empathy, but an act of analysis. In Schutz's words:[11]

> Meaning is not a quality of certain lived experiences [*Erlebnise*] emerging distinctively in the stream of consciousness. . . . It is rather the result of my explication of past lived experiences which are grasped reflectively from an actual now and from an actually valid reference schema. . . . Lived experiences first become meaningful, then, when they are explicated *post hoc* and become comprehensible to me as well-circumscribed experiences. Thus only those lived experiences are subjectively meaningful which are . . . examined as regards their constitution, and which are explicated in respect to their position in a reference schema that is at hand.

Meaning, therefore, is not a hypothetical entity which precedes the experience of an act. Meaning is, instead, constituted in retrospect, in the course of subsequent analysis, when the memories or the image of experience, and not the experience itself, is dissected and reorganized according to some 'reference schema' external to the experience. This applies to the professional student of social life in the same degree as it applies to ordinary members of the society in ordinary situations. This meaning which we seek in order to articulate our knowledge of 'how to go on' is only established in the process of interpretation. Even if we tend to phrase the products of interpretation in terms of 'intentions' or conscious ends of action ('surely, a reference is possible in principle to the original meaning-bestowing acts of "someone"'),[12] it is our interpretive activity which gives us the real understanding of whatever we experience.

Hence the proper subject-matter of an 'understanding' sociology, i.e. social science aimed at grasping the meanings of social phenomena, is the study of interpretive procedures in which meanings are being established in the world of everyday life. This is a statement of truly revolutionary consequences. It takes some effort to understand just how far-reaching the consequences are. They mean nothing less than a radical redistribution of roles assigned to the various units constituting sociological discourse. What has been unreflexively utilized as a resource of sociological work (as, for example, an explanatory referent) is now transformed into the topic of sociological study. Instead of employing the concept of class as an explanation of behaviour, one must analyse the behaviour which makes people consider their action in terms of class.

Interpretive procedures are the right objects for the effort of understanding since 'meaning' exists and can be found in no other place. Meaning is not an immanent feature of objects; neither is it a psychic event in the head of an actor. It is not, to be sure, the Husserlian intentional essence either. All meaning results from interpretation; it is something to be constructed, not discovered. There is no essential difference in this respect between the sense actors make of their action and the meaning assigned to this action by a sociologist, or any external observer for this matter: all of them are engaged in a basically similar process of meaning-construction-through-interpretation, and all of them use resources of the same type to do so. In this sense 'understanding' sociology in the Schutz style differs profoundl˙ from established academic sociology, which sharply differentiates the role claimed by sociologists (thinking, interpreting, selecting, testing, making sense, etc.) from that ascribed to the human objects of sociological study (determined by environment either directly or via rational assessment of environmental assets and ensuing adjustment). Again, like in Heidegger, it is suggested that there is only one kind of understanding, applicable to both 'ordinary' members of society and to their specialized and trained students; both cases of 'making sense' can be described in identical terms. The project of understanding sociology is feasible exactly for this reason; and remains feasible as long as it is conceived in a form which may be grounded on this essential identity. The superiority of sociologists over interpretive procedures operated matter-of-factly by the ordinary members of society may consist only of their operating the same procedure consciously and in a methodical way. This difference, however, is not of the kind on which a claim to a privileged access to truth could be founded. Truth, as it were, is not an issue. As all the meanings have the interpretive procedures which established them for their sole foundation, they are void outside the context of these procedures and have nothing else to be measured against in order to decide their validity. All meanings are 'objective' thanks to the interpretive procedures which produced them; no meaning, however, can survive its abstraction from the natural context. This is a new argument in favour of the old cultural sciences' idea of the 'rational' nature of all objectivity, as expressed, for instance, by Florian Znaniecki: 'Cultural system is really and objectively as it was (or is) given to those historical subjects themselves when they were (or are) experiencing and actively dealing with it.'[13]

The other way of expressing the same features of Schutz's concept of understanding is to say that it presents, in a sense, a sociological version of Kant's 'transcendental analytical logic'; or, rather, that it presents an attempt to construct a transcendental analytical logic of the life-world. As we know, Kant was concerned not with the actual contents of experiences (which was to be left to empirical cognition, based on sentient impressions) but with the principles which 'are the indispensable basis of the possibility of experience itself'. Such principles must logically (though in no other sense) precede all experience and be (in a 'structuring' sense) present in all experience. They must, therefore, be truly *a priori*, bear the character of verdicts of reason and not of empirical generalizations, which must remain, however all-embracing, forever contingent and arbitrary. Transcendental logical principles, on the contrary, are not arbitrary; they contain ideas of necessity and unqualified universality in their very conception. Kant called his transcendental propositions, concerned with indispensable conditions of all cognition, 'critique of pure reason'. In his view, its use 'will be only negative, not to enlarge the bounds of, but to purify our reason, and to shield it against error — which alone is no little gain'. In this sense, Schutz's doctrine may be properly called a 'critique of sociology'. It consists fully of transcendental propositions, if, following Kant, we apply the term 'transcendental' 'to all knowledge which is not so much occupied with objects as with the mode of our cognition of these objects, so far as this mode of cognition is possible *a priori*'.[14]

Schutz's criticism is aimed against a sociology which naïvely assumes that the meaning of a social phenomenon is 'given' as an object in its own right and that it can therefore be 'found' instead of constructed. According to the pattern established by Kant, criticism ought to consist of producing a sort of 'transcendental analytic' of meaning-production; in spelling out the conditions which must be always met for meaning-production to be possible at all. If we substituted 'meaning' for 'conception' and 'sociology' for 'philosophy', we would find in Kant the following apt characterization of Schutz's project:[15]

By the term 'analytic of meanings' I do not understand the analysis of these, or the usual process in sociological investigations of dissecting the meanings which present themselves, according to their content, and so making them clear; but I mean hitherto little attempted dissection of the faculty of understanding itself, in order to investigate the possibility of meanings *a priori*, by looking for them in the understanding alone, as their birthplace, and analysing the pure use of this faculty.

Just as Kant showed that space, time, or causality are not, as we uncritically suppose, properties of objects 'out there', but organizing principles of knowledge (transcendental conditions of 'things being known' rather than of 'things existing'), so Schutz intends to show that many an aspect which we uncritically attribute to 'social realities' are in fact organizing principles of our being-in-the-world (transcendental principles of life-world rather than the world on its own). That is to say, Schutz's critique of sociological reason consists in spelling out the transcendental conditions of the meaningful world as we know it.

These transcendental conditions must be of two kinds, assuming that 'the life world is a reality which we modify through our acts and which, on the other hand, modifies our actions'.[16]

First is the 'stock of knowledge', 'which serves me as the reference schema for the actual step of my explication of the world'. The stock of knowledge must contain a certain minimum of information without which action would not be possible, i.e. which cannot be acquired in the course of action itself. How this information came to be possessed in the first place is a question not in the focus of cogitation. The only thing which counts is that it must be 'at hand' for the model of action to be operative. Perhaps parts of the stock are elements of 'natural endowment' of a human agent, Kant-like; perhaps other parts are societally-induced and sedimented from initial stages of socialization. This is, by and large, irrelevant to Schutz's problem. The frequently repeated phrase 'from the outset' does not refer to the moment of birth of either the individual or his society. It does refer to the beginning of meaningful action, whose model is, naturally, extended in time.

'Types' are an indispensable element of the stock of knowledge. Our impressions are not analysable if chaotic, they are thinkable only if they are from the start organized into objects and events which belong to classes, each with its distinctive features and clues facilitating their recognition. Types have a lasting quality; an important feature of the natural attitude is the 'and so forth' generalization, implying that things will continue to be what they are at the moment, and that, consequently, I will be able to repeat in the future the same operations which I have committed on things in the past. All this I accept uncritically; not that I have been convinced in the course of reasoning and argument that things and events are really the types I deem them to be; on the contrary, they serve as an unquestioned starting-point for my action because I never ask about the foundation of my acceptance. Types, 'and so forth' generalizations, etc., are self-evident – obvious 'facts of life' which do not require any proof.

These 'self-evidencies' of which stock of knowledge is composed constitute the brick and mortar of this feature of life-world which, as Schutz tells us, has been given by Max Scheler the name of the 'relative-natural world view'. Natural, because accepted as nature normally is: taken for granted, as a ground whose existence cannot be sensibly put in doubt. Relative, because ultimately founded on the act of acceptance. Though acceptance as such is a necessary act without which no life-world can emerge, there is nothing necessary about the content of accepted axioms. Typification, for instance, is unavoidable, a truly transcendental condition of the life-world; but the way in which reality is actually 'split' into types is not, and must remain the irremovable element of relativity in any conceivable set of self-evidencies.

Typification is, of course, a two-pronged process; on the one hand, it solidifies some aspects of reality into an incorrigible, self-evident field of 'un-problems'; on the other hand, it draws the line which renders everything left on the other side potentially problematic. That is to say, the process of typification determines, by the same token, what is to be determined and what is to remain indeterminate.

The stock of knowledge, as we already know, includes the information that other people like us exist and that their conduct has the same structure which we 'know' from the experience of our own behaviour. This knowledge renders other people potential partners in communication viewed as a 'trade in meanings', as a mutual effort to grasp the message conveyed by words, gestures, facial expressions, etc. Other people (again a piece of knowledge being an indispensable part of natural attitude) differ from all other types, and from inanimate objects in particular, in that they are to be understood; that is, their conduct is to be interpreted as a basically voluntary and purpose-orientated action.

Once defined by the natural attitude as, above all, potential partners of communication, other people are typified according to their accessibility to this function. Some enter 'the world within actual reach';[17] these are people with which I actually communicate, to whom I talk and who talk to me, who react to the stimuli generated by my own conduct; people with whom I am engaged in an inter-action which requires constant vigilance as to the meaning of their behaviour, a perpetual 'reciprocal interpretation'. All other people are typified in my life-world according to their distance from this essential model of communication as founded on the 'world within actual reach'. Thus some people belong to the 'world within potential reach' (either 'restorable' or 'attainable'), in as far as they may enter time and again the central circle of the life-world, namely the world 'within actual reach'. But they are not there all the time, hence a sub-stantial part of their activity runs without my having either the need or the possibility to interpret it; and vice versa, only a fraction of my conduct comes under their scrutiny. This partiality of interaction is, of course, a matter of degree. As we move from the almost full and all-embracing communication to increasingly sporadic and fragmen-tary contacts, the world of other people becomes stratified. The further the given layer is from the centre of the 'world within actual reach', the thinner the slice of shared experience with agreed inter-pretation. Fewer and fewer people are seen as partners in actual or potential communication; less and less interpretation and under-standing seems to be the indispensable modes of dealing with them. Individuals, so rich and full-blooded when remaining inside the 'world within actual reach', turn gradually into specimens of types, while the tendency to 'causal explanation' of their behaviour (attuned to the mode of inanimate objects) gets on top of the urge to interpret it in terms of meaning and purpose.

I have tried to convey the flavour of Schutz's theorizing rather than its contents. I hope, however, that the meaning of 'transcen-dental analytic' is now sufficiently clear. The stock of knowledge, together with the life-world 'from the outset' stratified and divided into stable types and indeterminate margins, is a typical product of 'transcendental analytic'. Indeed, once the question has been asked 'without which life-world would be inconceivable', it becomes evidently and necessarily true that the stock of knowledge, as frag-mentarily sketched above, must be the first part of the answer. The second part is the already briefly mentioned 'interpretive procedures'. Indeed, once the initial stock of knowledge is given, the next question is its application to the production of actual life-worlds in the process of daily interaction between members of a community of men and women. This is exactly the notorious 'how' question which consti-tutes the gist of sociology as designed by Schutz's 'transcendental analytic'.

Schutz's writings are replete with 'how' questions. The following are examples selected at random:[18]

How the typifications are constituted in the stock of knowledge is a problem which is still to be investigated in detail.

How the transformation of a possible problem into an actual one comes about, how I become motivated to an explication of the horizon, is a question whose solution must now concern us.

How it ever happens that these stocks of knowledge are developed. It need hardly be stressed that we do not want to be concerned here with the formulation of historical-causal hypotheses or schemata of meaning. That task comes within the province of the empirical sociology of knowledge. Rather, we are interested in the basic question of what the general presuppositions are for the constitution of a social stock of knowledge.

(The answer to this question is that subjective stock of knowledge must be 'prior' to the social one; but this is explicitly posited not as an empirical, but transcendental analytic proposition:

A subjective stock of knowledge independent of the social one is conceivable without contradiction. In contrast, to imagine the latter as developed independently of the subjective acquisition of knowledge is sheer nonsense.)

What are the presuppositions for the acceptance of subjective knowledge into the social stock of knowledge?

In one sphere in particular 'how' questions are imperative. It is easy to see that this sphere overlaps, by and large, with the field traditionally occupied by sociological research. Schutz defines this sphere as 'habitual knowledge' which occupies[19]

a hybrid position between the basic elements of the stock of knowledge and the stock of knowledge in the narrower sense. The former elements are universal and in principle invariant. . . . The basic elements of the stock of knowledge are at hand for everyone; they are the same in whatever relative-natural world view he was socialized.

The latter, presumably, is not the one Schutz's project is particularly concerned with; Schutz gladly leaves it to the already mentioned 'historical-causal hypotheses'; questions 'why' are typically empirical questions, asking for causal or quasi-causal explanations, and Schutz has nothing of interest to add to the techniques of answering them developed elsewhere. But the intermediate field, that of 'habitual knowledge', is taken for granted much too often to be seriously explored. The ordinary sociologist rarely goes beyond reaping its conceptual fruits; seldom is he genuinely concerned with the processes of their fruition. While behaving in this manner, the ordinary sociologist fails to emancipate himself from the natural attitude and to set it in front of himself as an object of theoretical analysis. In the natural attitude, elements of habitual knowledge 'are a necessary component of each experiential horizon, without themselves becoming the core of experience'. Hence 'it is only through reflection in the theoretical attitude that I can get them in the grip of consciousness'.[20] But to bring them 'in the grip of consciousness' is exactly the paramount task of sociological study as Schutz sees it. Only when this is done can we say that we truly understand human action. The task of understanding boils down, therefore, to the question of how the habitual knowledge comes to be formed and then employed in generating human action.

Schutz's sociology is, by design, formal. It is not suitable (neither does it wish to be) for understanding why this or that element of a given relative-natural world (one of the many possible) happens to be as it is and not different, as it clearly could. Schutz's sociology is unconcerned with the 'whatness' of things, the major preoccupation of Husserl. Neither is it particularly excited by the urge to understand a historically given cultural object in its individual uniqueness, which was the meaning of understanding as conceived by traditional historical hermeneutics. Instead, Schutz's sociology takes the same stance toward social world as Kant took toward knowledge in general: it wants to cogitate the conditions under which any object may acquire its 'whatness', or any cultural fact may attain its individuality. Thus it is programmatically neutral toward any typifications of which the natural attitude may happen to piece together its reality. Like the anthropologist who so infuriated Popper, it will insist on spelling out the pattern of the typifying process, rather than trying to grasp its objectified products immanently or explain them genetically. To understand a cultural object means, in Schutz's sociology, to articulate the presuppositions without which the object in question would not be able to appear.

This is not simply an arbitrary choice of his field of interest, to which every scholar is entitled. Schutz believes that this is the only road an 'understanding' sociology could follow. Indeed, the only ground of meanings is the life-world in which they are embedded; they retain their objectivity only in as far as the 'relative world view' of which they are a part remains the 'natural' world for a given community; and the only place in which one can study them is the very location in which they have been born and sustained. A sociologist bent on understanding, and not just describing, social phenomena, faces two possibilities only; he can take his human objects' preoccupations to his heart and try to assist them in their constant testing and re-testing the consistency and coherence of their images of reality; or, alternatively, he can tell them that what they take for 'objectivity', 'truth', etc., derives all the sense it may possess from their own activities, and therefore the only sensible way of approaching it is to illuminate the socially organized setting in which it is produced and kept alive. In Garfinkel's words, '*recognizable* sense, or fact, or methodic character, or impersonality, or objectivity of accounts are not independent of the socially organized occasions of their use'. Or, more emphatically still, '"Really" made unavoidable reference to daily, ordinary, occupational workings.'[21] In a somewhat different context Alan Blum analysed the actual meaning of the term similar in use to 'really' – the often employed phrase of 'We agree that', and suggested that it 'comes to signify our agreement not to address what the "we agree" leaves unsaid, and it appears not as a limitation or failure of the programme but as a positive and constructive feature'.[22] 'We agree', one would say, is a term preferred by scholars or other people to whom the possibility of the 'left unsaid' being problematic occurred, but has been suppressed. 'Really' would be an expression used more often by people candidly ignorant of all these things they must ignore in order to believe in reality of the 'really'. In both cases, however, the spotlight of 'objectivity' may fall on X only because P, Q, and R have been left in shade. The area of routine everyday life and habitual knowledge left in shade is the one in which the vital processes take place which accord the rank of objectivity to some cultural constructs and banish others into the forbidden land of unspeakables. Ethnomethodology is about bringing this shaded area into the limelights of theoretical analysis, to show that[23]

'shared agreement' refers to various social methods for accomplishing the member's recognition that something was said-according-to-a-rule and not the demonstrable matching of substantive matters. . . . To assign exclusive priority to the study of the methods of concerted actions and methods of common understanding.

Schutz supplied theoretical foundations to what ethnomethodology posited as a programme of empirical study. Once engaged in the 'transcendental analytic', one could reach, by deduction alone, the 'basic elements' of the stock of knowledge. One could as well deduce that between these basic elements and specific, historically-causally explicable knowledge, there must be an intermediate zone in which universal, basic elements are at work producing historically diversified 'relative-natural' world-views. But one could hardly describe the structure of this intermediate zone ('habitual knowledge', in Schutz's vocabulary) while employing deduction alone. One has to have a close look at the actual situations in which people interact and 'find out' how they go about it, rather than build an axiomatic system accounting for the possibility of their interaction. And this is what ethnomethodology set out to do.

Ethnomethodology is, therefore, an essentially empirical activity. It aims at understanding human interaction by throwing light on the procedures through which meanings are produced in practice. As several of its most prominent practitioners recently declared, 'our interest [is] in what we call the grounds or auspices of phenomena rather than in phenomena themselves'.[24] But these grounds or auspices can be reached only via phenomena; they may be recovered only by a process guided by the theory of the life-world, but starting from its practice.

Ethnomethodology is, however, formal knowledge. Like Heidegger's theory of understanding and of its place in existence, like Schutz's theory of the life-world, it articulated its project in terms which exclude all taking of attitudes to phenomena in the real world. The radical moral neutrality of ethnomethodology has been achieved by limiting its cognitive apparatus so that it can be used only to describe the 'technology' of life rather than life itself, of the 'technology' of meaning-production rather than meanings themselves. Its moral neutrality, therefore, reflects the neutrality of technology they describe.

Indeed, the striking feature of empirical research by ethnomethodology is that it never leads to the explication of phenomena on which, at least at the first sight, it is focussed. On the contrary, it tends to make the phenomena under investigation as 'transparent' as possible. Phenomena best serve the purposes of ethnomethodological empirical activity if reduced to window-panes through which one could look directly into the intricate clockwork which they hide rather than disclose in daily life. But then the ethnomethodologist would not be interested in specific, non-universal and contingent, shapes of cog-wheels and catches which made the phenomena as they are; he would try instead to model the 'general', indispensable properties of the clockwork purified as much as possible of all specific content. One would say that ethnomethodological research is not *of* phenomena, but *through* phenomena. It is therefore determined to ignore everything which deprives phenomena of their transparency, everything which solidifies phenomena in historically specific, individual entities.

The empirical activity of ethnomethodology is, therefore, subordinated to the task of 'transcendental analytics'. As all transcendental analytics, it turns out an essentially negative knowledge: it dissolves the apparently solid phenomena to the point where their processual foundations become visible. It discloses 'members' work in the world' as these phenomena's only foundation.

If, however, phenomena (and what we reify as their 'meanings') have members' work as their sole foundation, one question which makes no sense within ethnomethodological discourse is the question of truth. Indeed, ethnomethodology has no tools with which to distinguish between 'true' and 'false' meanings, 'true' and 'false' understanding. The success or failure of interaction hinges on members' agreement as to the topic of their conversation; but at no point does it depend on a correspondence between the meaning the members assign to the topic and certain intrinsic features of the topic grounded on something other than the agreement itself – for instance, 'a real object out there' referred to in the conversation. For Durkheim, moral criticism of a social reality could be questioned only from the position of another society; for ethnomethodology, the validity of an agreement can be challenged and put in doubt only from the position of another communal agreement. But there is no ground on which our preference for one rather than the other of the competing agreements could be conclusively vindicated: that is, no ground which is not, ultimately, another agreement.

From the point of view of ethnomethodology, the reference to 'real objects', 'objective indicators', etc., is no more than a manner in which members negotiate and account for their agreement. To pretend that one could gain a direct access to the objects themselves while using resources which are not communally grounded would involve an absurd notion of knowledge without meanings and of speech without language. The only reality one can be aware of, have a notion of, be able to give account of, is constructed in the course of members' work.

In the form it is posited by ethnomethodology, the problem of understanding is radically divorced from the problem of truth. More precisely, truth (at least in the sense of the correspondence between what is being said and what it has been said about) is rendered irrelevant for the account of the origin, the foundation, the construction and the sustenance of understanding.

To Dilthey, as we remember, the location of the act of understanding in a historical tradition (Dilthey's version of communal grounding) presented itself as a most difficult problem for the obstacles it raised on the way to objective, truthful knowledge of meaning. Dilthey conceived of no conclusive solution, short of the 'end of history', to the paradox of a history-free, objective capture of meaning expected to be reached from an inescapably historical vantage-point. Husserl sought the way out of the predicament of understanding through a reason capable of purifying itself from historical limitation. This purification would result – Husserl hoped – in a radical divorce of the search for true meanings from the empirical activity of understanding, incurably relativistic as it is and will forever remain. Heidegger denied the possibility of such purification. To him, understanding can be nothing but an endless projection and re-projection, a never-ending process of recapitulation, in the course of which tradition provides both the foundation and the object of knowledge. We saw that to account for the validity of such understanding Heidegger had to re-phrase the concept of truth. Understanding is true not in the sense of the correspondence between a statement and reality it says something about, but in the sense of the self-disclosure of existence; the self-understanding of existence, 'the truth about existence' (or, rather, 'of existence') cannot be, therefore, less historical (and therefore less 'relative') than the existence itself. Ethnomethodology shed the subtler trappings of Heidegger's argument, but retrieved the gist of the message: the process of understanding, for the sake of its self-awareness, ought to be divorced from the problem of truth as constructed and given prominence by the advance of positive science.

This bold decision raises, of course, the question of the status of ethnomethodology itself as a reliable knowledge of understanding activity. If the 'communal relativism' is the predicament of all knowledge, ethnomethodology cannot be exempt from the universal rule. Hence the charge of 'infinite regression' frequently levelled against the ethnomethodological attitude. And yet ethnomethodology cannot but treat the charge lightly; indeed, it can easily take it into its stride. Of course, ethnomethodology is 'communally grounded';

all knowledge is, and cannot but be so. Being communally grounded does not detract from ethnomethodology's validity more than the fact that, say, physics is a discussion of goings-on in a modern physical laboratory detracts from the validity of physical knowledge. As it were, the accusation of 'infinite regression' carries weight only for people whose discourse entails already the notion of reality as separate from the life-world and truth as separate from communal agreement. But these are precisely the notions for which ethnomethodology has no use.

Not so for everybody, though. The equanimity with which ethnomethodology faces the accusations of relativism is often viewed as obtained at a price too high to be acceptable. Ethnomethodological serenity requires that the hope for true (objective, apodictically binding, conclusive) knowledge be abandoned. This requirement defies two powerful expectations generated and fed by our era. First, that the conflict between contradictory beliefs can be settled by reference to a view which is more reliable and a better guide for action because it is non-partisan and 'above conflicts'. Second, that human emancipation can be reached only through the destruction of false beliefs, deception, and misunderstanding. Both expectations can retain their vigour only in so far as the belief that true knowledge in general, and true understanding in particular, is – in principle – achievable, is sustained ('true' meaning corresponding to something tougher, and therefore more reliable, than the moving sands of communal agreement). This is, perhaps, the paramount reason for which ethnomethodological tranquillity, however attractive for the trouble-freedom it offers, is unlikely to become a universal attitude. The search for the true understanding and its grounding will continue. What Schutz and ethnomethodology disclose behind daily routine are invariant universals thoroughly cleansed of all historical specificity. Their disclosure 'debunks' the reality behind which they hide, but so, in view of their universality, it debunks all reality, including the one postulated by the emancipatory tasks at hand.

It is not that Schutz's universals are, in actual fact, historically limited. They are indeed transcendental conditions of all human life. Something else seems to be wrong with Schutz's project and its ethnomethodological implementation: they seem to act at cross-purposes with the original urge for understanding.

Having posited the task of understanding as that of elucidating the conditions of all meaning and agreement, Schutz deprived it of this content which alone could be of service to the understanding with 'practical consequences'. People begin to feel the need to understand when their intentions are defied and hopes dashed. The demand to understand arises from the hopelessness experienced when the meaning of human plight is opaque and the reason for suffering impenetrable. Schutz's detailed explanation why such an opacity is a transcendental condition of life-world helps as much as a painstaking description of the technology of making nooses helps the convict to overcome his fear of the gallows. When we ask about the meaning of our experience, we are above all interested in the meaning not of suffering as such but of the suffering experienced here and now; if we want to know why our fate is so opaque we are above all interested in penetrating the reasons for a particular opacity here and now, in order to dispose of a particular form of suffering which we experience most painfully at this particular moment, and which therefore constitutes 'objectively' an indispensable stage in the endless process of emancipation: the only 'meaning' of emancipation which in the given situation really counts. But these interests can be hardly satisfied by means of transcendental analysis alone, or by empirical research aimed only at formal properties of life-process. These interests cannot be satisfied by any intellectual programme which considers historicity or historical specificity of its object as irrelevant.

Emancipation, always historically determined and historically specific, being the constant source of our urge for understanding, one has to conclude that Schutz's penetrating analysis left the practical problem of understanding where it was.

9 Understanding as expansion of the form of life

Of suffering and happiness, Arthur Schopenhauer wrote:[1]

> Just as a brook forms no eddy so long as it meets with no obstructions, so human nature, as well as animal, is such that we do not really notice and perceive all that goes on in accordance with our will. If we were to notice it, then the reason for this would inevitably be that it did not go according to our will, but must have met with some obstacle. On the other hand, everything that obstructs, crosses, or opposes our will, and thus everything unpleasant and painful, is felt by us immediately, at once, and very plainly. . . . On this rests the negative nature of well-being and happiness, as opposed to the positive nature of pain. . . .

If I talk of happiness, it is because something makes me suffer. My dream of happiness is a dream of the absence of suffering. My image of bliss is the negative of my experience of chagrin. My Garden of Eden is freedom from everything which harrows me in the Vale of Tears. Happiness is the act of liberation from suffering. Suffering is always specific. The image of happiness is always generalized, as the elimination of specific suffering is seen as eradication of all suffering.

This being an illusion (elimination of a specific suffering is only elimination of a specific suffering), happiness is possible only as a purpose, an urge, an effort. In Freud's words, 'we are so made that we can derive intense enjoyment only from a contrast and very little from a state of things'.[2] Though we tend to project happiness into the state of fulfilment, happiness is to be found entirely in its programme and the exertion it prompts. There is no state of happiness; there is only struggle against the state of suffering.

Misunderstanding is one of the obstructions which force the brook of life to form eddies. Incomprehension is a most common form of suffering. It makes our situation uncertain, unpredictable, full of dangers. It prevents us from seeing through this order which 'decides when, where and how a thing shall be done, so that . . . one is spared hesitation and indecision'.[3] In the state of incomprehension we do not know 'how to go on' (Wittgenstein). Our life process, therefore, threatens to come to a halt.

Incomprehension is a state which calls for an effort to make the uncertain certain, the unpredictable predictable, the opaque transparent. We call this effort 'understanding'. We project it as a state at the end of our effort. But there is no such state. There is no state of understanding. There is only struggle against incomprehension. The image of understanding is the negative of the experience of incomprehension.

It is only the experience of incomprehension which makes us, in a flash, aware of the task of understanding. In as far as we are engaged in routine, orderly activities, in which events follow each other with the regularity of night and day, in which rules are unambiguous and choices habitual, we cannot discover understanding as a work in its own right, a work which calls for a separate set of skills of its own. Only when the routine is broken can we, in retrospect, rearrange our memories of allegedly matter-of-fact conduct to show it contains a constant and complex activity of understanding. We perceive the knowledge of 'how to go on' as a task only when we do *not* know how to go on.

Incomprehension, however, is as common as the daily routine. It is being continually generated on the two frontiers where rules reveal their ambiguity and habits show themselves poor guides. The first is the frontier of the 'outer reality', the second the frontier of the 'inner' reality.

Both 'realities' are potential sources of incomprehension because they resist, on occasion, our intention and bar us from behaving the way we otherwise would. They may resist our intentions because they are, so to speak, independent sources of action: independent, that is to say, from our will. The other name for their independence is our lack of control over them. Reality is something whose next state only partly depends on what I am doing or what I intend to do. This is an 'ontological' articulation of what in pragmatic terms is 'lack of control'.

We try first of all to deal with the tendency of reality to be uncertain in a preventive way. We try to reduce the probability that uncertainty will be generated. This can be done, obviously, by submitting reality to our control. Collectively, we constantly attempt to do this, and the artificial order called 'civilization' is the testimony of our efforts. We erect barriers between the enclaves of 'civilized world' and untamed nature. We try to keep the air inside the walls free of the germs and viruses abounding outside; we build houses inside which rain does not fall and temperature is kept steady within a narrow range. Since we lack the resources to submit all nature to such control (to enclose all of it inside the civilized enclaves), control takes above all the form of separation. The task is to keep out the part of nature we cannot submit to our will.

The other form our effort to prevent uncertainty may take is agreement. Only a part of 'outer reality' is potentially amenable to this form of control, the part which consists of other people. Since we see them as replicas of ourselves, we suppose that they, like ourselves, can, if they only try hard enough, abstain from behaving haphazardly, i.e. from creating a situation of uncertainty for the others. That is to say, we suppose that they can, by and large, control their 'inner reality'. This is why we can agree to assign specific ranges of behaviour to specific situations. Instead of separating the part of reality incapable of self-control, in the case of agreement we separate parts of possible conduct of the – human – elements of reality whom we deem to be 'responsible', i.e. capable in principle of controlling their own behaviour. We see to it that they will not resort to physical force in order to obtain something which the 'rules' refuse. We see to it that they will respond to our openings in one of the few ways which the rules permit. Of course, it is not enough to be a human to be treated as one. Normally we do not trust all human beings to be capable of abiding by the rules. Normally there are types of people whom, like intractable nature, we prefer to keep out of bounds. We usually prefer to separate alien races, criminals, mentally insane, sometimes children or women.

Daily routine, in so far as it runs smoothly, gives no justification for the positing of understanding as a problem to be solved by a separate set of theoretical or practical methods. 'Running smoothly' means, above all, a match between typified expectations and actual conduct of the people who constitute a part of the setting in which the daily routine is running. For most of human history, this was being achieved by severely limiting the number and types of people who, for all practical and therefore theoretical purposes, were a part of that setting.

The setting can be kept small in many ways. Everywhere until quite recently and on much of the globe today, the setting was small 'naturally', thanks to the technical constriction of geographical mobility. Then, for most people, the frontiers of their 'homeliness' (the cosy enclosure inside which they could proceed in a matter-of-fact way, without distancing themselves from their own acts and turning these acts into objects of analysis) closely approximated, if not coincided with, the frontiers of their *oikoumene* – the known inhabited world. The warning signs – Roman navigators scattered '*hic sunt leones*' on the fringes of their maps – were erected in walking distance from their homes; one does not expect to communicate with *communitas leonum*, much less to understand them in the unlikely case of their attempting to communicate.

More importantly, the pocket-size *oikoumene* could be, and in most cases was, easily managed with a single set of meanings and values which were rarely if at all challenged. It is always the case that the socially available definitions of the world are 'taken to be "knowledge" about it and are continuously verified for the individual by social situations in which this "knowledge" is taken for granted. The socially constructed world becomes the world *tout court* – the only real world, typically the only world that one can seriously conceive of.'[4] Inhabitants of the pocket-size *oikoumene* were never, in addition, confronted with the possibility that there might be other conceivable worlds and that their 'knowledge', therefore, could be partial or otherwise inadequate. The whole of the *oikoumene* was subject to the same cultural authority; definitions this authority produced and guarded therefore enjoyed the sturdiness and solidity of nature and could hardly ever disclose their 'merely conventional' foundation, which we now associate with man-made rules, as distinct from nature-determined laws. Conventional foundations of definitions, meanings or values can be discovered only in the clash of several mutually autonomous authorities vying with each other for the truth and binding force of their pronouncements.

Restricted geographical mobility alone could support the monopoly of cultural authority only in the most primitive of societies. At very early stages of history it was supplemented by other, positive, factors: man-made prescriptions and proscriptions whose common task was to distinguish between physical and cultural proximity; in particular, to prevent cultural communication which physical communication made feasible. Thus the manor and the village remained for centuries within each other's reach; there is no doubt that their respective 'world definitions' and behavioural codes were sharply distinct; still, the highly ritualized and otherwise restricted communication between the two, cast into a tight and stiff frame of inviolable etiquette, effectively prevented the possibility of the clash of meanings from ever actualizing in a way which could jeopardize the smoothness of mutual exchange. The village was allowed glimpses only of the outer, 'public' fringes of the manor; manor and village spoke different languages; the manor could be approached and addressed only on special, strictly determined occasions and in equally strictly defined matters. These and many other simple cultural rules kept the manor and the village, however close to each other physically, in watertight compartments; on the whole, leakages which could spill meanings kept in one container over the content of the other were effectively controlled.

Natural limitations of communication were, therefore, assisted and strengthened by social-structural barriers. Both were topped by cultural principles which positively discouraged 'morbid curiosity' of alternative ways of life, and particularly the temptation to emulate styles prescribed for others. The idea of perfection, taken over by the Christian doctrine from Aristotle's *Metaphysics*, demanded agreement with one's own type and branded cultural miscegenation as execrable impurity.[5] In both Aristotle and Plato the word 'perfect' (*teleos*) was used almost synonymously with 'total' and 'complete' (*pan, holos*). According to Aristotle, perfect is what is full, what contains all its components; perfect is what in its own kind cannot be better, what serves well its purpose. Underlying all these descriptions is the idea of the variety of ways in which a thing, or a person, can be perfect; each type has its own model of perfection, determined by its purpose and the kind to which it belongs and which it cannot either choose or change at will. This notion of perfection measurable only in relation to a type, rather than against an absolute standard common to all human beings, persisted practically unchallenged throughout the middle ages. Hence the trained blindness to the alien way of life, so striking in medieval pilgrims to the Holy Land, and the tardiness with which Europe came to consider freshly discovered civilizations and cultures as a challenge to its own smugly assumed righteousness.

With the border traffic thereby reduced to a minimum, and travellers equipped with foolproof blinkers, a variety of forms of life could coexist within each other's reach without generating the mood of uncertainty of which the problem of understanding is born. This could continue as long as the authority of each cultural pattern remained unchallenged in its own domain.

Cultural separation would not, however, always prevent uncertainty unless assisted, When and where it was imposed on groups whose mutual contacts were more than sporadic and marginal, it had to be supported by force. As long as it remains unchallenged, a dominance attained and guarded by force allows the dominant group to dispose of the problem of cultural variety by viewing other styles of life as either condemnable deviations from the right pattern, or patterns as inferior as they are strange. This view – the point demands repeated emphasis – would never suffice unless supported by the actual superiority of power or physical force. Viewing a pattern as superior can remain effective as a means of suspending communication (and, consequently, minimizes the chance of understanding being posited as a task) only as long as it supplements and reflects the actual relation of subordination. Alternatively, though for a relatively brief period, a similar view may draw its strength from the aspirations of a group aiming at establishing its own dominance.

One or other situation normally accompanies the 'hierarchical' notion of culture.[6] The first situation obviously provided foundation for aristocratic cultural patterns, whose dominance effectively forestalled the articulation of the problem of communication as that of negotiation and agreement. The aristocratic form of domination is, in this respect, prominent for the insoluble contradiction with which it is burdened: on the one hand, it presents the aristocratic pattern at the top of the cultural hierarchy as the only one whose emulation can be, in principle, squared with the moral ideal of perfection; on the other hand, it reflects hard and fast social division in a society ruled by an aristocracy, and so makes what is already difficult to achieve infamous in addition. The aristocratic network of values and behavioural patterns is tantamount to the noblest and morally most accomplished style; it is an ideal which can be reached only through diligent effort and exercise; at the same time, it is maintained that the propensity to such an effort is itself not obtainable through its exercise, but given by birth to some people and, by and large, denied to others. In an aristocratic society, the hierarchical view of culture thwarts and confounds aspirations to which it itself gives moral foundation. Aristocratic society is built more of dams than bridges. The two most important dams have been described by Weber under the names of *commercium* and *connubium*, the twin institutionalized exclusions: the second reinforced with endogamic rules what the first achieved by circumventing undesirable social contacts between physically close but culturally distant groups. As the result, the estates or castes of such a society had many, if not all, of the earmarks of 'intra-breeding' populations, whose internal 'cultural mutations' were slow in crossing group boundaries.

And yet the very hierarchical nature of aristocratic society undermined the effectiveness of restrictions imposed upon inter-group communication. Aristocratic society could not help encouraging imitation, which it fought by insisting on the unequal value of lifestyles. By the same token, it underlined the asymmetrical, nonreciprocal nature of cultural communication. Such cultural traffic as took place between the estates could better be described as 'trickling' rather than 'floating' of cultural patterns. Univocal hierarchy channelled and streamlined the possible cultural borrowings. Tarde even defined aristocracy as a group whose most prominent feature is its 'initiating character'.[7] While McDougall tried to apply the 'downward' tendency of cultural imitation, as engendered by the hierarchical view of cultural ideals, to the explanation of the vigour or tardiness of cultural change.[8] In Russia, for example, the impetus which the aristocracy could give to cultural innovation was largely ineffective for the lack of middle classes to act as middle men. There is no imitation, said McDougall, if the distance between groups is too large. In England, where the space between aristocracy and lower classes was tightly filled by dense and ramified middle classes, imitation was prompt and cultural change vigorous.

If the communication between cultural patterns was asymmetrical, so was, and perhaps to a greater extent still, curiosity about strange ways of life. The patterns marked as most noble and refined could, time and again, be closely watched and diligently copied (if not studied) by those below who aspire to social promotion; the late medieval literature is full of reprimands of those rich and arrogant *burghers* who did just that. But there was hardly any incentive to turn curiosity downwards. Styles and patterns branded as inferior were not considered 'cultures' in their own right, complete with axial values and logic of their own. They were rather perceived as imperfect or corrupt (immature at best) versions of patterns higher in the hierarchy. They tended to be described in terms of what they 'lacked', or what they 'fell short of', rather than in terms of their positive, but indigenous, traits. Their dissimilarity was not conceived as the testimony of the relativity of all and any cultural superiority; rather, their 'imperfections' were seen as living proof of the advantages of the pattern defined as ideal. The evaluating posture had, so to speak, an inbuilt self-corroborating mechanism. It could remain immune to the mere accumulating of knowledge of cultural variety, as long as the structure of social dominance which underlied it remained intact and unassailed.

It was not until the rule of aristocracy, and inviolability of estate boundaries, had been shaken that the single-dimensionality of life-modes could be seriously questioned. Not that the hierarchical notion of culture (as well as its foundation: social and political dominance) failed to try to reassert itself in a new form. But it was through the cracks in the hitherto monolithic authority of the nobility that the European mind first described the same alien ways they looked at for centuries, as entities in their own right, as self-sustained life-forms which could and ought to be approached in their own terms.

Misgivings about the wisdom of patterns whose true or imaginary timelessness was adduced to justify their rule opened Montaigne's eyes to the relativity of all and any cultural style: 'He who would rid himself of this violent prejudice of custom will find that many things are accepted with undoubting resolve, which have no support but in the hoary beard and wrinkles of the usage which attends them.' With scorn he wrote of his less thoughtful contemporaries who, 'when they are out of their village, they seem to be out of their element'. In actual fact, 'not only every country, but every city and every profession has its particular form of civility'. The verso of each custom is blindness and incomprehension of any other custom that differs from one's own. Hence our propensity to intolerance, as well as our unwillingness and inability to grant virtue to alien images of good life. 'We all call barbarism that which does not fit in with our usages.'

These discoveries led Montaigne, the first among modern thinkers, to condemn custom as that which 'dulls the senses'. Following the custom meant being steeped in one's own life-style unreflectively; never to distance oneself from one's own style, never to conceive of this style as an object of impartial description and scrutiny. The cultural blindness and conceit are born of lack of reflection:

The principal effect of the force of custom is to seize and grip us so firmly, that we are scarcely able to escape from its grasp, and to regain possession of ourselves sufficiently to discuss and reason out its commands. In truth, since we imbibe them with our mother's milk, and the world shows the same face to our infant eyes, we seem to be born to follow the same path; and the common ideas that we find current around us, and infused into our souls with the seed of our fathers, appear to be general and natural. Whence it comes that what is off the hinges of custom we

202 Understanding as expansion of the form of life

believe to be off the hinges of reason: God knows how unreasonably for the most part.

A hundred years later Blaise Pascal, developing Montaigne's seminal ideals, would bluntly declare that our natural principles are nothing 'but principles of custom', and that 'a different custom will cause different natural principles'.[9] The difference, therefore, between our own ideals and ideals apparently approved of by other peoples is not that between nature and its corruption or negligence, but between several equally well-, or equally ill-founded customs. Each set of customs derives its resilience from its own consistency and its self-corroborating capacity. One has to arise intellectually above the level of daily life, ruled by habit and offering no occasion for self-reflection, in order to reduce the all-powerful human nature to its true, customary, size. This intellectual detachment, which posits all 'particular forms of civility' as external objects, whose content and structure is to be investigated in order to be grasped, puts forth a pattern of thought which makes the articulation of understanding as a problem possible.

More than mere intellectual detachment is, of course, involved. Both Montaigne and Pascal speak of other customs as possessing their own validity and meaning. People who have bestowed on those customs their meanings are, by the same token, posited as subjects. This is another way of saying that they are respected as autonomous beings, allowed the sovereign right to select, and to hold to, their own concepts of right and wrong, the desirable and the undesirable. Positing another person or another culture as a subject to be understood, rather than an object whose behaviour is to be causally explained (i.e. reduced to external, objectified, circumstances), presupposes a degree of respect, and acceptance of an equality, however relative.

Both respect and acceptance of equality were missing in the attitude towards strange cultures as distortions of the natural pattern, or deviations from the ideal. They were absent again in the era of the 'white man's mission', when Europe seemed to be gaining worldwide domination fast. Military and economic superiority was intellectually reflected as the perfection of cultural patterns. 'The natives' were now perceived as immature, or infantile forms which European civilization passed and left behind at some stage of its development. 'Natives' were looked at, therefore, as more or less 'underdeveloped' forms of what, in its developed shape, was to be seen in European civilization. Most adults see children in much the same way: as beings on the way to become adults themselves, who still are ineptly striving to bring this end about, and ought to be assisted in their effort. Rather than subjects of a separate kind, children are imperfect miniatures of adult subjectivity. Hence the child's behaviour can be explained by reference not to the child's meanings and intentions, but to the temporary lacunae in those meanings and intentions, and the ensuing incapacity to act in an adult way.

The problem of understanding is fully grasped only as 'the other' is capable of sustaining his autonomy and his autonomy is, with or without enthusiasm, recognized. It is then that 'the other' is recognized as a subject endowed with authority in the negotiation which follows.

The task of understanding then becomes the task of attaining concerted action of autonomous subjects under conditions in which concerted action is not automatically assured. Concern with understanding comes in response to disagreement which is recognized as such and not, for instance, taken as mere obstinacy or ineptitude.

At the first analytical extreme we find the clerk trying to penetrate the obscure intentions of his boss in order to oblige his whims, escape his wrath or earn his favour. Or a student struggling through recondite locutions of an authoritative textbook, in order to grasp the meaning which he believes to be there but which eludes him. Or an immigrant trying hard to learn whether, 'Drop in some time to see me', is an invitation for tonight or a device to terminate the conversation. Or a lover watching attentively subtle hints in their partner's behaviour in order to monitor the effectivity of advances. What all these cases have in common is the recognition that the other side has the authority to guide the subject's action: the acceptance of the 'in-order-to' motives of the alter as the 'because' motives of the ego. Wishing to learn 'how to go on', the ego accepts the alter's intentions as essentially unalterable conditions of action. He treats them as one treats natural phenomena, except for the acknowledged symbolic status of observable human acts and, consequently, an allowance for possible deception, insincerity, or technical ineptness. The motive which triggers off the effort of understanding in this sense is the ego's intention to adjust his or her behaviour to requirements laid out by the alter's unquestionable power over the ego. This remains true even if, in the end, the ego seeks to use the acquired knowledge of the alter's intention to manipulate the alter's conduct in his own interest.

The other extreme response stems from an opposite intention: the ego wishes to transform his own 'in-order-to' motives into the 'because' motives of the alter. The autonomy of the alter is still acknowledged; the alter is still recognized as the rightful owner of meaning, as the ultimate authority in deciding what the meaning of his action is. But now the ego's action does not stop at 'deciphering' this meaning. The ego's intention is to induce the alter to change the meaning he assigns to the situation. It is not the ego's, but the alter's action which is to be adjusted; and not the alter's, but the ego's authority which is to be accepted as legitimate and unquestionable. This intention gives sense to the negotiation in which new or modified relations of power are sought. The form negotiation may take varies all the way from the unconcealed struggle for domination (Weber's sword) through the use of inducements unrelated to the topic at hand (Weber's purse) up to the most sublime of forms – in which only the power of persuasion is resorted to (Weber's pen).

It has become customary, though by no means universal, to distinguish between the efforts we make when confronted with incomprehensible 'natural' events, and the efforts most likely and appropriate in confrontation with incomprehensible human conduct. Sometimes it is suggested that the term 'understanding', at variance with common usage, ought to be reserved for the latter. The systematic study of human behaviour and its artefacts is then 'understanding science'. It is clear that the term 'understanding' in this proposition appears in a sense different from the one we assumed thus far. Its use suggests that 'understanding' is an activity significantly distinct from that which Karl Popper presented as universal to all science, including science of the social.

In Karl Popper's view, science aims at the causal explanation of reality, constructed in such a way that explaining offers from the start means of predicting (and, therefore, controlling, if only we possess the necessary resources) the phenomenon under study:[10]

There is no great difference between explanation, prediction and testing. The difference is not one of logical structure, but rather one of emphasis; it depends on *what we consider to be our problem* and what we do not so consider. If it is not our problem to find a prognosis, while we take it to be our problem to find the initial conditions or some of the universal laws (or both) from which we may deduce a *given* 'prognosis', then we are looking for an explanation (and the given 'prognosis' becomes our 'explicandum'). If we consider the laws and initial conditions as given (rather than as to be found) and use them merely for deducing the prognosis, in order to get thereby some new information, then we are trying to make a prediction.

If, finally (so may we add), we use our resources to create the 'initial conditions' in which the general law will cause the phenomenon to happen, or, on the contrary, we prevent conditions being fulfilled to obviate the occurrence we consider undesirable, then we are trying to control the phenomenon. Which amounts to recognizing that, 'by virtue of their logical structure, scientific theories are technically utilizable theories'.[11] The identification of the state of incomprehension with inability to control, and the admission that the urge to control is the initial motive of scientific investigation, are both made explicit in the structure of scientific explanation. To overcome incomprehension is to know how, in principle, to control a phenomenon.

At first sight it is difficult to see why understanding of the human part of reality ought to differ in its strategy. Whether the reality we confront at the moment consists of human, or of inanimate objects, we find ourselves in the state of incomprehension from which we are keen to escape, if our plans are confounded and no good course of action comes 'naturally' to our mind. In other words, in both cases we perceive the task called 'understanding' as that of regaining the control over the situation which has been lost. Mental 'knowledge' and practical ability to act are in both cases closely intertwined. (As Gadamer recently brought to our attention, the German term '*Verstehen*', commonly used to indicate the uniqueness of humanities as 'understanding' sciences, is used in its original German language 'also in the sense of a practical ability', e.g., *er versteht nicht zu lesen*, he cannot read.[12]) In both cases, as well, we want such knowledge as can, in principle, be applied in order to get on the top of the situation. In view of this striking similarity between the two cases which 'understanding' sociology wishes to present as distinct from each other, we have to ask for the possible foundation of such distinction.

It is being said that sociology must be an 'understanding' science since human behaviour is 'symbolic'. Symbols are objects which send us to something other than themselves. They, so to speak, have a meaning which resides outside them; only the person who is aware of the 'invisible link' between the symbol and the object for which it stands can grasp this meaning. Thus, for example, only a person who knows the Highway Code 'understands' a white triangle with walking silhouettes on it as a warning that children are crossing the road. Only a peasant of East Poland, well versed in local customs, will understand that his offer of marriage has been turned down when he is served a bowl of black gruel. The argument from symbols seems, however, unconvincing. Symbols may serve the twin purposes of understanding and control only if the link with the objects they symbolize is regular and reasonably stable. But the same applies to symptoms which help us to comprehend natural events. Thus for everybody but a permanent dweller of a desert a wet pavement 'means' recent rainfall. For every person versed in basic chemistry the redness of a litmus strip 'means' acidity of a solution.

A likely rejoinder to this objection is that 'symbols', unlike 'symptoms', are man-made. That is to say, it is people who fixed the connection between a symbol and its referent; without this act of fixing there would be no link between the two. In other words, symbols are arbitrary. They could differ if only the original decision had been other than it was. It is easy to see, however, that this argument, though undoubtedly true, bears no immediate relevance to the problem of understanding. It is an argument from history: it points to the origin of the significance of symbols in distinction from symptoms, and not to a difference between the processes involved if understanding one or other. It well could be that the meaning of symptoms, just like that of symbols, is a historical phenomenon, that it was established at some specific point of time by God. This is, however, irrelevant as far as our efforts to grasp the information the symptom contains are concerned. What is relevant is that, at least for the duration of the effort itself, the link between the symptom and its referent is well established and unchangeable. The same applies to understanding symbols, however keenly aware we are of their human origins.

Indeed, when I say, 'I do not understand', when confronted with an unfamiliar human gesture, a sentence of a strange language, or an implement I cannot attach to any known function, I tacitly assume that there is something to understand, that I would be led to its referent if only I knew the link between them. I assume, in other words, that the link exists in much the same objective way as between the wet pavement and rainfall. It is exactly because of this assumption that understanding becomes a viable project. It is true that symbols have not been symbols since the beginning of the universe; but they became symbols, and therefore potential objects of understanding, only when their link with referents ceased to be random and therefore arbitrary.

It was Ferdinand de Saussure, the great Swiss linguist and the father of modern linguistics, who indicated that arbitrariness is the paramount distinctive feature of human signs; unlike natural symptoms, the link between *signifiant* (the sentient form of the sign) and *signifié* (its content, or meaning, or referent) is purely conventional. It appears and disappears together with the community of people who abide by this convention. This is undoubtedly true, in as far as we are interested in the historical dynamics of signs, yet it is still not clear in what way, if any, this peculiarity of signs' provenance should make their understanding different from understanding other signs of a comparatively longer history. One is rather inclined to agree with the argument advanced by Émile Benveniste:[13]

The link between *signifiant* and *signifié* is not arbitrary; on the contrary, it is necessary. The concept [*signifié*] '*boeuf*' is compellingly identical in my consciousness with the phonetic syndrome [*signifiant*] *böf*. How could it be otherwise? The unity of the two has been imprinted in my mind; they appear united in all circumstances.

The emphasis in Benveniste's argument is on 'all circumstances'; the sign and its referent are linked in as far as they *always* appear together. Only from the historical point of view is the link arbitrary; what makes the sign a sign, i.e. a potential object of understanding, is the necessary, not arbitrary, character of the link, whatever its historical beginnings. In the words of A. Meillet we can understand words at all only because they form a system which 'does not exist apart from the individuals who speak (write) the language. It nevertheless exists independently of each one of them, for it imposes itself on them.'[14] From the point of view of every person confronted with the task of understanding, the meaning of human signs is as objective and external as that of natural symptoms. Because of this similarity, and not in spite of it, he hopes that understanding will give him the desired ability 'to go on'.

Thus the original arbitrariness of symbols does not, in itself, provide for the alleged distinctiveness of 'understanding' as the mode of knowing human behaviour rather than inanimate events. One has to look for other foundations. One can say, for instance, that there is a difference in kind between laws, which ground the identity of natural symptoms, and rules, which guarantee the identity of human symbols. Often it is said 'mere rules', implying a comparative feebleness and somewhat less regularity with which symbols are tied to their meanings. And so, according to Peter Winch, 'it is only in terms of a given *rule* that we can attach a specific sense' to words.[15] Again, it is not immediately obvious why this should signify a situation essentially distinct from the one conveyed in the sentence, 'It is only in terms of a given law that we can attach a specific sense to an event.' It seems that the difference between the two situations is interpretive rather than immanent. It is the ways in which we account for the regularity which make them look different. We call one regularity a 'law', and the other a 'rule'. If the argument concerning arbitrariness was one from history, the argument concerning 'rule' is one from authority; it refers to the difference between powers who stand behind, respectively, rule-governed and law-governed sequences. Thanks to several centuries of scientific development, we have disposed of the notion of 'law giver' in the realm of natural phenomena. That is to say, we have acquired a set of procedures and a vocabulary which allow us to describe the regularity of natural events without continually referring to its authorship; we can meaningfully discuss natural phenomena without being concerned with the question which worried our ancestors: who laid the laws of nature in the first place. Apparently we are not prepared to shed this question of authorship or authority when discussing human phenomena. It may be interesting to look at the reasons why.

One possible reason is that we envisage the anonymous author of the rules as less self-disciplined, orderly and systematic than the legislator of the laws of nature. Having agreed with, say, Spinoza[16] that 'God could not create things in any other form or sequence than He did', one could stop worrying about God's will and dedicate one's effort entirely to the study of necessities. In order to generate the notion of the law as the major tool of comprehending (and controlling) nature, scientists had to agree that, whether God does or does not exist, He could not create the world (i.e. lay its rules) in a different way, and things must obey His rules in every case. With these two assumptions accepted, the existence of God has become irrelevant to scientific pursuits. On both counts, however, social scientists shun similar assumptions regarding the anonymous authors of social rules. First, since they know of many contending rules, they cannot be sure that any given set of human rules could not be different from what it is. Secondly, they believe the rules to be much less apodictic and 'exceptionless' than, in their view, natural scientists consider their laws to be.

Thus, in Winch's words,[17]

The notion of following a rule is logically inseparable from the notion of *making a mistake*. If it is possible to say of someone that he is following a rule that means that one can ask whether he is doing what he does correctly or not. Otherwise there is no foothold in his behaviour in which the notion of a rule can take a grip; there is then no *sense* in describing his behaviour in that way, since everything he does is as good as anything else he might do, whereas the point of the concept of a rule is that it should enable us to *evaluate* what is being done.

That is to say, rule is a norm (and to say that something 'occurs normally' is to say that it occurs with somewhat less than an unfailing regularity); it is a standard of behaviour, perhaps with mechanisms attached which cause the actual conduct to approximate the standard, but a standard it is all the same. The actual behaviour may come up to it, but then it may not. This, we are told, is the essential difference between rule-governed human action and the boringly monotonous, law-subordinated behaviour of natural phenomena or, for that matter, machines:[18]

It is said that hi-fidelity phonographs have been perfected to the point where blindfolded music critics are unable to distinguish their 'playing' from that of, let us say, the Budapest String Quartet. But the phonograph would never be said to have performed with unusual brilliance on Saturday, nor would it ever deserve an encore.

That far the difference between rules and laws looks as one of degree rather than of kind. We have been told that human behaviour is somewhat less repetitive and monotonous and, therefore, less amenable to predictions. But this 'less' makes sense only if related to a somewhat dated notion of scientific laws. Few natural scientists today would agree that the laws they formulate are as exceptionless as social scientists seem to believe. Laws of natural science are mostly statistical, and they can specify only the degree of probability that a given phenomenon will occur in one instance, rather than any 'necessity' of its occurrence. The existence of a rule, presumably, indicates a similar statistical probability; it would make little sense to speak about a rule in the case of behaviour which occurs only in minority of instances. The apodictic concept of natural laws was perhaps indispensable for the declaration of independence from theological explanations; as a manifesto of self-sufficiency of a 'Godless' discourse. Once it had, however, acquired its independence, science obtained its own momentum and now it needs 'exceptionless' laws not much more than the smooth run of bourgeois society needs a daily reading of the 'declaration of rights of man and citizen'. As the question of the authorship of laws was long ago rendered irrelevant, the discovery of the statistical, probabilistic nature of laws was not seen as an occasion to revive long-forgotten metaphysical concerns. Scientists manage to deal with 'merely statistical' laws without referring them to a 'legislating authority' of any kind. Obviously, the lack of full certainty does not, in itself, show that the question of authorship has to be taken into account in the case of the rules of human behaviour.

Setting the rules apart becomes understandable if we agree that their implementation can be only mediated by conscious decisions of men. They must be 'applied' in order to become real, and 'known' in order to be applied. Thus their distinctive character is grounded in certain psychical events which take place in the minds of people; nothing of a similar nature can be predicated upon natural pheno- mena or machines (however similar their overt behaviour may resemble that of the humans).

This, indeed, seems a valid argument. We are prepared for its acceptance by the whole of our daily thinking and acting. Whenever we do not grasp 'directly' the meaning of other people's behaviour (i.e. whenever we cannot go on without thinking how to go on), whenever it comes to a need to interpret this behaviour, we tend to do our mental job by using concepts like 'he wants to imply', 'he intends', 'he wants me to believe that', etc. – all referring the meaning of what has been said or done to mental processes of one kind or another. This we do only in the case of human behaviour. We would certainly resent somebody's using similar terms to describe conduct of a machine. This resentment was very well expressed by Jefferson, as quoted by A. M. Turing:[19]

Not until a machine can write a sonnet or compose a concerto because of thoughts and emotions felt, and not by the chance fall of symbols, could we agree that machine equals brain – that is, not only write it but know that it had written it. No mechanism could feel (and not merely artificially signal, an easy contrivance) pleasure at its successes, grief when its valves fuse, be warmed by flattery, be made miserable by its mistakes, be charmed by sex, be angry or depressed when it cannot get what it wants.

Two very different things are confused in the above statement. One is a statement of fact: indeed, no machine to date can write a sonnet (though, in principle, such a machine could be constructed). The second, however, is a statement of interpretation: writing a sonnet *because* of thoughts and emotions felt. Jefferson presents here as an attribute of the machine what is, in actual fact, an attribute of his own interpretation (however many people may share it). What Jefferson tells us is, in the last account, that he is not prepared to account for a sonnet the machine will eventually write by adducing thoughts and feelings to it.

This is a good example of the circular reasoning normally underlying the argument 'only men think and feel . . . ': natural phenomena or machines would be like men only if I were to predicate on them thoughts and feelings as causes of their behaviour. But I would not do that. Therefore, I have proved that they are not like human beings. I explain the behaviour of people by reference to their thoughts and feelings. I refuse to do that in case of natural phenomena or machines. What I posit as intrinsic qualities of phenomena are projections of my decision as to how to interpret them.

Thus the belief that 'men, and men only, act because of thoughts and feelings' is ultimately grounded in our habit of interpretation. Jefferson is a man, and he is naturally inclined to assume that other men are like him (i.e. that he is right in ascribing to them attributes he ascribes to himself). Jefferson, however, is not a machine. Never having been a machine, he naturally has no foundation to ascribe to machines features which are 'knowable' only from 'inside'. The question, 'How does it feel to be a machine?' can obviously be answered only by a machine; and even if a machine were to answer, humans would have no reason to believe it; and perhaps no faculty to understand it. As Wittgenstein wrote, if lions could speak, we would not understand them.

Let us be quite clear of what is involved in reasoning of Jefferson's type: human behaviour is unique not because no other behaviour is quite like it, but because it is only about humans that we make suppositions of a special kind, and consequently ask about their behaviour questions we would not ask of any other conduct. We split, for the purposes of interpretation, our 'outer' reality into two; to the second we ascribe features we 'know' from different sources.

These 'different sources' are located in the 'inner' reality. 'Understanding' other humans' behaviour, as against merely 'explaining' the conduct of inanimate objects, means ultimately extrapolating the method we use to account for our own action on to our accounts of the behaviour of other objects whom we recognize as human. Recognizing them as humans, and extrapolating the method, mean in fact the same thing.

Thus perceiving an object as human boils down to assuming that the object has its own 'inner reality' structured in the same way as ours. That is to say, that the object sets purposes to its activity, intends to 'express' something in the fashion of results of action, controls the course of action in thoughts, reacts emotionally to situation and the changes introduced by the action, etc. Above all, we believe that the object's control over its own 'inner' reality is as limited as ours; that is, that the link between his 'overt' purposes, i.e. purposes as he sees them and gives account of, and the actual content of his action is somewhat less than perfect; that he cannot give a full and cogent account of the 'true' motives which guide his action; that he is incapable of conceptualizing all the contents of his 'inner' reality. Whenever account is given of the impact of 'inner' reality upon the actual conduct, the question of 'veracity' arises, different from the question of 'truth' in that it can be answered (if at all) by discourse and negotiation only, rather than by objective testing.

This indeed is the way in which other human beings as entities unlike inanimate objects are conceived. There is little chance that we could conceive of them without predicating upon them all those manifold attributes we know from our 'inner experience' (or, rather, the way we account of the experience of our 'inner' reality). We will in all probability always think of human behaviour as distinguished by psychic events which take place in the actor's head before and in the course of his action.

To the question why, we expect different answers, depending on whether it is applied to humans or to inanimate objects. If a pebble falls from the top of a cliff, we seek, as the answer we need, some information about a 'general law' and certain conditions in which this law may 'produce' the event which actually took place, i.e. the falling of the pebble. The general law is, by and large, an inductive statement which tells us that events like the one we are trying to explain tend to take place whenever specific conditions occur; the general law, in other words, informs us of a regularity of which the single event in question may be portrayed as a particular case. In our example, the general law is the law of gravitation; the conditions, heavy and prolonged rains, or strong wind, or a high-pitched sound, are things which can overcome the 'counter-force' of friction and inertia which kept the pebble in place.

If, however, it was John Smith who tumbled down the slope, we would not take the law of gravitation as answer to our why. Instead, we try to account for his falling by referring to some inner states of his mind, which could 'make sense' of the happening. He could have soberly assessed his life as unworthy and decided to opt out by committing suicide. Or he could have acted in a fit of despair when his love proved to be unrequited. Or he could be absent-minded when engrossed in working out the plot for a new book. In all these cases, we attempt to 'make sense' of John's fall by plunging into the invisible depth of his mind, into what we call 'intentions', 'motives', 'frames of mind', 'emotions', etc. We do not need such an exercise to satisfy our curiosity as to the causes which led to the fall of a pebble.

Do we in fact need insight into the psychical process in the mind of the actor in order to *understand* his behaviour? Do we actually reconstruct this mental process when engaged in the effort of understanding? It is true that we normally refer to such mental processes when accounting for our *interpretation*. We articulate our version of other people's conduct in terms like 'he thinks that', 'he does not like it', 'he does not wish', 'he wanted to', 'what he meant was', etc., all implying that we have penetrated the 'inside' of our partner's mind and found the meaning of his behaviour there. The question is, however, whether these are only the terms which we use to couch our interpretation, or whether they are a true expression of what we have actually done.

The latter is, of course, what our common sense suggests. The verbal expressions we use imply that we have indeed explored and revealed what was going on in other people's minds, what other people actually thought, intended, meant, etc. It is only when we begin to analyse the grounds of such beliefs that doubts start to arise. We realize that, after all, we 'know' only that *we* think, intend, mean; it is from this 'inner' experience that the framework in which we put other people is forged. We ascribe to them what we know about ourselves. As a matter of fact we do not know what '*they* think', 'intend', 'mean'. Or, at least, we do not know it in the same way as we know our own thinking, intending, meaning. What we know is only their action, the sentences they utter, the prosodic features which accompany their speech, the 'paralinguistic' aspects of their behaviour (combinations of physiologically grounded parameters with pitch, loudness, duration and silence being variable in relation to their identification; for example, different degrees of loudness distinguish 'ordinary' from 'stage' whisper).[20] All these refer to what we can see and hear. When we speak of their thinking, intending, meaning, we do not refer to what we see or hear, but to the manner in which we interpret what we see or hear.

According to Ludwig Wittgenstein, this common-sense-grounded manner of speech is regrettable, as it beclouds rather than reveals the true nature of understanding. It suggests that the activity of understanding needs what in actual fact it can well (and must) do without: knowing something which is essentially 'unknowable'. When I ask you to give me a red pencil, I can reasonably expect you to give me one. Yet I have no idea how you experience the 'redness' of the pencil; whether your experience of redness is 'like' mine. The point is, however, that this knowledge is unnecessary for our interaction to take place to mutual satisfaction. We both 'know how to go on' in spite of the fact that both of us have only our private, uncommunicable experiences of 'redness'. The only thing which really matters is that both you and me use the word 'red' in the same way, i.e. we both use it as the name for the same set of objects. The worry, therefore, over just what you 'feel' when looking at a red object is entirely redundant from the point of view of my 'knowing how to go on', of that control over the situation which is the substance of my urge to understand. The 'sameness' of your and my usage of the word 'red' is grounded in our knowledge of language, and not in the 'sameness' of our experience of 'redness'. Consider:[21]

The sentence has sense only as a member of a system of language. . . . There is no more point in *postulating* the existence of a peculiar kind of mental act alongside of our expression. . . .

If we scrutinize the usages which we make of such words as 'thinking', 'meaning', 'wishing', etc., going through this process rids us of the temptation to look for a peculiar act of thinking, independent of the act of expressing our thoughts, and stowed away in some peculiar medium. . . .

The meaning of a phrase for us is characterized by the use we make of it. The meaning is not a mental accompaniment to the expression. Therefore the phrase, 'I think I mean something by it,' or, 'I'm sure I mean something by it,' which we so often hear in philosophical discussions to justify the use of expression is for us no justification at all. We ask, '*What* do you mean?', i.e., 'How do you use this expression?'

Thus we understand a sentence because it is a part of language (or a symbol because it is a part of a symbolic system), and not because we grasp intuitively the invisible link between the sentence and the speaker's intention which has accompanied it. This understanding which is the indispensable condition of communication is assured (or not) by our knowledge of language (or lack of it).

We know, however, how unsatisfactory language is, all its practically unlimited richness notwithstanding, as a vehicle of expression. If 'being understood' really matters but at the same time we are aware that it is not easy, we often 'struggle for words' and despair their noxious ambiguity. We realize that even the most carefully chosen words fail to cover exactly the ground we wish to express, that their borderlines are blurred, and that they leave residues which cannot be easily classified and are doomed to linger on the fringes of the expressible. In Wittgenstein's words again,[22]

We might, by the explanation of a word, mean the explanation which, on being asked, we are ready to give. That is, if we *are* ready to give any explanation; in most cases we aren't. Many words in this sense then don't have a strict meaning. But this is not a defect. To think it is would be like saying that the light of my reading lamp is no real light at all because it has no sharp boundary.

This is, indeed, a splendid analogy. Words are lamps which shed light on parts of our experience. Words of natural languages, like light in natural atmospheric conditions, have no sharp boundaries. Like the atmosphere which disperses light beams, surrounding the brightly lit spots by a shaded area melting gradually into darkness, so the words of our natural language bring into sharp relief some bits of our experience, the clarity of the picture they illuminate decreasing the further we move from the focus. There are no half-shades on a planet without atmosphere. Perhaps it is possible to achieve a perfect clarity of conceptual boundaries in an artificial language designed to account for the limited and fully controlled 'experience' of scientific experiment. But such a clarity is unattainable in natural languages. This adds importance to Wittgenstein's analogy. We are reminded, with its help, that just as the blurred boundaries of light do not deprive a reading-lamp of its usefulness as a 'light', the lack of a strict definitional meaning does not disqualify words as useful tools of communication.

The opposite is true. A language cleansed of all equivocality could be used only by a group whose every member fully participates in the same, relatively narrow set of activities, and only in reference to aspects of these activities which have been fully 'objectified', i.e. reduced in their relevant meaning to the one determined by the definition. This is how formal languages of highly structured sciences attain the unequivocality they rightly boast. This is, however, also why none of those languages is flexible and pliable enough to be used for communication in situations less strictly controlled and by people who have not acquired the 'trained incapacity' to look beyond the aspects such a given language allows them to notice. For other people and in other situations only a language of polysemic words with blurred boundaries can be used as a vehicle of communication.

I can hope to be given the red pencil when I ask for one not because your experience of redness and mine are identical (how would I know, if no amount of words could fully convey the contents of these experiences?), but because the fulfilment of my hope does not depend on that identity. It really depends on your and my knowledge of the way to use the word 'red', 'pencil', and 'give'. The possibility of successful communication, i.e. interaction which does not give us occasion to experience miscomprehension, hangs on our ability to detach the symbols we use from private, subjective, idiosyncratic 'mental states' which accompany them 'inside' this or that actor; to make their use independent of possible differences between those mental states.

Sociologically, in order to grasp the meaning of a symbol as unproblematic, we do not need to know what 'he actually meant when he used it'. What we really need to know is the context in which the symbol is commonly used, and the kind of conduct with which it is commonly associated. Understanding a symbol consists in referring it not to the unknown intentions of the user, but to its communally grounded usages. In Wittgenstein's words, to understand a language means to know 'a form of life'. Conversely, when I say, 'I do not understand', I refer not to my inability to penetrate the unfathomable depths of the other's mind, but to the subjective strangeness of the form of life of which the given symbol has been a part.

This strangeness may manifest itself on many levels, and accordingly lack of understanding may emerge on various levels of social organization. Often 'I do not understand' refers to disturbances in the communication between individuals. A couple of very intimate friends can develop a hermetic system of hints and clues which nobody but themselves would understand; though physically accessible, these symbols remain, nevertheless, semantically remote to others. A person promoted to a higher position in his organization's hierarchy is likely to commit many a blunder before the meaning of the words and the silences exchanged 'on high' cease to escape him. An ethnologist stops, bewildered, in front of a strange rite which makes no sense against the background of all his previous knowledge. Seemingly different, all the three cases are, in fact, variations on the same theme: one 'form of life' encounters another one, with which not enough points of contact have been established to make possible control over the situation which involves the 'strange' form.

Faced with this, we tend (for the reasons spelled out above) to articulate it as piercing through the symbols in order to reach the intentions, values, ways of thinking of the persons whose behaviour strikes us as inexplicable. Were we aware of the technical terminology, we would articulate the task as that of 'empathy', an effort to think those persons' thoughts and feel their feelings. We know now, however, that this is not possible; or, rather, that what we take as 'putting myself into his mind' can only remain forever an interpretation of overt conduct, referring to our own introspective experience. Does this mean that the barrier between strange forms of life is doomed to remain impermeable? In order to understand a West Indian boy from Leicester, I have to be like the West Indian boy from Leicester; but I cannot be like the West Indian boy from Leicester. Therefore, I cannot understand the West Indian boy from Leicester. The syllogism seems impeccable.

The point is, however, that the first premise is false. I need not be a West Indian boy from Leicester in order to understand a West Indian boy from Leicester. I am not my wife; neither am I my friend Michael; yet we understand each other very well. At least we never have any difficulty in communicating with each other and dissolving misunderstandings as they arise. Understanding, as it were, is not about 'feeling the feelings' and 'thinking the thoughts' of others, but about sharing in a form of life. Or, in the case of an encounter between hitherto alien forms – *about constructing a form of life of a 'higher order', which will incorporate the previous two as its sub-forms.* This form of life of the higher order will contain all those 'contiguous points' where the previous two become elements of each other's situation.

In phrasing the problem of understanding between initially alien forms of life in this form of establishing a form of life of a higher order, I follow the ideas of Claude Lévi-Strauss regarding the tasks and the limitations of historical and ethnographic study. Historians and ethnographers are the two professions which face the task of communication between forms of life separated by time or by distance. They are, as well, the two professions who have to perform this task *for* the society; they struggle to produce translatability which has not yet been accomplished 'matter of factly', in the process of diffuse intercourse, as it normally happens in the case of new neighbours coming from distant places but 'getting to know each other' by sharing in each other's life. Historians and ethnographers are perhaps the only people who, by the nature of their task, have to achieve understanding 'all alone', and by a purely intellectual effort ('anthropology is the science of culture as seen from the outside'). This is why in the context of their work understanding appears most often as a theoretical problem and tends to be discussed in most general methodological terms. This is why, as well, their cogitations may illuminate the practices of other social scientists less alive to the issues at stake:[23]

> Both history and ethnography are concerned with societies *other* than the one in which we live. . . . What constitutes the goal of the two disciplines? Is it the exact reconstruction of what has happened, or is happening, in the society under study? To assert this would be to forget that in both cases we are dealing with systems of representations which differ for each member of the group and which, on the whole, differ from the representations of the investigator. The best ethnographic study will never make the reader a native. The French Revolution of 1789 lived through by an aristocrat is not the same phenomenon as the Revolution of 1789 lived through by Michelet or Taine. All that the historian or ethnographer can do, and all that we can expect of either of them, is to enlarge a specific experience to the dimensions of a more general one, which thereby becomes accessible *as experience* to men of another country or another epoch.

That is to say, one can achieve understanding of alien forms of life not by immersing oneself in their specific uniqueness or re-living them as if 'from inside', but by following an exactly opposite strategy: by spotting the general in the particular, by enlarging both the alien and one's own experience so as to construct a larger system in which each 'makes sense' to the other.

The usual objection to this proposal is that the strategy it suggests would inevitably 'distort' the meaning intrinsic to the alien form of life. The meaning, so the argument goes, is not a product of communication between forms, an end-result of the effort of understanding, but something which was already there in the alien form of life (distant past, remote culture) before even the need to understand it arose. This meaning was bestowed upon the era or the culture by their 'members'. To reveal the meaning therefore means to discover and record faithfully those members' representations. We have already met this objection. We have seen that this is, on the whole, an imaginary worry as far as daily, matter-of-fact understanding-through-interaction is concerned (it is only my representation of redness that I know when I ask you to help me to find a red pencil). Is the worry more serious and real when the search of meaning of alien times and cultures is at stake?

Lévi-Strauss recalls the case of a Kwakiutl Indian whom Boas invited to New York to obtain information about Kwakiutl culture. This Indian[24]

was quite indifferent to the panorama of skyscrapers and of streets ploughed and furrowed by cars. He reserved all his intellectual curiosity for the dwarfs, giants, and bearded ladies who were exhibited in Times Square at the time, for automats, and for the brass balls decorating staircase banisters. For reasons I cannot go into here, all these things challenged his own culture, and it was that culture alone which he was seeking to recognize in certain aspects of ours.

Is this a case of a mind particularly obtuse, an eye trained to be blind to what is 'really' important in a cultural reality? Or is this rather what we all do all the time, bizarre only for the reversal of usual roles? We find phenomena intelligible only when they conform (or when we succeed in presenting them as conforming) to what our own experience prepared us to expect and not to be bewildered by. We dig up in ancient epochs the true 'class' meaning of events, which for contemporaries could be only invisible. We are bound to bring into relief the dynamism of the past webs of human relations in order to grasp their meaning; again an aspect which could be only obscure to the generations who subjectively lived 'outside history'. Speaking of the changing fashions in the brief history of the modern study of totemism, Lévi-Strauss suggested that 'the theory of totemism is set up "for us", not "in itself", and nothing guarantees that in its current form it does not still proceed from a similar illusion'.[25] Similarly, our present coming to terms with myths as cultural products pregnant with respectable meaning, an attitude so opposite to the one taken a few dozen years ago by scholars so profound as Frazer or Lévy-Bruhl: is not this, to an extent at least, an achievement possible only thanks to the transformation of our sensitivity accomplished by the surrealist revolution? And if we are not any more, when visiting distant cultures, interested in brass balls decorating staircases, but rather in the routine of the quotidianity – this is a by-product of our own internal development, which made evident to us the oddity of the usual and the mysteriousness of the routine.

In the practice of the ethnographer, Lévi-Strauss tells us,[26]

it is never either himself or the other whom he encounters at the end of his investigation. At most he can claim to extricate, by the superposition of himself on the other, what Mauss called the facts of general functioning, which he showed were more universal and had even more reality.

Rather than forgetting his own specific form of life (as he often mistakenly thinks), the ethnographer (or the historian, for that matter) can only grasp the meaning of another form by unfolding the general which is hidden in the two particularities of his own and the alien culture. In so doing, his own culture is an asset, rather than a liability. It is his own culture, distinct as it is from the one under his scrutiny, which offers him a pole, distant enough from the other, to magnify the projected 'facts of general functioning' as much as is needed in order to make them visible. The larger the distance between the ethnographer's (or historian's) own and the investigated form of life, the more general features of human life may be necessary for, and revealed in the course of, understanding.

Lévi-Strauss is not engaged here in the effort to construct an ingenious methodology of ethnographic or historical research. What he attempts to do is to unveil the structure endemic to any effort of understanding an unfamiliar and 'practically unconnected' form of life. It is not that we ought to master methods hitherto neglected in order to change our deplorable habits; it is rather that we ought to become aware of what we are doing anyway, all the time, and inevitably. There is simply no other way of understanding. It suffices, in Lévi-Strauss words, 'for history to move away from us in time or for us to move away from it in thought, for it to cease to be internalizable and to lose its intelligibility, a spurious intelligibility attaching to a temporary internality'.[27] The intelligibility attached to the 'internality' (by definition temporary), the intelligibility of the 'insiders', is spurious, since it exists in as far as it has never been brought into the focus of attention. We call it intelligibility when we look from the outside at people who clearly do not experience the agony of miscomprehension; who clearly 'must understand', since they move around their reality with such facility and since they never complain of misunderstanding. It is, therefore, a strange intelligibility; one which holds as far as its need is not felt. When I am immersed in this kind of 'internality', distancing myself from it is beyond my power. The most I can do is to know[28]

(but in a different register) that what I live so completely and intensely is a myth – which will appear as such to men of a future century, and perhaps to myself a few years hence, and perhaps will no longer appear at all to men of a future millennium.

The kind of intelligibility which is given to the insiders could not survive the attempt to forge it into a tool of 'objective understanding', just as the deep-sea fish, so tenacious and versatile in its natural habitat, would not survive transfer to a laboratory tank. The totality with which any historical era becomes matter-of-fact for those who live it disappears when looked at by an outsider; it splits into a multitude of facts, and the links between them which we call their meaning no longer enjoy pristine self-evidence. In order to make sense of the pile of raw data which the past presents to me, I have to perform first an operation of selection:[29]

In so far as history aspires to meaning, it is doomed to select regions, periods, groups of men and individuals in these groups and to make them stand out, as discontinuous figures, against a continuity barely good enough to be used as a backdrop. . . . What makes history possible is that a sub-set of events is found, for a given period, to have approximately the same significance for a contingent of individuals who have not necessarily experienced the events and may even consider them at an interval of several centuries. History is therefore never history, but history-for.

History for – what? History for the pattern of meaningfulness which is upheld by people engaged in the effort of understanding. They can reach understanding only by trying to find the smallest common denominator between the experience of the era whose meaning they want to capture and of their own. However small, this common denominator can never be smaller than either of the original two.

That 'generalizing', rather than a mere evolutionary 'superseding', is the way to get through to alien forms of life is a most important contribution made by structuralism to the on-going struggle of social science with the challenge of hermeneutics. This point has been recently made forcefully by Anthony Giddens, and shown to be a strong argument in favour of the thesis that the endemic relativity of all meaning (its 'insidedness' in relation to a given form of life) does not have to result in the relativism of interpretation. Giddens rightly castigates some over-enthusiastic interpreters of Wittgenstein (notably Winch) for treating universes of meaning as 'self-contained' or unmediated.[30] Winch, in Giddens's words, exaggerates the internal unity of forms of life 'and consequently does not acknowledge that the problem of mediation of different frames of meaning has to be treated as the *starting-point* of analysis'.[31] Such a mediation, as we have already seen, could arise out of a level of analysis wider, or more general, than that of the two forms of life facing each other in the task of mutual comprehension. The mundane understanding, the one out of which the daily interaction is constructed, is grounded already on such mediation (or, rather, generalization) accomplished matter-of-factly, by reference to objectivized points of reference whose comprehension is shared; such points of reference form an interpretive scheme which must underlie every act of understanding. The distinction of the interpretive schemes generated by sociology, and indeed by all 'understanding' sciences, is in their taking the form of a social-scientific discourse. It is the availability of such an interpretive scheme, which spans one's own and the alien forms of life, rather than the romantic 'immersion' in the alien subject, which enables the sociologist to understand the alien form of life *as* a form of life, instead of dismissing it as a perverted, or infantile, version of his own.

The generalizing elucidated by the work of structuralists seems to provide the escape from the twin dangers of ethnocentric conceit and relativistic humility we are seeking.

As we have seen, various responses given by the social sciences to the challenge of hermeneutics (developed, above all, as a methodological reflection on the work of historiography) can be best understood as efforts to reconcile the recognition of the essentially subjective nature of social reality with the attainment of objective (universally acceptable or/and apodictically binding) description of this reality. It has been widely accepted that such reconciliation depends upon demonstrating that it is possible to grasp the meaning of social phenomena without exercising empathy, 're-living', 're-experiencing', or otherwise plumbing the inaccessible 'inside' of individual psyche.

Prompted by the same urge, the responses differed however in the factors they chose as decisive. By far the most radical has been the division between 'historicist' and 'rationalistic' strategies. The first counted on the advent of an era of 'universal intersubjectivity', as a consequence of already accomplished or impending transformations of society. Short of this expectation coming true, they could however offer little practical advice for a somewhat less absolute, but perhaps more realistic interpretive consensus attainable in less favourable historical circumstances. The second pinned its hopes fully on analytical reason, subject to its own logic and largely independent of the vicissitudes of the wider historical development. It failed, however, to show the way in which the findings of such reason, however refined and methodologically elegant, could be fed back into social consensus and therefore contribute to the promotion of interpretive consensus. Both strategies viewed the attainment of true understanding as essentially distinct from the themes and resources of mundane, commonsensical understanding; both considered critique of common sense as their essential task. Both, however, failed to engage in practical dialogue with the common sense they criticized and thereby could deal with practical understanding only as a problem of the theory of interpretation and truth.

This lack of communication with the routine understanding of daily life was held against both historicist and rationalistic responses to hermeneutical challenge by the existentialistically inspired critique. This critique denied the qualitative distinction between scientific and mundane understanding and reduced the task of theory to the investigation of the way in which mundane understanding is attained; in other words, to the reflection on the 'generative grammar' of mundane understanding. The renewed interest in the routine and the ordinary led, however, to the dissolution of the problem of truth in the concept of existence. The approaches which posited understanding as the work of daily life could deal with interpretation and truth only as a problem of a practical, on-going accomplishment of communal consensus.

The lasting contribution of the existentialist critique to the problem of understanding was its exposure of understanding as a task arising out of disturbances in communal agreement. Understanding emerges as a problem, i.e. as a task which cannot be resolved unreflectively, when (a) clues or directions for conduct are equivocal, (b) removal of this ambiguity (i.e., acquisition of knowledge of 'how to go on') appears to depend on the attainment of agreed interpretation of such clues or directions, (c) this agreement is to be reached by negotiations with others who are recognized as autonomous subjects. Concern with understanding comes, in short, in response to disagreement arising in conditions of relative equality and assumed observance of democratic rules of conduct.

It could be concluded from our survey of the existentialist and the structuralist contributions to the debate that the unproblematic, unreflective agreement is attainable thanks to the shared participation in a 'form of life' – communally shared life experience and communally supported language. Negotiated agreement is required when forms of life in which respective partners are embedded differ. It consists of the expansion of each of the two or more forms of life involved; it results, if successful, in constructing a new, wider form of life; the progress of communally agreed understanding consists in generalizing, rather than superseding, successive forms of life.

The rules of achieving agreement (or communal consensus) are not, however, identical with the rules that guide the pursuit of truth; the problem of objective, or true, understanding cannot be, therefore, collapsed into that of consensus. *Objective* understanding is sought as a safeguard against imposed consensus, as an appeal against unacceptable outcome of communal negotiation. Objective understanding is sought, in a sense, as a surrogate of the control over the practical conditions of agreement. The urge for objective understanding as distinct from simply communal consensus is generated by the restrictions imposed upon equality and democracy by the structure of domination which underlies the negotiating process.

The rules which guide the attainment of objective, as opposed to merely consensual, understanding will therefore have to focus upon the conditions of genuine equality of the forms of life involved in the negotiation and the genuine democracy of proceedings. Rules of truth-attainment are, above all, the rules of criticism which allow exposure of the imperfections of practical conditions in which consensual agreement takes place, and thereby exposure of the content of such agreement falling short of the ideal of objective understanding. Rules of truth-attainment, like all methods of scientific activity, can be only conceived as a method of criticism. This we will attempt to demonstrate in the last chapter.

10   Consensus and truth

In the short story, 'Averroes's search',[1] the great Latin American writer Jorge Luis Borges considers a case of understanding which fails; an effort to comprehend which has been defeated. It is neither the complexity of universe, nor its notorious amenability to contradictory interpretations, which in this case defies the power of intellect. It is the partiality of intellect itself, its tendency to see some of the things rather than others, which is responsible for the defeat. Any intellect, however powerful, sets about its work loaded with its own past; this past is simultaneously its liability and its asset. Thanks to its past, the intellect is able to see; because of it, it is bound to remain partially blind.

Averroes's is not a story 'of the archbishop of Canterbury who took it upon himself to prove that there is a God; then, of the alchemists who sought the philosopher's stone; then, of the vain trisectors of the angle and squarers of the circle'. These would-be heroes engaged in their lost battles as, so to speak, representatives of the human species as a whole, as yet unaware that the paths they were exploring are forever closed to humans. Their defeat has, so to speak, a species-wide significance; it brands some tasks as unrealistic, a verdict which will remain valid for all time. Averroes's story is different; it tells of the 'case of a man who sets himself a goal which is not forbidden to others, but is to him'. Moreover, Averroes's defeat can in no measure be ascribed to his own 'private' intellectual weakness: Averroes, as other giants of the same breed, represented the very peak a human could reach under conditions circumscribed by history's accumulated achievement. If Averroes failed, so would anybody else in his place. The goal, therefore, was 'forbidden' to him solely because the tradition which constituted his intellect offered him no object to which to refer the meaning of an alien cultural product. However hard Averroes tried to understand what the two curious words used by Aristotle could mean – he, 'closed within the orb of Islam, could never know the meaning of the terms *tragedy* and *comedy*'; he could not 'imagine what a drama is without ever having suspected what a theatre is'. Using the only torch he had – that of Islamic cultural experience – to disperse the darkness of an alien text, Averroes wrote in his manuscript: 'Aristu (Aristotle) gives the name of tragedy to panegyrics and that of comedy to satires and anathemas. Admirable tragedies and comedies abound in the pages of the Koran and in one *mohalacas* of the sanctuary. . . . ' These were not dictionary troubles. Words, if understood, tell us how to go on. But Averroes had nowhere to go.

This is Borges's message: there is no understanding without experience to which the object can be referred. But the obverse relation holds as well: the meaning is accessible only together with experience. Hence with varying experience, the meaning varies. Is not the meaning, therefore, subject to a 'double bind', constrained simultaneously by the text and by the reader? And if this is so, can the meaning ever be conclusive, final, ultimately borne out once and for all?

Pierre Menard, the hero of another Borges story,[2] decided to produce a few pages of Don Quixote, which would coincide, 'word for word and line for line', with those of Miguel de Cervantes. The most obvious way of performing the task was to 'know Spanish well, recover the Catholic faith, fight against the Moors or the Turk, forget the history of Europe between the years 1602 and 1918, *be* Miguel de Cervantes'. This solution, however, though the most obvious and the simplest, was, alas, impossible: 'It is not in vain that three hundred years have gone by, filled with exceedingly complex events. Among them, to mention only one, is the *Quixote* itself.' What has been left to Menard was a much more arduous and challenging task: 'to go on being Pierre Menard and reach the *Quixote* through the experiences of Pierre Menard'. This was the only thing Menard could do, and that is what he did; or, at least, that is the only way in which one can conceive of his accomplishment.

Indeed, Menard produced a number of fragments identical 'word for word and line for line' with those which had come from Cervantes's pen. But were the meanings of the two identical? They could hardly be. After all, the second text came from Menard, through the experience of Menard. And we simply cannot conceive of Menard's experience forgetting that Menard lived three hundred years after Cervantes, that he was a Symbolist from Nîmes, a devotee of Edgar Allan Poe, of Baudelaire, Mallarmé, Valéry. We know all this. For this very reason we cannot understand Menard's text in the same way we understood Cervantes's. Let us follow Borges to see how the two understandings diverge.

Three centuries divide Menard from Cervantes; Menard's text had to be subtler, richer and more ambiguous than Cervantes's. The images, the phrases, the words of *Don Quixote* soaked and absorbed new emotions and entered new associations. To start with, Cervantes 'in a clumsy fashion, opposes to the fictions of chivalry the tawdry provincial reality of his country'. Not so Menard: he 'selects as his "reality" the land of Carmen during the century of Lepanto and Lope de Vega'. The 'objective alternatives' confronting Menard in the twentieth century were not those faced by Cervantes in the seventeenth; thus identical choices could not but have different meanings. A choice owes its meaning to the chances it leaves behind, 'objectively rejects'. When Menard wrote, sixteenth-century Spain wore many masks which Cervantes could not discard for the simple reason that they had been put on her face long after his death. If these masks are, however, ignored in Menard's work, we can understand this only as the author's artistic decision. We *see* in Menard's *Quixote* (though not, of course, in Cervantes's) – the conspicuous absence of 'gipsy flourishes or conquistadores or mystics or Philip the Seconds or autos da fé' – all those clichés into which later centuries tightly wrapped Quixote's Spain. Cervantes's clumsy naturalness turned into Menard's refined subtlety.

Similarly, Cervantes's straightforwardness became Menard's enigmatic equivocality. Both authors' Don Quixote enters a debate during which he commends arms and derides letters. As for Cervantes, one could hardly expect a different attitude from a former soldier. Menard, an intellectual 'naturally' suspicious of everything military and coercive, 'a contemporary of *La trahison des clerks* and Bertrand Russell', *must* be a different matter. No wonder, Borges tells us, his curious attitude has inspired numerous interpretations. No one, however, came forward with a reason as cogent and simple as that which enables us to understand Cervantes with such facility. Menard's interpretations are doomed to remain controversial; we perceive this uncertainty of ours as 'richness' or 'ambiguity' of Menard's text.

To underline still stronger this crucial feature of interpretation, let us – following Borges again – compare two views of history:

It is a revelation to compare Menard's *Don Quixote* with Cervantes'. The latter, for example, wrote (part one, chapter nine):

... truth, whose mother is history, rival of time, depository of deeds, witness of the past, exemplar and adviser to the present, and the future's counsellor.

Written in the seventeenth century, written by the 'lay genius' Cervantes, this enumeration is a mere rhetorical praise of history. Menard, on the other hand, writes:

... truth, whose mother is history, rival of time, depository of deeds, witness of the past, exemplar and adviser to the present, and the future's counsellor.

History, the *mother* of truth: the idea is astounding. Menard, a contemporary of William James, does not define history as an inquiry into reality but as its origin. Historical truth, or him, is not what has happened; it is what we judge to have happened. The final phrases – *exemplar and adviser to the present, and the future's counsellor* – are brazenly pragmatic.

Perhaps Menard was an avid reader of William James and his ardent follower; perhaps he never held James's book in his hand. Whichever was the case, the meaning of Menard's statements would not be affected. It was not Menard's own convictions which filled his statements with pragmatic content. Though we present this content as if it derives from Menard's intention, as a meaning existing 'for him' – we can only 'read out' this intention from what we know about the phase of historical discourse in which the statement was conceived or in which we suppose it to have been conceived. Menard's phase, as we know, was dominated by the powerful mind of James. It seemed, at least to his contemporaries, that James once and for all discredited the naïve, reflective view of history, and that no one's view of history after James can be the same as before. The simple phrase 'truth, whose mother is history' could not claim any more the a-philosophical innocence which only the 'objective absence' of James's argument can offer. The old phrases have been given new meaning by the sheer act of their being seized by a new philosophy. One could use them only together with the new meaning. The sheer presence of James turned Menard, without much further action on his part, into a pragmatist. And so on. For example, the literary style. The contrast between Cervantes's and Menard's style, so Borges tells us, is 'vivid. The archaic style of Menard – quite foreign, after all – suffers from a certain affectation. Not so his forerunner, who handles with ease the current Spanish of his time.' The unadorned conventionality of Cervantes's vernacular turned into affectionate archaism under Menard's pen.

The whole idea of a Menard writing anew a book composed centuries ago seems, to say the least, bizarre. But there is more to it than another of Borges's amazing feats of literary fantasy. Menard, of course, is a product of Borges's imagination; but not the problem Menard's story has revealed. Menard helped Borges to reach the problem of understanding and interpretation in its purest form. As the result, aspects have been revealed which in 'real', and therefore 'impure', cases may well elude our attention.

What it exposes, above all, is the endemic fluidity of meaning. Far from being once and for all fastened to the text by the author's intention, meaning keeps changing together with the readers' world. Of this latter world it is a part, and only inside can it be meaningful. The text the author has produced acquires its own life. True – the text derives its meaning from the setting in which it has been conceived. In this setting, however, the author's intentions are just a factor among many others; and surely the one factor of which we know least. No less significant are those other constituents of the setting which the text absorbed, and those the text could absorb but did not: the absence is as vociferous as the presence. On the other hand, the reader is no more free than the author in determining the meaning of the text. It is true that he has an edge on the author. He may know more about the setting in which the text was born. He knows, or at least can know, all these things the author could be aware of and (by design or by default) was not. But the reader as well is a child of his age. He understands as much as his knowledge allows him. His attempt to detach himself from this knowledge would result not in a better understanding, but in blindness. The text would lie in front of him obscure and impenetrable, as a statement made in an unknowable language (when we learn a foreign language, we try to assimilate its structure into the syntax and semantics of the language we already know). If the author sends his signals from an island whose interior he had not and could not explore in full, the reader is a passenger who walks the deck of a sailing ship he does not navigate. The meaning is the instant of their encounter.

This fluidity of meaning, so unlike the alleged solidity of its textual 'container', has been brought into prominence thanks to the artful transparency of Menard's case. But the profundity of discovery is by no means confined to the laboratory of Borges's imagination. Consider carefully the following:

Menard (perhaps without wanting to) has enriched, by means of a new technique, the halting and rudimentary art of reading: this new technique is that of deliberate anachronism and the erroneous attribution. This technique, whose applications are infinite, prompts us to go through the *Odyssey* as if it were posterior to *Aeneid* and the book *Le jardin de Centaure* of Madame Henri Bachelier as if it were by Madame Henri Bachelier. This technique fills the most placid works with adventure.

Tongue in cheek, we are reminded of a very serious matter indeed: that what transforms the 'looking at the text' into understanding is the act of placing the text in a context. Anachronistic attribution is not such a new technique as Borges pretends. As a good caricature, it only magnifies the features of its object: the ordinary, and the only possible, technique of understanding. Wrongly viewing Homer as a successor to Virgil is not technically different from rightly locating Madame Henri Bachelier. Both must be located somewhere in order to be understood. Measuring them against alternative contexts only reveals what was already there, in the very project of understanding: the intrinsic variability of possible meanings and their interpretations. Above all, it reveals the intimate bond between the meaning and the reader's world. The text is a dumb object which only the act of interpretation-by-placement can force to speak.

The conclusion one can draw from Averroes's and Menard's experiences is not to everybody's liking. Indeed, what follows is that the concepts of 'right' or 'wrong' understanding make sense only in a given context. The fullest understanding one can think of is still context-dependent and context-confined. It is not immediately clear why this conclusion ought to be disturbing. After all, as long as we remain in a given context, we can as well remain satisfied that nothing in the meaning of the text eludes us; we cannot miss something of whose possibility we are not aware (remember Averroes). The dependence on context seems only a minor irritant in most purposes of practical communication. So why are we worried? Why does the hypothesis of the irrevocably 'relational' nature of all understanding tend to generate endless efforts at its theoretical refutation or methodological neutralization? Why did it inspire generations of thinkers to search frantically for context-free meanings?

The reason can be found not so much in the intrinsic superiority of context-free over context-bound understanding, as in the urge for control which no context-bound understanding can satiate in as far as no context is fully controlled. As it is bound to a context whose dynamics are beyond my control, the meaning cannot satisfy the need of control which is the original source of the understanding effort. Only if I can be sure that what I have grasped is from now on immutable and immune to contingencies of fate, can my knowledge give me the feeling of genuine mastery over the object. The real trouble, therefore (the real reason of our anxiety) is not the endemic structure of theoretical understanding, but *the practical lack of control over the life situation* which a most perfect interpretation will still be helpless to redress. *Objective understanding appears*, so to speak, *as a substitute for practical control over the situation*; as an 'intellectual socialization' of the conditions of actions which in reality are privately owned. *This is why attempts to gain objective understanding will always be repeated: and this is why they will be never successful.* That is, unless an entirely different situation of action deprives them of their goal. Paradoxically, *a truly objective understanding would be accessible only in conditions which do not require it: which do not posit such an understanding as a problem.*

Theories which do posit understanding as a problem of methodology set out to discover, or to design, a method of interpretation which can be seen as leading to objective, i.e. universally acceptable, results. Grounded in that methodology, results would be apodictically true; they would, therefore, have to be accepted by all sides. The negative impact of the current balance of power between sides would be neutralized. The assets arising from the access to the powers of the sword or purse would be outweighed and superseded by the advantages offered by the access to an unfailing methodology. The outcome of negotiation, and the substance of resulting agreement, will be largely independent from factors of power different from those directly possessed and operated by interpreters.

Most of the approaches to the problem of understanding we have surveyed belong to this category. (Heidegger, Schutz, and the ethnomethodological currents inspired by them provide the few exceptions which refused to discuss truth as an authority external to the process of reaching agreement. They allow the interpreter no tools for evaluating the validity of meanings he has determined. In particular, he is denied the means with which to distinguish a 'true' from a 'false' basis of communal agreement.) They are relatively less interested in the anatomy of routine understanding, on which Heidegger or Schutz focus attention. The lack of interest comes from a disbelief that the rules guiding the pursuit and the attainment of truth can be found in mundane inter-action. Both types of approaches agree, as it were, that communal agreement, through which under-standing in daily life is achieved, does not depend on the truthfulness of views the community agrees about. The pursuit of true under-standing, as distinct from ordinary agreement, must therefore detach itself from everyday discourse and seek its own rules else-where. What counts is not the way in which an interpretation has been reached, but the way in which its objective validity may be defended and – ideally – proved. Only if this way is found can the interpretation be awarded the authority required in relation to alter-native interpretations which cannot be so defended. The rules which guide the process of reaching agreement in routine interaction are admittedly not the rules which guide the pursuit of truth. Hence the pursuit of specifically *true* understanding calls for a separate set of rules which would constitute this activity as an autonomous, self-sustained and self-governed realm.

This postulate has been pushed to its extreme in Husserl's pheno-menology. This method hermetically seals the pursuit of true mean-ing from the potentially distorting influence of socio-historical context. Even the interest in meanings held by actual empirical individuals or groups is considered potentially polluting; insight into the content of ideas present in pure consciousness is left as the only safe haven where true understanding may be anchored. We have seen that even if such a haven, unruffled by the tides coming from the open sea, were more than a fiction born of despair, its imperme-ability would be a curse as much as a blessing. No products of 'true understanding' so conceived could be taken beyond its confines without losing all they gained from isolation. There is no clear way in which phenomenological findings could be fed into ordinary discourse and exert an influence upon meanings produced and embedded in daily life.

Other theorists were careful never to present the rupture between methodical pursuit of truth and mundane understanding as complete and irreparable. On the contrary, the hope of rational organization of society (Weber) or scientific politics (Mannheim) was never lost from their sight as the ultimate end of their efforts. The intention to feed their methodically attained results back into the texture of social life was integral to their strategy. True understanding was therefore portrayed not as a negation of mundane understanding, but as its correction; as a rationalized, purified version of meanings which members of society strive to reach, but fail if not assisted. The wager was on the preference members of society would accord to views able to show scientific credentials. In the times of Marx, Weber or Mannheim the prestige of science was securely entrenched (inside the western civilization) and the role of experts institutionalized. It was hoped that communally anchored, relative outlooks would give way to the universal pronouncements of science with the same inevitability with which folk healing gave way to scientific medicine. The pattern would be repeated without fail if only the methodic interpretations worked out within social sciences were to claim and gain the rights already accorded to other sciences. In other words, the agreement reached by the community of social scientists would become the basis for universal agreement.

So far, this hope seems to come nowhere near fulfilment. The proliferation of methodically construed interpretations offered in the name of social science seems, if anything, to contribute further to the dispersion of opinions and resulting disagreements. In addition to conflicting interpretations of the meaning of modern society or social inequality, which have been with us for a considerable time, we have witnessed recently the birth of 'black' or 'feminist' sociologies. Not that society at large failed to follow an agreement reached by its social-scientific experts – that remains a rather remote prospect, as rifts and cleavages inside the social-scientific community show unabated tenacity.

The lack of consensus, particularly conspicuous if compared with the sciences of nature, seems to have deeper roots than the human and professional frailties of social scientists.

Each science is constituted by the practices of its practitioners. To say this is to admit a considerable autonomy for science, which provides social foundation to the authority of its findings. In this sense Galileo's reaching for the telescope and using it to challenge the popular view of celestial bodies may be viewed as the birth-date of science. From then on, and to an ever-growing degree, instruments managed and operated by scientists gave them access to realities which naked eye and unarmed ear could not reach. The conversation between men of science and laymen turned from a continuous battle of wits, in which a balance of power had to be established anew in each successive skirmish, into a teaching and learning process within an institutionalized framework of clearly defined roles and statuses. Each science which followed this path of development turned increasingly into a continuous discussion of events taking place in the scientific laboratory, events inconceivable without instruments operated and controlled by scientists. A particle accelerator is not standard equipment in the ordinary home. But the modern physicist's view of the structure of the atomic nucleus is thinkable only as an interpretation of events produced with the help of accelerators. The authority of interpretations proferred by physicists is socially founded on the autonomy of the practices to which these interpretations refer. Gaston Bachelard in his *Applied Rationalism* (1949) called the 'givens' of modern physics or chemistry 'reified theorems'. Indeed, the phenomena modern scientists investigate would not be present in nature if not for the scientific technology; they are not even natural consequences of the extra-laboratory universe. The 'new scientific intellectualism' has as its foundation '*la cité scientifique*' confined and tightly locked.

But this is clearly not (with a few exceptions) the situation of social sciences; in particular, not the situation of sociology as 'understanding' activity. It is not just that the 'laboratory' of sociologists is the wide society upon which they have little, if any, control. More importantly, the phenomena they study – the meanings – are facts to which they have no more privileged access than do laymen. No monopoly control of instruments makes an 'understanding sociologist's' field of study inaccessible to an ordinary member of the society. The pronouncements of the sociologists have the practice of such ordinary members, and not their own, as their referent. In addition, sociology is a reflection on practices which are themselves self-reflective (compare Giddens's notion of 'double hermeneutics'). *Understanding sociology, therefore, cannot help but be permanently engaged in a discourse with its own object: a discourse in which the object and the subject of study employ essentially the same resources.* If the truth of physicists is the derivative of agreement reached by the physicists regarding phenomena fully controlled by physicists, the truth of sociology is the derivative of an agreement reached (if at all) in the debate between sociologists and the objects of their study regarding phenomena whose control is shared between sociologists and their objects to the clear disadvantage of sociologists. *The truth of sociology has to be negotiated in the same way the ordinary agreement is*; more often than not, it is not the sociologists who set the rules of negotiation.

This seems the essential reason why the search for truth in the context of meaning-understanding seems to present problems immensely more complicated than a similar search in the context of causal explanation. This seems also the reason why a great number of sociologists tried (and still try) to disengage from common discourse by constructing a language which excludes references to meanings, or a language in which terms which apparently refer to meanings derive their sense fully from their logical relation to other terms of the same self-enclosed language (we have seen one attempt in the case of Parsons). For the same reason, however, accounts produced within such a language stop far short of gaining recognition similar to this of physicists' accounts. Unlike physical discourse, they have an 'outside' as well as an 'inside'; they are looked upon from this 'outside' and then perceived as just one of many competing interpretations none of which can make the case for its superiority apodictically convincing.

Sociologists who agree that the reference to meaning must be an integral part of any acceptable account of social phenomena may still insist on a privileged access to 'true understanding', claiming superiority for the analytical means employed by sociologists in comparison with those employed by laymen. We have surveyed different arguments which can be used to support this claim. For many theorists the thesis of the interpreter's privileged access to truth is equivalent to the proposition that the mundane relativism of outlooks and meanings can in principle be overcome. One of the first expressions of this belief was Schleiermacher's proposition concerning the hermeneutic superiority of the interpreter over, say, an artist in deciding the true meaning of the work of art. When subjected to further elaboration by Dilthey, the proposition revealed its weakness as an attempt to transcend relativism. From the idea of an ever-widening hermeneutic circle, or the equally evident fact that interpretations of cultural facts tend to be replaced sooner or later by interpretations which invoke a broader set of cultural phenomena, no clear way leads to a certainty that the hermeneutic circle will ever stop rotating and that some interpretation will be not just relatively 'broader' than the preceding one, but the broadest possible, and therefore final. This is a case of the general impossibility of arguing from even the best-tested empirical generalizations to apodictic truths. It is difficult to see how one can justify the belief in the end of relativity of understanding by arguing from the relative superiority (comprehensiveness, utility, dominance) of later over earlier interpretations.

In this respect, there has been little change since the times of Schleiermacher. We can see this in Ernest Gellner's recent argument against Winch's view that cultural facts can be understood only within their own 'forms of life' and that, therefore, correct interpretation of meanings must always remain relative. In order to prove that the seemingly insoluble problem of relativity of understanding has a solution, Gellner starts with 'the world as it really is' – and then proceeds from this empirical reality, allegedly exempt from hermeneutical treatment, thus:[3]

> The philosophical significance of the scientific-industrial 'form of life', whose rapid global diffusion is the main event of our time, is that for all practical purposes it does provide us with a solution of the problem of relativism. . . . The cognitive and technical superiority of one form of life is so manifest, and so loaded with implications for the satisfaction of human wants and needs – and, for better or worse, for power – that it simply cannot be questioned.

A number of objections can be raised against this argument. First, Gellner seems to assume that the technical-instrumental superiority of a civilization spills over its less technical aspects and assures, among others, its hermeneutic pre-eminence; but this is to beg the question not to answer it. Secondly, he seems to assume that the 'scientific-industrial form of life' is unified culturally as it is in its technical-scientific accomplishment, and that it offers therefore a homogeneous point of view from which one can observe and assess other forms of life; he overlooks the fact that inside one technical-scientific framework numerous, often conflicting, forms of life coexist which stubbornly resist 'scientific arbitration'. Thirdly, the argument begs other troublesome questions it was expected to solve: the superiority of the scientific-industrial form of life is defended in terms of values (satisfaction of human wants, power, global diffusion) which precisely this 'form of life' cherishes and considers superior. Its superiority, which was to be proved, has been therefore accepted as the central premise.

Most important, however, for our topic is another objection. The gist of Gellner's argument is that in so far as we accept the values of our civilization as measures of progress, we consider its current world dominance as confirmation that the historic conflict of outlooks and meanings tends to be resolved by the attainment of truth. This argument, however, could be used by any civilization with ecumenical tendencies, whatever its cognitive patterns and interpretations. Gellner's argument against relativism as such has been launched from the relative superiority of one historic form of life; in an indirect way, it can be read as a confirmation, rather than refutation, of relativity. It is not impossible to imagine the super-session of western civilization in its current form by another at present subordinate, and therefore, by Gellner's standard, considered inferior and left behind (remember 'barbarians' stealing ecumenical dominance from sophisticated Roman 'heathens'). As much as one cannot prove the apodictic validity of induction inductively, one cannot claim solution of the 'relativism problem' using proofs whose status clearly is historically relative.

We have not moved far beyond Schleiermacher's earnest but specu-lative hope. In order to pass from historically, socially and culturally relative understanding to an interpretation which can be accepted as conclusively and apodictically true, we need standards by which the validity of such understanding could be judged, standards which by definition ought to be external to any particular culture. It is not easy, however, to suggest standards which cannot be shown, with some effort, to be internal to a specific form of life. It seems as if we were moving in a vicious circle. It seems that under-standing is doomed to remain forever transient and relative. It seems that the roads of truth and understanding are unlikely ever to meet. It seems that interpretive sociology is condemned to relativism.

These suppositions are, to be sure, less shocking than the first impression they make on a reader used to the awe-inspiring image of science as a conversation with the absolute. They largely overlap with the findings of perhaps the most sophisticated of the available accounts of science, as presented by Karl Popper. According to Popper, science has developed only 'negative' standards: standards of procedure which may lead to a convincing refutation of a scientific theory. 'We can determine at most the falsity of theories.' The scientist is interested in theories not-yet-refuted because 'some of them *may* be true'. The progress of science consists, however, as far as its lasting and conclusive results are concerned, in discarding theories as untrue and at odds with new experience. The progress of science is, in its core, an endless effort to expose and eliminate false theories:

> By this method of elimination, we may hit upon a true theory. But in no case can the method *establish* its truth, even if it is true; for the number of *possibly* true theories remains infinite, at any time and after any number of crucial tests.... The actually proposed theories will, of course, be finite in number; and it may well happen that we refute all of them, and cannot think of a new one.

On the other hand, *among the theories actually proposed* there may be more than one which is not refuted at a time *t*, so that we may not know which of these we ought to prefer. . . .

The method which underlies the spectacular accomplishment of western science is negative rather than positive. Construction of new theories is essentially uncodified, and often unmethodical; one can arrive at a new theory by hunch, by a lucky coincidence, by an inexplicable flash of inspiration. (In Jacoby's words, discovery is a 'rape followed by seduction'.) Only the process of refutation is subject to strict and codifiable methods: 'The method described may be called the *critical method*. It is a method of trial and the elimination of errors, of proposing theories and submitting them to the severest tests we can design.' All this said and done, *'there is no assurance that we shall be able to make progress toward better theories'*. The best status a theory can hope for is to be a statement thus far unrefuted; never a statement unrefutable. What we can be sure of is that we have done our best to show that our theories are not true, but we have not succeeded; we can never be sure, with the same degree of certainty, that our theories are indeed true and will not be found to be false in the future. A supersession of a specific theory is not necessarily a step towards truth and, even if it happened to be, we would have no means of proving this.

The important point, however, is the following one: rejecting the naïve view of science as an activity not only hitting upon true theories but 'knowing for sure' that this is exactly what has happened in a given case, does not entail the denial of the crucial role played by the idea of truth in whatever practical success (however logically tentative) science can rightly boast. One could almost say that there would be no science if it were not for the ubiquitous presence of the idea of truth. This idea, however, makes its presence tangible as the constant pressure of an ideal; as, so to speak, an utopian horizon with an inexhaustible force of attraction. It remains a powerful factor guiding scientific activity (in line with other utopian ideals) as long as it is seen as an objective and not mistaken for a description of a specific state of things reached here and now. In Popper's words, the rules on which the activity called science are founded 'may be regarded as subject to the general *aim of rational discussion, which is to get nearer to the truth'*.[4]

So conceived rules of scientific activity, as long as they remain in the generalized form given in the above quotations, seem to apply to the search for 'true understanding' as well as they fit the pursuit of scientific laws. In both cases truth is an unrealistic objective if posited as a predicate of a hypothetical set of specific propositions about reality. In both cases, however, truth is crucial as the guiding principle of the on-going rational discussion, resulting every once in a while in rationally substantiated agreements. As a matter of fact, *if it were not for the ideal of truth as the supreme standard of belief, no agreed interpretation of meaning would be conceivable.* Truth is perhaps unachievable as a state of knowledge. But truth is indispensable for knowledge to exist.

Truth is indispensable as it guides the rules of rational discussion; while the pursuit of scientific laws, as well as the pursuit of objective understanding, can take place only within the context of their respective rational discussions, and only within these contexts have both function and sense.

Whatever passes for truth in each of the two contexts can only be relative to the historical, cultural and social parameters of a given discussion. This relativity is not, however, an attribute of the discussion as such and its structure. The pursuit of truth and objectivity, as guiding principles of human technical and practical activity – human work and communication – are anthropological, not historical features of human existence: they are transcendental conditions of the specifically human mode of existence.

The above idea has been forcefully articulated by the most prominent living heir of the 'Frankfurt School' in German social sciences – Jürgen Habermas. In Habermas's view, the notorious logical difficulties we encounter whenever we try to account for the relation between truth and understanding (as well as the relation between truth and empirical inquiry) stem from the fact that the rules which validate our interpretations and causal explanations are mistakenly located on the level of transcendental logic – conditions of pure theoretical reason in Kant's style. It has been repeatedly demonstrated that his 'conditions of knowledge as such' are insufficient to ground either the procedure of the hermeneutic circle or the subtle dialectic of theory and 'facts'. The difficulty ceases to be overwhelming, however, when one realizes and accepts that the validity of propositions turned out in the course of human technical and practical activity is grounded on transcendental conditions somewhat less abstract and apodictic than those of pure reason: on the conditions of specifically human being-in-the-world, which is predicated on human work and communication, the two unique, but universal features of the human species. In Habermas's words,[5]

Unlike transcendental logic, the logic of the natural and cultural sciences deals not with the properties of pure theoretical reason but with methodological rules for the organization of processes of inquiry. These rules no longer possess the status of pure transcendental rules. They have a transcendental function but arise from actual structures of human life: from structures of a species that reproduces its life both through learning process of socially organized labour and processes of mutual understanding in interactions mediated in ordinary language. . . . A transcendental subject is replaced by a *species* that reproduces itself under cultural conditions. . . .

These 'species transcendental' conditions have the structure of interests. The specifically human mode of self-reproduction or, rather, self-constitution, can be sustained only if two interests are consistently pursued: the technical and the practical.

The first manifests itself in the activity of work; the second in the activity of communication. The first is aimed at the control of nature, more specifically, at eliminating, or reducing, or counterbalancing the contingency contained in overwhelming natural forces. It tries to penetrate the order hiding behind the surface of contingency, with the possibility of predicting, and eventually of controlling, as the guiding objective. The truth is the norm which guards the pursuit of this objective. The cognitive reflection of the technical interest as manifested in work takes the shape of empirical-analytical sciences:[6]

Empirical-analytical sciences disclose reality insofar as it appears within the behavioural system of instrumental action. . . . They grasp reality with regard to technical control that, under specified conditions, is possible everywhere and at all times.

The second, practical, interest finds its cognitive reflection in cultural, 'understanding' sciences. This interest is continually generated by a situation in which many different forms of life co-exist, each providing its own framework for the interpretation of reality; the term 'form of life' is here understood widely, as any relatively distinct framework of interpretation starting from broad cultural systems and reaching up to biographically determined and unique 'selections of forms'. If empirical-analytical sciences are possible only on the assumption of the essential regularity and recurrence of certain patterns of work practice and its effects, *cultural sciences are possible only on the assumption that there is a broader basis of intersubjectivity which forms of life could share, that argument and eventually agreement between forms of life is therefore attainable*. The truth, in this case, is the norm which guides the search for agreement. As Habermas put it, hermeneutic statements 'grasp interpretations of reality with regard to possible intersubjectivity of action-orienting mutual understanding specific to a given hermeneutic starting point'.[7] If empirical-analytical sciences facilitate technical control over processes of work, hermeneutic sciences assist the practice of communication and the effort of reaching agreement.

We have seen already that the methods of empirical-analytical sciences cannot guarantee the truth of scientific propositions; they can only guarantee that false statements will eventually be exposed and rejected. What scientific method – the method of criticism – demonstrates beyond all doubt is that under certain conditions related propositions are invalid; and the method consists, above all, in spelling out these conditions of invalidation. The method of sociological hermeneutics cannot hope for more. It will not guarantee the truth of intersubjective agreement; it will not ground the faith that the concerted action evidently resulting from the process of negotiation reflects a true consensus regarding meanings. *The method of sociological hermeneutics*, like that of empirical-analytical science, *can serve the practice of communication only in its negative capacity, as the method of criticism. It can expose some conditions of communication which lead to an invalid, untrue consensus.*

To understand is to 'know how to go on'; the intersubjective effort of mutual understanding is aimed objectively at a reciprocal acceptance of norms which will eventually guide the behaviour of negotiating partners. If the discourses which constitute empirical-analytical science are concerned with grounding (providing validity, legitimations of) assertions, practical discourses are, ideally, concerned with grounding (providing a rational argument in favour of) norms of conduct. We have seen how ethnomethodology demonstrated this conduct-forming objective of meaning-negotiation: a verbal exchange, apparently concerned with objects 'out there', leads to the establishment, between the conversationalists, of a pattern of mutual relations. Discussing the same matter in a different theoretical context, Gregory Bateson described the human system of communication as using 'a syntax and category system appropriate for the discussion of things that can be handled, while really discussing the patterns and contingencies of relationship'.[8] If the subject-matter of the two types of discourse differ, the conditions of their rationality do not. In both cases, the results of the discourse have to be rejected as invalid if the discourse fails to provide rational grounds for the acceptance of its propositions.

Rational discourse, in particular, means that

validity claims of assertions, recommendations, or warnings are the exclusive object of discussion; that participants, themes and contributions are not restricted except with reference to the goal of testing the validity claims in question; that no force except that of the better argument is exercised; and that, as a result, all motives except that of the cooperative search for truth are excluded.

Unless these conditions are present in full, one cannot accept the resulting consensus as reflecting 'rational will'.[9] In other words, one cannot accept the manifest understanding as 'true' if the preceding negotiations glossed over the validity ground of the advocated (and eventually accepted) norms of conduct; if those grounds were 'bracketed' and not allowed to come under the argumentative scrutiny of the participants. If, for example, participants have been exhorted to obey the advocated norms not on their merit, but because of the support lent by a powerful authority, or if the participants were prevented from considering alternative norms and interpretations.

The second group of conditions of rational discourse refer to the quality of participation:[10]

Since all those affected have, in principle, at least the chance to participate in the practical deliberation, the 'rationality' of the discursively formed will consists in the fact that the reciprocal behavioural expectations raised to normative status accord validity to a *common* interest ascertained *without* deception. The interest is common because the constraint-free consensus permits only what *all* can want; it is free of deception because even the interpretations of needs in which *each individual* must be able to recognize what he wants become the object of discursive will-formation. The discursively formed will may be called 'rational' because the formal properties of discourse and of the deliberative situation sufficiently guarantee that a consensus can arise only through appropriately interpreted, *generalizable* interests, by which I mean needs *that can be communicatively shared.*

It is only the equal chance to participate in the discourse which can, at least potentially, prevent a consensus being based on deception. No alleged interest, whether public or private, is exempt from a discussion in which all the affected have the right to participate on an equal footing (differentiated only by the power of relevant argument). In a rational discourse, there are *only* participants – and all those concerned *are* participants.

It is only too easy to demonstrate the unreality of the 'rational discourse' as described by Habermas. No such discourse has ever taken place, except for, perhaps, small 'primary groups' little advanced on the road to institutionalization. It is particularly difficult to visualize a discourse which answers Habermas's description, taking place on the scale of a modern complex society. To those eager to dismiss the description on the ground of its unreality, two comments are, however, in order.

First, the 'rational discourse' model is no more 'utopian' (or, alternatively, no less 'realistic') than, say, the model of ideal experiment or canons of inductive reasoning. Actual experiments approximate the ideal model in various degrees, but never meet in full the stern requirement of full control over conditions or of 'other things being equal'. Similarly, inductive conclusions are in practice reached and provisionally accepted long before the 'uniqueness' of a difference, or the commonality of a common factor, has been (if at all) proved. The rational discourse model, like all other model descriptions of postulated rules of science, is not a generalization of practice, but the definition of its idealized horizon. It is the ensuing re-projection of this ideal upon actual practices which provides the standard of evaluation of results, as well as exerting pressure towards further improvement.

Secondly, Habermas's model is admittedly a statement of the transcendental conditions of rationally attained consensus (understanding which can be considered true). Its role does not consist of informing us what the actual meaning-negotiations are like, but what the circumstances are in which intersubjective negotiations could lead to a rational agreement. In practice, the model brings into focus the empirical gap between actual communication and the ideal conditions of rational debate. Its heuristic power, like the power of all scientific methodology, lies ultimately in its role of a recipe for criticism. *Only thanks to the painstaking analysis of the transcendental conditions of rational agreement can we perceive actual consensus as resulting from a distorted communication: as, consequently, a false consensus.* Thanks to the same analysis, we know how to attempt to bring the actual debate closer to the conditions of rationality.

Habermas's model of rational agreement is not, therefore, to be dismissed lightly. On the contrary, it brings the methodology of understanding sciences as close to the ideal of truth-guided criticism as the rules of experimental practice brought empirical-analytic sciences.

It puts, however, the problem of 'true understanding' and its grounding in a different light. The search for such a grounding has been heretofore guided by a rather superficial similarity with the status of empirical-analytic sciences: it has been hoped that the truth of understanding will eventually be grounded fully in the practices of the interpreters, who will therefore acquire a well-nigh monopolistic authority in the matters of true interpretation, akin to the authority enjoyed in their field by natural scientists. Habermas's model dashes such hopes. The model demonstrates that the rationality of discourse in cultural sciences, comparable to that of empirical-analytical sciences, cannot be codified without reference to the social dimensions of the debate; that, in other words, *the epistemology of hermeneutics cannot be detached from the sociology of communication.* If social scientists were to usurp the right to judge the veracity of meanings and then to present their decisions as verdicts supported by the authority of science, there would be just another case of distorted communication, i.e. a violation of the only rules which could, in the conditions of hermeneutics, lead to truth. Achievement of true understanding depends on much more than the methods operated and controlled by hermeneuticians. It depends, in the first place, on the structure of the social situation in which the negotiation of meaning takes place and from which the ensuing consensus results. It requires, above all other things, that the grounds of validity of the action-oriented meanings are discussed openly and that they are discussed, with equal rights, by all concerned. It requires, in other words, an operation committed upon society, and not just upon practices of the experts.

The paramount obstacle standing in the way of true consensus is the structure of dominance, which defies both conditions of rational agreement. The discussion of the grounds of validity of behavioural norms is suppressed, replaced by sacred or secular, but always ideological legitimations of the authority of the source. (According to Michel Foucault, constitutive parts of the 'discursive formation' responsible for the socially accepted meanings are the question, 'Who is speaking? Who, among the totality of speaking individuals, is accorded the right to use this sort of language?' and the 'institutional sites' from which contributions to the discourse are made.[11] This is, in Habermas's theory, an attribute of a distorted communication; an attribute which most ethnomethodologists tend to leave out of sight altogether.) And the active and passive, sender's and recipient's, roles in the debate are clear-cut and kept separate. The situation, on the whole, is far from the ideal one in which 'no force except that of a better argument is exercised'.

Important conclusions follow for a sociology which wants to be of service to the civilization whose foremost value is the attainment of rational consensus – agreement grounded in truth. Sociology will not live up to this standard if it collapses the 'upper floor' of its 'double hermeneutics' into the lower: if it confines its task to the comprehending and elaborating upon the current societally attained consensus, that is a consensus attained and sustained in conditions unpropitious for rational discourse. Neither will it live up to its standard if it forgets about the 'ground floor' of its hermeneutics and regards its own activity as unconfined by mundane consensus and, consequently, by social conditions which do not provide for rational discourse; that is, if it regards its own activity as the sole grounding against which the standards of truth could be measured. The universal validity (truth) of agreed understanding, as the compelling ideal of our civilization, can be well served by such a sociology, which aims at an evolutionary theory showing the way which the society could follow toward conditions progressively emancipated from obstacles to rational agreement.

The role of social scientists can be crucial not only in developing such a theory (obviously their task). They can play a prominent role in facilitating its actualization, i.e. bringing into being conditions of true understanding. Again, their role will not be essentially unlike that played by natural scientists. The most spectacular contribution made by empirical-analytical sciences to human life is in the constant scientific critique of human technical-instrumental activity. Understanding sciences' contribution can consist in a critique of social practice. Laying bare the elements of distortion in the situation of discourse, these sciences can play their part in the ever-growing approximation to the conditions of rational society.

Standards of truth by which the content of consensus can be judged (as distinct from the standards of acceptance internal to a given cultural, historical and social setting) *can be only the ideal standards of rational discourse.*

To sum up: Methods of the scientific activity known as sociology have to take into account the fact that – unlike in sciences which treat their object as nature – negotiation of agreement in sociology includes its objects as 'recognized autonomous subjects'. Sociology cannot help but be permanently engaged in discourse with its own object; in the course of this discourse, both 'objects' and 'subjects' employ essentially the same resources. Consensus in sociology is, therefore, pursued in a communal negotiation whose scale extends beyond the boundaries of professional sociology proper.

Sociology's concern with objective (true) understanding entails, consequently, not only preoccupation with the rules of agreement between sociologists, but an intense interest in the conditions which underlie the attainment of consensus in society at large. Sociology is 'socially engaged' not in spite of, or in violation of, its truth-seeking motives, but in consequence of those motives. Conversely, sociology may pursue its aim of true, as distinct from merely consensual, understanding only thanks to its active engagement with the task of promotion of equal opportunity and democracy.

The specifically sociological form of such an engagement can only consist in the application of the general scientific method of criticism to the scrutiny of the consensus reached in society. In the same way as science employs the model of ideal experiment to expose and eventually eliminate flaws in the practice of scientists, so sociology employs the model of ideal communication to lay bare and eventually help to eliminate the flaws in the practice of societal consensus.

When absorbed by social science and adapted to its tasks, epistomology of hermeneutics is transformed into sociology of communal agreement in general, spurious and true consensus in particular. Methodology of true interpretation – the major concern of hermeneutics – is transformed into the theory of social structure which ideally facilitates unimpaired communication and genuine universalization of forms of life. *The practical success of sociology so understood can be only measured by the degree to which the opposition between consensus and truth is gradually reduced, and the problem of understanding as an activity distinct from communal life gradually disappears.*

Notes

Some alternative US and UK editions, where appropriate, are indicated in square brackets: [   ]. The pagination of US and UK editions may differ.

Introduction: the challenge of hermeneutics (pp. 7–22)

1. Anthony Giddens, *New Rules of Sociological Method*, Hutchinson, London [Basic, New York], 1976, p. 12.
2. ibid., p. 13.
3. Sir Isaiah Berlin, 'Foreword' to Friedrich Meinecke, *Historism*, Routledge & Kegan Paul, London, 1972, pp. ix–x.
4. Georg Wilhelm Friedrich Hegel, trans. J. Sibree, *The Philosophy of History*, Dover, New York, 1956, pp. 25, 78, 456–7.

1 The rise of hermeneutics

1. cf. Karl J. Weintraub, *Visions of Culture*, University of Chicago Press, Chicago and London, 1966, p. 7.
2. Quoted after Hans Kohn, *The Mind of Germany*, Harper, New York, 1965, p. 60.
3. Fritz Stern, *The Politics of Cultural Despair*, Doubleday, New York, 1965, pp. 338–9.
4. Eric Newton, *The Romantic Rebellion*, Shocken, New York [Longman, London], 1964, p. 56.
5. Joachim Wach, *Das Verstehen, Grundzüge einer Geschichte der hermeneutischen Theorie in 19. Jahrhundert*, 3 vols., J. C. B. Mohr (Paul Siebeck), Tübingen, 1926.
6. cf. Wach, vol. 1, p. 33.
7. ibid., p. 38.
8. ibid., p. 92.
9. Hans Georg Gadamer, trans. Garren Burden and John Cumming,

Truth and Method, Sheed & Ward, London [Seabury, New York], 1975, p. 164.

10. Wilhelm Dilthey, *Der Aufbau der Geschichtlichen Welt in den Giesteswissenschaften*, in *Gesammelte Schriften*, vol. 7, B. G. Teubner, Leipzig and Berlin, 1927, p. 191.

11. Rudolph A. Makkreel, *Dilthey, Philosopher of the Human Studies*, Princeton University Press, Princeton, 1975, p. 248.

12. Fritz Medicus, 'On the objectivity of historical knowledge', in Raymond Klibansky and H. J. Paton (eds.), *Philosophy and History; Essays Presented to Ernst Cassirer*, Clarendon, Oxford, 1936, p. 138.

13. Dilthey, p. 259.

14. Jose Ortega y Gasset, 'History as a system', in *Philosophy and History*, p. 300.

15. Dilthey, p. 191.

16. ibid., p. 205.

17. ibid.

18. ibid., p. 206.

19. ibid., p. 212.

20. ibid., p. 214.

21. ibid., p. 215.

22. ibid., p. 225.

23. ibid., p. 227.

24. ibid., p. 233.

25. Benedetto Croce, trans. Cecil Sprigge, *Philosophy, Poetry, History; An Anthology of Essays*, Oxford University Press, Oxford and New York, 1966, pp. 561, 563.

26. Raffaello Franchini, *La teoria della storia di Benedetto Croce*, Morano, Naples, n.d. (*c.* 1968), pp. 96, 98.

27. Benedetto Croce, trans. Douglas Ainslie, *Theory and History of Historiography*, Harrap, London, 1921, pp. 12, 26.

28. R. G. Collingwood, *The Idea of History*, Oxford University Press, Oxford and New York, 1946 (1973 ed.), pp. 218, 219, 230.

29. ibid., p. 230.

30. ibid., p. 248.

31. Johann Huizinga, trans. D. R. Cousin, 'A definition of the concept of history', in *Philosophy and History*, p. 7.

32. ibid., pp. 8–10.

2   Understanding as the work of history: Karl Marx

1. Karl Marx, trans. Rodney Livingstone and Gregor Benton,

Early Writings, Penguin, Harmondsworth [Random House, New York], 1975, p. 209.

2. ibid., p. 384.

3. ibid., p. 393.

4. ibid., p. 87.

5. ibid., p. 191.

6. ibid., p. 354.

7. ibid., p. 366.

8. ibid., p. 124.

9. ibid., pp. 137, 145.

10. ibid., p. 356.

11. Marx, trans. Martin Nicolaus, *Grundrisse*, Penguin, Harmondsworth, 1973 [Random House, New York, 1974], pp. 163–5.

12. Karl Marx and Friedrich Engels, trans. T. B. Bottomore, in Karl Marx, ed. T. B. Bottomore and Maximilian Rubel, *Selected Writings in Sociology and Social Philosophy*, Penguin, Harmondsworth, 1963 [McGraw-Hill, New York, 1964], p. 95.

13. Karl Marx, *Capital*, vol. 1, in *Selected Writings*, pp. 97–8.

14. *Early Writings*, pp. 158–9.

15. ibid., pp. 244–5.

16. ibid., p. 393.

17. ibid., p. 252.

18. Karl Marx, 'Preface to *A Contribution to the Critique of Political Economy*', in *Selected Writings*, p. 68.

19. Marx, *Grundrisse*, p. 104.

20. Marx, *Capital*, vol. 1, in *Selected Writings*, p. 100.

21. Marx, *Grundrisse*, p. 351.

22. Marx, 'German ideology', in *Selected Writings*, p. 72.

23. Marx, *Grundrisse*, p. 107.

24. Marx, *Early Writings*, p. 350.

25. ibid., p. 350.

26. ibid., p. 335.

3 Understanding as the work of history: Max Weber

1. Max Weber, trans. Guy Oates, *Roscher and Knies; The Logical Problems of Historical Economics*, Free Press, New York, 1975, pp. 128–9, 142, 147–8, 151.

2. Max Weber, ed. Talcott Parsons, *The Theory of Social and Economic Organization*, Free Press, New York, 1969, p. 101;

Wirtschaft und Gesellschaft, J. C. B. Mohr (Paul Siebeck), Tübingen, 1956, vol. 1, p. 6.

3. Weber, *Theory of Organization*, p. 103.

4. ibid., p. 104.

5. Max Weber, ed. Eduard Baumgarten, *Werk und Person; Dokumente ausgewählt u. kommentiert von Eduard Baumgarten*, J. C. B. Mohr (Paul Siebeck), Tübingen, 1964, p. 404.

6. ibid., p. 107.

7. Max Weber, ed. H. H. Gerth and C. Wright Mills, *From Max Weber*, Routledge & Kegan Paul, London, 1970 [Oxford University Press, New York, 1946], p. 145.

8. Weber, *Werk und Person*, p. 121.

9. ibid., p. 653.

10. Weber, *From Max Weber*, pp. 155–6.

11. Talcott Parsons, in Otto Stammer (ed.), *Max Weber and Sociology Today*, Blackwell, Oxford [Harper & Row, New York], 1971, p. 38.

12. ibid., p. 33.

13. Max Weber, *The Protestant Ethic and the Spirit of Capitalism*, Allen & Unwin, London [Scribner, New York], 1930, p. 13.

14. Ephraim Fischoff, 'The history of a controversy', *Social Research*, vol. 11, 1944, pp. 61–77.

15. Wolfgang J. Mommsen, *The Age of Bureaucracy*, Blackwell, Oxford [Harper & Row, New York], 1974, pp. 12–13.

16. Weber, *Protestant Ethic*, pp. 16–18.

17. Weber, *From Max Weber*, p. 155.

18. Max Weber, trans. Edward A. Shils and Henry A. Finch, *The Methodology of the Social Sciences*, Free Press, New York, 1949, pp. 37–8.

19. ibid., p. 57.

20. ibid., pp. 52–3.

21. Weber, *Theory of Organization*, pp. 90, 92.

22. ibid., p. 93 (Weber, *Wirtschaft und Gesellschaft*, p. 3).

23. ibid., pp. 98, 99.

24. ibid., pp. 114–15.

25. ibid., pp. 112–13.

26. ibid., p. 95.

27. ibid., p. 96.

28. ibid., pp. 112, 111, 97.

29. ibid., p. 92.

30. Arun Sahay, 'The importance of Weber's methodology in

sociological explanation', in Arun Sahay (ed.), *Max Weber and Modern Sociology*, Routledge & Kegan Paul, London and Boston, 1971, p. 68.

31. cf. John Rex, 'Typology and objectivity, a comment on Weber's four sociological methods', in *Max Weber and Modern Sociology*, pp. 17–18.

32. *Max Weber and Sociology Today*, p. 52.

33. ibid., p. 53.

34. ibid., p. 65.

4 Understanding as the work of history: Karl Mannheim

1. Karl Mannheim, *Essays on the Sociology of Knowledge*, Routledge & Kegan Paul, London [Oxford University Press, New York], 1952, p. 44.

2. cf. ibid., p. 53.

3. Karl Mannheim, *Essays on Sociology and Social Psychology*, Routledge & Kegan Paul, London [Oxford University Press, New York], 1953, pp. 85–6.

4. Mannheim, *Essays on the Sociology of Knowledge*, p. 55.

5. ibid., pp. 55–6.

6. ibid., p. 60.

7. ibid., p. 61.

8. ibid., p. 62.

9. ibid., p. 78.

10. Mannheim, *Essays on Sociology and Social Psychology*, p. 75.

11. Ernst Grünwald, 'Systematic analyses', in James E. Curtis and John W. Petras (eds.), *The Sociology of Knowledge, a Reader*, Duckworth, London [Praeger, New York], 1970, p. 206.

12. Mannheim, *Essays in Sociology and Social Psychology*, p. 241.

13. ibid., p. 239.

14. Karl Mannheim, *Ideology and Utopia; Introduction to the Sociology of Knowledge*, Routledge & Kegan Paul, London, 1960 [Harcourt Brace Jovanovich, New York, 1955], p. 1.

15. Karl Mannheim, *Essays on the Sociology of Culture*, Routledge & Kegan Paul, London [Oxford University Press, New York], 1956, pp. 117–18.

16. ibid., p. 101.

17. Mannheim, *Ideology and Utopia*, pp. 7–8.

18. ibid., p. 10.

19. ibid., p. 11.

20. ibid., p. 141.
21. ibid., p. 71.
22. Florian Znaniecki, *Cultural Sciences: Their Origin and Development*, University of Illinois Press, Urbana and London, 1963, p. 133.
23. Mannheim, *Ideology and Utopia*, p. 74.
24. ibid., p. 84.
25. ibid., pp. 86, 87.
26. ibid., p. 69.
27. ibid., p. 26.
28. ibid., p. 105.
29. ibid., pp. 52, 117.
30. ibid., p. 72.
31. ibid., p. 93.
32. ibid., pp. 139, 140.
33. Mannheim, *Essays on the Sociology of Culture*, p. 105.
34. Mannheim, *Ideology and Utopia*, p. 143.
35. Mannheim, *Essays on the Sociology of Culture*, p. 106.

5 Understanding as the work of reason: Edmund Husserl

1. Karl R. Popper, trans. Glyn Adey and David Frisby, 'The logic of the social sciences', in Theodor Adorno *et al.*, *The Positivist Dispute in German Sociology*, Heinemann, London, 1976, p. 9.
2. ibid., p. 104.
3. Leszek Kolakowski, *Husserl and the Search for Certitude*, Yale University Press, New Haven, 1975, pp. 28, 29.
4. Plato, trans. W. H. D. Rouse, *The Republic*, 514 a–517 b.
5. Rene Descartes, trans. Elisabeth S. Haldane and G. R. T. Ross, *Meditations on First Philosophy*, Meditation 1.
6. cf. Edmund Husserl, 'Ideen zu einer reinen Phänomenologie und Phänomenologischen Philosophie (Ideen I)', first published in *Jahrbuch für Philosophie und Phänomenologische Forschung*, 1913, part 2, para. 30.
7. Hans Blumenberg, trans. Theodore Kisiel, 'The life-world and the concept of reality', in Lester E. Embree (ed.), *Life-World and Consciousness, Essays for Aron Gurwitch*, Northwestern University Press, Evanston, 1972, p. 431.
8. ibid., p. 432.
9. Edmund Husserl, *Erste Philosophie* (orig. 1923–4), *Husserliana*, vol. 8, Martinus Nijhoff, The Hague, 1959, pp. 344, 154.

10. cf. Husserl, *Ideen* . . . , part 2, para. 32.
11. cf. Edmund Husserl, *The Paris Lectures* (orig. 1907), Martinus Nijhoff, The Hague, 1967, pp. 5–9.
12. Marvin Farber, *The Aims of Phenomenology*, Harper & Row, New York and London, 1966, p. 76.
13. Emmanuel Levinas, trans. André Orianne, *The Theory of Intuition in Husserl's Phenomenology*, Northwestern University Press, Evanston, 1973, p. 149.
14. cf. Husserl, *Ideen* . . . , part 2, para. 57.
15. Quentin Lauer, *Phenomenology, its Genesis and Prospects*, Harper & Row, New York, 1965, p. 36.
16. cf. Husserl, *Ideen* . . . , part 2, para. 29.
17. Edmund Husserl, trans. Quentin Lauer, *Phenomenology and the Crisis of Philosophy*, Harper & Row, New York and London, 1965, pp. 141–2.
18. ibid., p. 143.
19. Robert Sokolowski, 'Husserl's protreptic', in *Life-World and Consciousness*, p. 72.
20. Husserl, *Phenomenology and the Crisis of Philosophy*, pp. 166–7.
21. Quoted by Lauer, p. 69.
22. Kolakowski, p. 54.
23. Marvin Farber, 'On the meaning of radical reflection', in *Edmund Husserl 1859–1959, recueil commémoratif à l'occasion du centenaire de la naissance du philosophe*, Martinus Nijhoff, The Hague, 1959, p. 156.
24. Alfred Schutz, 'Husserl's importance for the social sciences', in *Edmund Husserl, 1859–1959*, p. 88.
25. There is more on this subject in Z. Bauman, *Towards a Critical Sociology*, Routledge & Kegan Paul, London and Boston, 1976, pp. 49–52.
26. cf. Edward G. Ballard, 'On the method of phenomenological reduction', in *Life-World and Consciousness*.
27. Schutz, p. 93.
28. Maurice Natanson, *Literature, Philosophy, and the Social Sciences*, Martinus Nijhoff, The Hague, 1962, pp. 157, 165.
29. Paul Ricoeur, trans. Kathleen McLaughlin, *The Conflict of Interpretations, Essays in Hermeneutics*, Northwestern University Press, Evanston, 1974, p. 9.

6 Understanding as the work of reason: Talcott Parsons

1. Talcott Parsons, *The Structure of Social Action*, Free Press, Glencoe [Allen & Unwin, London], 1949, p. 59.
2. ibid., p. 64.
3. ibid., p. 67.
4. ibid., pp. 44–5.
5. ibid., p. 589.
6. ibid., p. 46.
7. ibid., p. 47.
8. ibid., p. 48.
9. ibid., p. 49.
10. Talcott Parsons and Edward A. Shils (eds.), *Toward a General Theory of Action; Theoretical Foundation for the Social Sciences*, Harper & Row, New York and London, 1962, p. 4.
11. Talcott Parsons, *The Social System*, Routledge & Kegan Paul, London, 1970 [Free Press, New York, 1964], p. 4.
12. Parsons, *Structure of Social Action*, pp. 701, 700.
13. ibid., p. 733.
14. ibid.
15. ibid., p. 24.
16. Parsons and Shils, pp. 24–5.
17. Parsons, *Structure of Social Action*, pp. 750–1.
18. Parsons and Shils, p. 14.
19. ibid., p. 16.
20. ibid., p. 23.
21. Parsons, *Social System*, pp. 5–6.
22. Parsons, *Structure of Social Action*, pp. 752, 753.
23. Parsons and Shils, p. 24.
24. ibid., p. 25.
25. ibid., p. 54.

7 Understanding as the work of life: Martin Heidegger

1. Martin Heidegger, *Sein und Zeit*, 6th ed., Neomarius Verlag, Tübingen, 1949 (first published in the *Jahrbüch für Philosophie und Phänomenologische Forschung*, 1926), para. 28.
2. Martin Heidegger, trans. Ralph Manheim, *An Introduction to Metaphysics*, Yale University Press, New Haven and London, 1959, pp. 14–15.

3. ibid., p. 102.

4. ibid., p. 191.

5. Samuel J. Thodes, 'Sensuous abstraction and the abstract sense of reality', in James M. Edie (ed.), *New Essays in Phenomenology*, Quadrangle, Chicago, 1969, p. 17.

6. Cornelis van Peursen, 'Some remarks on the Ego in the phenomenology of Husserl', in *For Roman Ingarden, Nine Essays in Phenomenology*, Martinus Nijhoff, The Hague, 1959, p. 39.

7. Martin Heidegger, trans. Terence Malick, *The Essence of Reasons*, Northwestern University Press, Evanston, 1969, p. 43.

8. Repeated in Heidegger, *Introduction to Metaphysics*, p. 49.

9. cf. M. H. Abrams, *The Mirror and the Lamp*, Oxford University Press, Oxford, 1953. Quoted in R. Furst, *Romanticism in Perspective*, Macmillan, London, 1969, p. 128.

10. M. Bowra, *The Heritage of Symbolism*, Macmillan, London, 1959 [St Martin, New York, 1943], p. 230.

11. Quoted in Hoxie Neal Fairchild, *The Noble Savage*, Columbia University Press, New York, 1928, p. 504.

12. Magda King, *Heidegger's Philosophy*, Basil Blackwell, Oxford, 1964, p. 93.

13. Michael Gelven, *A Commentary on Heidegger's 'Being and Time'*, Harper & Row, New York and London, 1970, pp. 126, 128.

14. Heidegger, *Sein und Zeit*, para. 24.

15. Arland Ussher, *Journey through Dread*, Devin-Adair, New York, 1955, p. 80.

16. cf. Vincent Vycinas, *Earth and Gods*, Martinus Nijhoff, The Hague, 1969, pp. 36–7.

17. Heidegger, *Sein und Zeit*, para. 18.

18. cf. ibid., paras. 35–8.

19. King, p. 48.

20. Ludwig Landgrebe, trans. Kurt P. Reinhardt, *Major Problems in Contemporary European Philosophy, From Dilthey to Heidegger*, Frederick Ungar, New York, 1966, p. 119.

21. Thomas Langan, *The Meaning of Heidegger*, Routledge & Kegan Paul, London [Columbia University Press, New York], 1959, p. 58.

22. cf. Heidegger, *Sein und Zeit*, paras. 58–60.

23. Hans Georg Gadamer, trans. P. Christopher Smith, *Hegel's Dialectic; Five Hermeneutical Studies*, Yale University Press, New Haven and London, 1976, p. 115.

8   Understanding as the work of life: from Schutz to ethnomethodology

1. Theodor W. Adorno *et al.*, *The Positivist Dispute in German Sociology*, Heinemann, London, 1976, pp. 93–5.
2. Harold Garfinkel, *Studies in Ethnomethodology*, Prentice Hall, Englewood Cliffs and London, 1967, pp. 27–8.
3. Alfred Schutz, *Collected Papers*, Martinus Nijhoff, The Hague, 1967, vol. 1, p. 127.
4. ibid., p. 132.
5. ibid., vol. 2, p. 10.
6. Alfred Schutz and Thomas Luckmann, trans. Richard M. Zaner and H. Tristram Engelhardt Jr, *The Structures of the Life-World*, Heinemann, London, 1974 [Northwestern University Press, Evanston, 1973], pp. 4, 5.
7. Schutz, *Collected Papers*, vol. 1, pp. 343–4.
8. Alfred Schutz, ed. Richard M. Zaner, *Reflections on the Problem of Relevance*, Yale University Press, New Haven and London, 1970, pp. 139–40.
9. Aaron V. Cicourel, *Cognitive Sociology*, Penguin, Harmondsworth [Free Press, New York], 1973, p. 40.
10. Ludwig Wittgenstein, trans. G. E. H. Anscombe, *Philosophical Investigations*, Blackwell, Oxford, 1953, pp. 27^e, 42^e, 61^e, 63^e.
11. Schutz and Luckmann, pp. 15, 16.
12. ibid., p. 17.
13. Florian Znaniecki, *The Method of Sociology*, Octagon, New York, 1968, p. 37.
14. Immanuel Kant, trans. J. M. D. Meiklejohn, *Critique of Pure Reason*, Dutton, New York [Dent, London], 1969, pp. 26, 27, 38.
15. ibid., p. 71.
16. Schutz and Luckmann, p. 6.
17. ibid., p. 36 ff.
18. ibid., pp. 7, 9, 261–2, 263, 264.
19. ibid., p. 109.
20. ibid., p. 101.
21. Garfinkel, pp. 3, 14.
22. Alan Blum, *Theorizing*, Heinemann, London [Humanities, New York], 1974, p. 21.
23. Garfinkel, pp. 30, 31.
24. Peter McHugh *et al.*, *On the Beginning of Social Inquiry*, Routledge & Kegan Paul, London and Boston, 1974, pp. 2–3.

9 Understanding as expansion of the form of life

1. Arthur Schopenhauer, trans. E. F. J. Payne, *Parerga and Paralipomena*, vol. 2, Clarendon Press, Oxford and New York, 1974, p. 291.

2. Sigmund Freud, trans. Joan Riviere, *Civilisation and its Discontents*, Hogarth Press, London, 1973, p. 13.

3. ibid., p. 30.

4. Peter L. Berger, 'Identity as a problem in the sociology of knowledge', in Gunther W. Remmling (ed.), *Towards the Sociology of Knowledge*, Routledge & Kegan Paul, London, 1973, p. 275.

5. cf. Wladyslaw Tatarkiewicz, *O Doskonalosci* (On Perfection), Panstowe Wydawnictwo Naukowe, Warsaw, 1976, p. 7.

6. There is more on this notion in Z. Bauman, *Culture As Praxis*, Routledge & Kegan Paul, London and Boston, 1973, chapter 1.

7. Gabrel Tarde, *Le Lois de l'imitation*, Alcan, Paris, 1890, p. 248.

8. W. McDougall, *An Introduction to Social Psychology*, Methuen, London [Milford, Kennebunkport], 1928 (orig. ed. 1908), p. 290 ff.

9. The quotations from Montaigne and Pascal, along with others relevant to the topic, can be found in the excellent anthology compiled by J. S. Slotkin, *Readings in Early Anthropology*, Methuen, London, 1965.

10. Karl R. Popper, *The Poverty of Historicism*, Harper, New York, 1964 [Routledge & Kegan Paul, London, 1960], p. 133.

11. Albrecht Wellmer, trans. John Cumming, *Critical Theory of Society*, Herder & Herder, New York, 1971, p. 20.

12. Hans Georg Gadamer, trans. Garrett Barden and John Cumming, *Truth and Method*, Sheed & Ward, London [Seabury, New York], 1975, p. 231.

13. Emile Benveniste, 'Nature de signe linguistique', in Eric P. Hemp, Fred W. Householder and Robert Austerlitz (eds.), *Readings in Linguistics*, vol. 2, Chicago University Press, Chicago, 1966, p. 105.

14. Quoted in Maurice Leroy, trans. Glanville Price, *The Main Trends in Modern Linguistics*, Blackwell, Oxford, 1967, p. 96.

15. Peter Winch, *The Idea of Social Science and its Relationship to Philosophy*, Routledge & Kegan Paul, London [Humanities, New York], 1967, p. 27.

16. cf. Spinoza, *Ethics*, Theorem XXXIII.

17. Winch, p. 32.

18. Keith Gunderson, 'The imitation game', in Alan Ross Andersson

(ed.), *Minds and Machines*, Prentice Hall, Englewood Cliffs, 1964, p. 64.

19. A. M. Turing, 'Computing machinery and intelligence', in *Minds and Machines*.

20. John Lyons, 'Human language', in Robert A. Hinde (ed.), *Non-Verbal Communication*, Cambridge University Press, London and New York, 1975, p. 53.

21. Ludwig Wittgenstein, *The Blue and Brown Books*, Blackwell, Oxford, 1975 [Barnes & Noble, New York, 1969], pp. 42, 43, 65.

22. ibid., p. 27.

23. Claude Lévi-Strauss, trans. Monique Layton, *Structural Anthropology*, vol. 2, Allen Lane, London, 1977 [Basic, New York, 1976], p. 55.

Claude Lévi-Strauss, trans. C. Jacobson and B. G. Schoeph, *Structural Anthropology*, Basic, New York, 1963 [Allen Lane, London, 1968], p. 17.

24. Claude Lévi-Strauss, trans. S. O. and R. A. Paul, *The Scope of Anthropology*, Cape, London, 1967 [Grossman, New York, 1968], p. 44.

25. ibid., p. 45.

26. ibid., p. 15.

27. Claude Lévi-Strauss, *The Savage Mind*, University of Chicago Press, Chicago [Weidenfeld & Nicolson, London], 1966, p. 255.

28. ibid.

29. ibid., p. 257.

30. Anthony Giddens, *New Rules of Sociological Method*, Hutchinson, London [Basic, New York], 1976, p. 18.

31. ibid., p. 158.

10   Consensus and truth

1. Jorge Luis Borges, *Labyrinths*, Penguin, Harmondsworth, 1970.

2. Jorge Luis Borges, 'Pierre Menard, author of *Quixote*', in *Labyrinths*.

3. Ernest Gellner, *Cause and Meaning in the Social Sciences*, Routledge & Kegan Paul, London and Boston, pp. 71–2.

4. Karl R. Popper, *Objective Knowledge, an Evolutionary Approach*, Clarendon Press, Oxford and New York, 1972, pp. 12–17.

5. Jürgen Habermas, trans. Jeremy J. Shapiro, *Knowledge and Human Interests*, Heinemann, London, 1972 [Beacon, Boston, 1971], pp. 194–5.

6. ibid., p. 195.

7. ibid. There is more on Habermas's theory of knowledge-generating interest, in Z. Bauman, *Towards a Critical Sociology*, Routledge & Kegan Paul, London and Boston, 1976, chapter 3.

8. Gregory Bateson, *Steps to an Ecology of Mind*, Paladin, London, 1973 [Ballantine, New York, 1975], pp. 341–2.

9. Jürgen Habermas, trans. Thomas McCarthy, *Legitimation Crisis*, Heinemann, London, 1976 [Beacon, Boston, 1975], pp. 107–8.

10. ibid., p. 108.

11. Michel Foucault, trans. A. M. Sheridan-Smith, *The Archeology of Knowledge*, Tavistock, London, 1974 [Irvington, New York, 1972], pp. 50, 51.

Index